Essay Ind P9-AGA-345

Masterful Images

Masterful Images

ENGLISH POETRY FROM
METAPHYSICALS TO ROMANTICS

A. E. DYSON
and
JULIAN LOVELOCK

M

First published 1976 by
THE MACMILLAN PRESS LTD
London and Basingstoke
Associated companies in New York Dublin
Melbourne Johannesburg and Madras

SBN 333 16622 1 (hard cover)
     333 16624 8 (paper cover)

Printed in Great Britain by
THE ANCHOR PRESS LTD
Tiptree, Essex

CONTENTS

PREFACE

This book is intended primarily for those who are making a serious study of poetry for the first time, whether as undergraduates, sixth-formers, or as 'mature' students seeking to broaden their minds. It is hoped that it might also have its uses as a refresher course, perhaps for readers or teachers who are exploring new ground, or filling gaps.

The main aim is to supply a sense of tradition, of the unfolding and continuity of our poetry, but to do this through close and careful reading of the texts. In essence, such 'practical criticism' is a personal response to poems, made by readers alive to their excitement and keen to explore. Inevitably, this turns on strong and living impressions, not on dogma – but on impressions which are trained, rather than random, and related precisely to texts. The study of literature should aid and encourage this activity, treating both readers, and poems, with honest respect.

Nowadays most teaching concentrates on individual poems and poets, or on very short 'periods', and this study of 'topics' seems basically sound. The older 'chronological' method tended towards superficial generalisations, as any attempt to cover fifty or a hundred years in one course surely must. The danger with 'literary history' is its tendency to vagueness, its gravitation away from the particularity, the uniqueness, of the works it exists to serve.

Yet the new methods, too, have their problems, one of which is that students are apt to swing to the other extreme. Poems may be isolated from their context, discussed in a vacuum, until all sense of history and tradition is lost. Can the gap be bridged? We attempt here to do so, by combining two approaches in a new way. The Introduction and the Appendix on 'Dating' attempt general information – very pared down and compressed – about literary 'periods', and the rest of the book studies particular works. In this way, the general can be checked against the particular, and the tension between the two can be underlined.

The generalisations in the Introduction and Appendix are offered, therefore, purely for their minimal usefulness, and the studies are the major part of the book. We hope that the generalisations will help students to grapple with 'dating' exercises – that is to say, with the challenge to look closely at poems or parts of poems removed from context, and to deduce where, in the history of poetry, they belong. This exercise is still the best general test of literary knowledge, since it depends upon wide and informed reading, and a true sense of the past. No one can 'teach' it as a skill, since it comes from experience, but there are certain hints, or tips, that students find useful to know. In the Introduction and Appendix, we restrict ourselves to those aspects which, in our own experience as readers and teachers, we have found most helpful, and which stand or fall by a pragmatic test.

In this context, we decided to visit the major poets in our 250-year period, and to concentrate on one work from each. When there is a famous 'long' poem, we have chosen it; otherwise, we have chosen a poem that seems typical and, inherently, 'great'. When discussing the 'long' poems, one typical passage has been chosen for close analysis, but in relation to the structure, tone and mood of the whole. In this way, it has been possible to include *Paradise Lost, Absalom and Achitophel, The Rape of the Lock,* 'The Ancient Mariner' and *The Prelude,* and to allow our title 'masterful images', its fullest scope. These poems are central to our culture, and among its greatest achievements; they are 'images' which no literary critic, indeed no historian, can afford to ignore.

A final word on dialogue. The present book arose out of teaching situations in the University of East Anglia, where the seminar method is used. The authors belong to different generations and differ widely in temperament, so no uniformity of response exists. In most of these essays the insights converge and are held in tension, often through an agreement on the *questions* that have to be asked. This method presupposes that readers will enter into the dialogue, either in groups (in formal seminars) or when reading alone. Once or twice, however, differences were highlighted, and then the original form of dialogue has been allowed to remain. Dialogue is, we believe, the essence of criticism – part of that chain of responses and explorations which poems need, and provoke.

A. E. DYSON
JULIAN LOVELOCK

INTRODUCTION

I MASTERFUL IMAGES

> Those masterful images, because complete
> Grew in pure mind, but out of what began?

In these well known words from 'The Circus Animals' Desertion'
Yeats refers to his own works as 'masterful images'. The phrase,
in context, is surrounded with ironies, yet Yeats knows that it
points to an important, and triumphant, truth. Any successful
poem stands finished and assured, in its own formal existence, a
unique object, made with words and containing power. In a sense
it is like a rune, as well as an icon; an object of beauty, with
mysteriously transformed energy locked in itself. The words on
the page may seem passive, as well as permanent, yet they are
full of vitality awaiting its release. What is needed? Clearly,
the close attention of ourselves and of other readers – of anyone
who is both willing, and able, to let the words work.

In 'Lapis Lazuli' Yeats himself works the magic, as he stands
looking at the lapis lazuli carving which gives his poem its name.
'I delight to imagine,' he says, towards the end of the poem; and
it is as if the carved figures come mysteriously yet vividly alive.
Yet another phrase from Yeats suggests the curious power of art,
and of poems notably, to transmit, from poet to reader, a dance of
life :

> These images that yet
> Fresh images beget

The whole poem from which this comes, 'Byzantium', points to
that process whereby the artist's experience is first locked into the
form and structure of his own creation, and then released,
through close attention, into the life of whoever attends. In the

word 'image', Yeats describes the work of art as a whole in its prime reality, and in 'beget' he points to the quality of response – from the whole self, not from the intellect merely – which art both requires and rewards.

It follows that reading poems is both a precise, and a dynamic activity, demanding a sustained and preferably a trained response. On the one hand we have to pay close attention to the poem in its formal existence, but then we have to clothe it with emotions and thoughts, with energy, drawn from ourselves.

If it is asked, 'What is the purpose of reading poems; or indeed of writing them?', Yeats's 'masterful images' provides perhaps our best clue. Men make images to articulate and clarify, to communicate, to enshrine and sometimes to heal experience, and these are human activities, known to us all. In one respect, as the Geneva critics asserted, all literature can be regarded as the history of human consciousness itself.* But, further, literature is an embodiment, and therefore a guarantee, of human resilience and creativity, in that it is part of the story of what men can make as well as of what they can say. Through art, men pass on their own wisdom often, to enrich others, but they do so by making new and permanent objects of beauty where none was before. These new creations of art are themselves experiences, and of the kind which build up civilisation in its richest form.

Reading can best be seen then as an exploration, in which literary criticism may be part a record, and part a guide. The poems themselves stand to one side of time now, potent with vitality, arrested yet available, for as long a period as their physical existence continues and there are minds to respond. The literary critic does not seek to pin them down, or to offer 'definitive' readings, but to share his own responses, and to indicate his awareness of the range of responses that can possibly be made. In this process it often happens that th'ngs we already

* For an account of this influential modern school see J. Hillis Miller, 'The Geneva School. The Criticism of Marcel Raymond, Albert Béguin, Georges Poulet, Jean Rousset, Jean-Pierre Richard, and Jean Starobinski', *Critical Quarterly*, vol. 8 (1966).

half-knew are clarified, as though the words of the poem were a sudden revelation of ourselves. What habitual reader has not sometimes come upon words which set up a marvellously liberating sense of familiarity, as if he had always been waiting for them, and only now is complete? Keats said of great poetry that 'it should strike the reader as a wording of his own highest thoughts, and appear almost as a remembrance' * – and undoubtedly, when poetry does strike us in this manner, we need less than the usual persuasion to call it 'great'.

2   PRACTICAL CRITICISM

The method used in this book is practical criticism, a method pioneered by I. A. Richards in Cambridge, and brought to fruition by a number of critics on both sides of the Atlantic; Cleanth Brooks's *The Well-Wrought Urn* (1949) is still perhaps the finest pure example. In essence, practical criticism is simply the applied perception that we have to attend closely to words and structure, neither skipping over things that really are part of them nor reading into them things that are not, but allowing them to come as powerfully alive as possible in our own response. Some people have feared that the method will kill poetry, substituting abstract intellectual analysis for emotional power. But this fear might well in the end be an insult to the poems, a suspicion that they are not fitted to bear close attention without suffering harm. Fortunately, great poems are not so easily diminished, but grow in power and stature, rather, with attention and time. They flourish from close acquaintance and become more rewarding, very much as any richly interesting thing, or person, taken seriously, is apt to do.

A fuller consideration of practical criticism has been offered

* Letter to John Taylor, 27 February 1818; reprinted in *The Letters of John Keats*, ed. Maurice Buxton Forman (1952) p. 107. The letter concerns Keats's 'axioms for poetry', and is important as a whole.

elsewhere by one of the present authors, and we have no wish
now to repeat.* But it may be worth glancing quickly at two of
the major areas of controversy which have developed around the
method, with our basic definition of poems as 'masterful images'
in mind.

(a) *Intention*

W. K. Wimsatt, in his excellent book *The Verbal Icon* (1973),
attacked (and named) 'the intentionalist fallacy', which is the
notion that practical criticism is a simple tracking down of the
writer's conscious aim. Northrop Frye expressed the objections
to naive intentionalism strongly in his brilliantly searching
Anatomy of Criticism (1957): 'the assertion that the critic
should confine himself to "getting out" of a poem exactly what
the poet may vaguely be assumed to have been aware of "putting
in", is one of the many slovenly illiteracies that the absence of
systematic criticism has allowed to grow up'. With the main tenor
of this, we are in entire agreement; obviously, the poet's sub-
conscious as well as his conscious self will influence his work. The
artefact is bound also to have its own autonomy, in that it belongs
to an order of literature as well as to an order of life. The words
used in it, the myths and archetypes, have their own lives and
directions, beyond the bending of any one writer's will. The nearer
a writer comes moreover to true and deep human experience, the
more his work will take on the complexities of 'life'. No doubt, if
you create a wish-fulfilment character for a romantic novel, you
can do with him, or her, very much what you will. But if you
create an Anna Karenina or a William Dorrit, you are bound by
the highest laws of reality itself. Your very success in launching
such a creation then becomes a discipline, ensuring that you
cannot get away with anything less than the truth.

But is poetry not different, it may be asked; is it not a more
'magic' world? In some aspects, yes; but not entirely; Milton's
Satan, Pope's Belinda, cannot be isolated from the great truths

---

* C. B. Cox and A. E. Dyson *The Practical Criticism of Poetry*
(1965) and *Modern Poetry: Studies in Practical Criticism* (1963).

they explore. After creating Belinda, Pope could not have changed either his insight into her as a person, or the tone and mood of his art, without putting his whole poem at risk. The poet's 'intention', in short, is at the service of his themes and subjects, which, in turn, may have depths and complexities beyond any he can personally control, or totally plumb.

When this has been said, however, as it must be, 'intention' has not disappeared entirely from sight. No poem drops from heaven, mysteriously; it comes from a human experience, and a human mind. Since the poet has trained himself to communicate and articulate, and to do these things precisely, then clearly, his conscious intention will be embodied in his work. The reader will then to some extent be engaged with him in communication, often at a highly subtle level, sometimes almost at the level of a battle, or a game.

It was this area of creation which Wayne Booth wrote about in his book *The Rhetoric of Fiction* (1961), a work illuminating to the reading of poetry, as well as of imaginative prose. All literature, Booth points out, has an element of 'rhetoric' – by which, he means precisely the artifice intended by the creating mind. 'Nothing the writer does can finally be understood in isolation from his efforts to make it all accessible to someone else – his peers, himself as imagined reader, his audience.' The reader of poetry, bearing in mind this simple precept, and the highly sophisticated criticism that it can lead to, will surely steer his way between 'intention' and 'effect' in art without too much strain.

(b) *Morality*

The sponsors of *Scrutiny*, writing in their first issue, said that 'there is a necessary relationship between the quality of the individual's response to art and his general fitness for a humane existence'. The positive thought underlying this is perhaps acceptable; presumably, it is that the study of art can, and should, civilise and enrich. But in itself the formula seems gravely misleading; perhaps because it appears to bypass free will? We can be subjected to any kinds of influence, good or bad, without 'necessary' consequences; the most that can be hoped is that good influences will have good effects. It seems likely that whenever the moral hopes attaching to the study of literature are pitched too high, then certain dangers both of cultural élitism, and of cultural pessimism, start to loom. A further danger is that these might then provoke a strong reaction, back to merely linguistic criticism, in which moral and experiential aspects of art suffer a new neglect.

The *Scrutiny* formula seems open in fact to two opposite dangers, which can both be put in a simple form. The first is that it appears to equate 'general fitness for a humane existence' with formal – even artistic – education; a notion which mercifully, we know to be wrong. Many intellectually simple and untutored people have qualities of wisdom, kindness, and occasionally profound goodness which far transcend any artistic, or educational, tests. If we forget this, we not only drop into snobbery, and the wrong claims for education, but we risk alienating those who are most acutely aware of the fallacy in what is claimed. On the other side of the picture we risk confusing appreciation of art, of literature and poetry, with virtue, and so of laying up further disillusionment when this, too, is seen to be manifestly untrue. In *Language And Silence* (1967) George Steiner noted that we now know that a 'man can read Goethe or Rilke in the evening, that he can play Bach and Schubert, and go to his day's work at Auschwitz in the morning', and, in the light of this, he asks : 'Has our civilisation, by virtue of the inhumanity it has carried out and condoned, forfeited its claims to that indispensable luxury which we call literature?'

What the problem amounts to is that some people who are neither able, nor sometimes perhaps willing, to enjoy poetry and literature, are morally admirable and at times holy, while some people (many people?) who do have this literary dimension to their lives are morally ordinary, or neutral, or in extreme cases profoundly evil. Should this surprise us? The crux does appear to be our freedom; which ensures that literature has no automatic power to make us virtuous if we choose to resist. In this, it is like religion, philosophy and all other conceivable influences, none of which has irresistible power. The simple truth is that literature can extend our awareness, refine our insight, appeal to our sympathies, give us wider perspectives on life and the hope that comes with these, but, in the end, it leaves us free.

What is needed, no doubt, is not to abandon the insight that literature can be morally elevating, but simply to return it to its more normal, and Christian, form. The definitive statement still seems to be St Paul's, in his letter to the Philippians : 'Whatsoever things are true, whatsoever things are honest, whatsoever things are just, whatsoever things are pure, whatsoever things are lovely, whatsoever things are of good report : if there be any virtue and if there be any praise, think on these things.' St Paul does not say that these things – which surely include art and poetry – will make us good necessarily; but he does say that their natural tendency will be to co-operate with good. The assumption will be that just as ugly or depraved things exert a strong influence upon men who are surrounded by and become absorbed in them, so also do works of creative beauty and exemplary truth. Wordsworth believed that a life lived among beautiful natural surroundings is influenced towards wholeness; the same intuition may be extended – with certain cautions – to a life surrounded by art.

We return therefore to our key concept, 'masterful images'. Poems which have a man's imaginative and spiritual life and energy locked in them are bound to have power over minds that respond. They will influence readers not only through their 'content' – which is to say, through their direct communication of meaning – but equally and perhaps more importantly by what they *are*. For, just as no literature can deny the intelligence, the creativity and resilience, often the compassion which inform it, so no reader who responds to these qualities can deny them, without telling a lie. The species which creates is not less than its own creations, at least in potential; nor can works which strike us as meaningful be finally 'absurd'. It is therefore certain that great poems reveal much of man's potential for sublimity, and that our study of them is *more likely* to do good than harm. With this proviso, the moral case for studying literature remains impressive; it is the study of men at their fullest and richest and most articulate stretch.

Our own understanding of the moral value of literature derives most from C. S. Lewis, among the critics of modern times. In *An Experiment in Criticism* (1961) he argues brilliantly the case for critical reading as homage to works of art which are in themselves objects of great beauty and significance, and which extend our consciousness by initiating us into the minds of other men, often greater, and certainly more articulate, than we can hope to be:

This, so far as I can see, is the specific value or good of literature considered as Logos; it admits us to experiences other than our own. They are not, any more than our personal experiences, all equally worth having. Some, we may say, 'interest' us more than others. The causes of this interest are naturally extremely various and differ from one man to another; it may be the typical (and we say 'How true !') or the abnormal (and we say 'How strange !'); it may be the beautiful, the terrible, the awe-inspiring, the exhilarating, the pathetic, the comic, or the merely piquant. Literature gives the *entrée* to them all. Those of us who have been true readers all our life seldom fully realize the enormous extension of our being which we owe to authors. We realize it best when we talk with an un-literary friend. He may be full of goodness and good sense but he inhabits a tiny world. In it, we should be suffocated. The man who is contented to be only himself, and therefore less a self, is in prison. My own eyes are not enough for me, I will see through those of others. Reality, even seen through the eyes of many, is not enough. I will see what others have invented.

The ordered patterns of literature and poetry have their own kinds of autonomy, and perhaps most men – certainly most of the poets now to concern us – see these as pointing towards supreme truths. Those who share this view, and the high view of man which is implied in it, should be willing to fight for the integrity of criticism, and for the integrity of those poems, and other works of literature, which criticism serves. The enemies of human dignity usually attack first our language, as many modern writers (Aldous Huxley in *Brave New World,* George Orwell in *1984,* for instance) have shown. If we diminish words, we diminish man himself – his potential for being – and, ultimately, we abolish freedom in any meaningful sense. In literary criticism any reductiveness, whether towards mere linguistics, or mere verbal ingenuity for its own sake, points in the wrong direction; it opposes rather than assists the power of art. At a time like our own, when images of destruction and violence proliferate on the media, we need the 'masterful images' of great art as seldom before.

3 LITERARY HISTORY AND 'DATING'

Just in so far as the studies which follow are concerned with the specific – with unique and complex poems – so they resist 'literary history', with its inevitably generalised ground. Yet major poems can often be seen to reveal something of the age they belong to, and may acquire a reputation as 'masterful images' in this context as well. Whole decades have sometimes been associated with the names of poets (Shakespeare, Milton, Dryden, 'the Romantics', and so on), and we find that historians, as well as literary critics, may take this view. The paradox is that while great works are nothing but themselves, both in their inner texture and in their particular tone and complexities, they may, none the less, seem to typify a whole ethos, or an entire mode of thought. Precisely here, we encounter the difficulty attending 'literary history'; most literary histories, by abstracting, end by falsifying the sources they must chiefly use.

It remains observable, however, that 'periods' do have general characteristics, which their great poems exemplify – so the abstractions of literary history are in no simple sense 'untrue'. Perhaps the great test of literary knowledge and sensitivity is the ability to 'date' unseen passages out of context; and those who

can do this realise that abstracted generalisations about 'periods'
often are among the best 'clues'. Certain verse forms *are* common
in one period, then used very little or not at all in another; the
same is true of certain themes, and certain approaches to themes.
A love poem written in 1590 differs from one written in 1690, or
in 1790, or in 1890 decisively, even though the author is human,
and the experience – romantic or sexual love – has not changed in
itself. Still more strikingly, all writers clearly belong to their period,
whether they set out consciously to express it, or consciously to
oppose. The very terms in which debates, arguments, feelings
themselves are defined, are recognisably of their period, whether
the writers thought of themselves as allies, or whether as enemies
fighting to the death. There can be little doubt that all readers
of this book will be dateable as 'late twentieth century' if they
leave writings behind them, whatever their views, and whether
they write badly or well.

It follows that generalisations, once perceived, have a real point
and justification : they prove themselves by *working,* as students
of literature come to know.

Our purpose in this book is not to write formal 'literary history',
though we hope that certain developments between the time of
Donne, and of Keats, will be perceived. With this in mind, we
have added an appendix, in counterpoint with the studies, and
with the needs of those fairly new to the study of literature chiefly
in view. This will not in any simple sense 'teach' dating – the
ability to date comes only with wide reading and practice – but it
might help students to locate the larger, and most pervasive,
symptoms of cultural change. Normally we should be totally
unwilling to abstract in this manner, if only because the tension
between the general and any particular poem whatsoever is
always so great. But, with the specific studies at hand to act as a
corrective, we risk concluding with a very small-scale map of the
vast terrain.

1 CONTRACTED THUS: DONNE'S 'THE SUNNE RISING'

The poem explodes into fiercely rhetorical argument, pursued through three stanzas of sustained exaltation. First the sun is rebuked as a kind of elderly voyeur; then sent about his business; then accused of vanity; then dispatched (unsuccessfully) to look for 'both the'India's'. Finally contempt gives way to patronage, and the sun is invited to perform his duties with the inertia more fitted to age, standing still.

Clearly, such an argument is provocative and, given the sun's normal role as king of the Heavenly bodies and divine emblem, even blasphemous; like Shakespeare's famous sonnet 130. 'My Mistres eyes are nothing like the Sunne', only more outrageously, it reverses the tradition of hundreds of Petrarchan and Elizabethan love poems in which the sun is a touchstone of ecstatic tribute. As an emotional attitude to the sun it verges on derangement, or at least on that excess of fancy divorced from normal perception and judgement which helped to make metaphysical poetry so generally uncongenial to the eighteenth century, and which to Dr Johnson's tormented mind bore a fearful resemblance to insanity.

Where, then, might a critic start? On a fairly simple level the exaggeration of language mimes the assurance of love. Time becomes 'rags', change, decay, and diminution all recede. But we see at once that the poem works not directly but obliquely, by indirections finding directions out. The sun is not its true subject; contempt and patronage for the sun are not its true emotional charge. Its true subject is the lady; its true emotion love. Every insult to the sun is a compliment to the mistress, every assertion of the sun's weakness attests her power. This is in no simple manner a split between thought and feeling, since both are involved, in the equation, on either side. The literal argument

is, in fact, a pseudo-argument (the term is I. A. Richards's):
it uses an apparent subject and emotional attitude which relates
to the real subject and emotional attitude by systematic inversion.
The pseudo-argument generates an apparent logic (the sun's
antics) and an appropriate emotion (contempt for the sun). The
true argument is also logical, with the familiar and simple logic
of love, and generates love's appropriate emotion, ecstatic homage.

It is precisely here, however, that we encounter the poem's
central complexity and chief strategy. The literal argument is
often more (though it is never less) than a pseudo-argument, and
circles back even in the first stanza to make a kind of sense in its
own right. If men are indeed exalted by love beyond the temporal,
are they not entitled to 'look down' on the sun and on its 'spheare'?

> Busie old foole, unruly Sunne,
>   Why dost thou thus,
> Through windowes, and through curtaines call on us?
> Must to thy motions lovers seasons run?
>   Sawcy pedantique wretch, goe chide
>   Late schoole boyes, and sowre prentices,
>   Goe tell Court-huntsmen, that the King will ride,
>   Call countrey ants to harvest offices;
> Love, all alike, no season knowes, nor clyme,
> Nor houres, dayes, moneths, which are the rags of time.

Any potentially comic effect is undercut by a note of seriousness,
or perhaps overplayed by a note of exhilaration. Donne's imagery,
though bizarre and exaggerated as pseudo-argument, asserts what
every Platonist and Christian really believes. At certain moments,
any man might be wrapt beyond mortality, in the eternal
intimations of spiritual love. Statements like

> Love, all alike, no season knowes, nor clyme,
> Nor houres, dayes, moneths, which are the rags of time

and (in the third stanza)

> She'is all States, and all Princes, I,
> Nothing else is

ride triumphantly over their assumed contempt for the sun, attesting that the world fittingly symbolised in the 'schoole boyes, and sowre prentices', the 'Court-huntsmen' and 'countrey ants' is indeed tinged with illusion, and at one remove from the truth. In calling the material world (in normal speech, the 'real' world) unreal, the poem is saying, with Plato, that even the world's princes and potentates are mere shadows, an imitation in time of the time-less ideals. Such lines as

> Princes doe but play us; compar'd to this,
> All honor's mimique; All wealth alchimie

(stanza 3)

are not, on this showing, even paradoxical: Donne is a true Platonist, and perhaps unusually daring only in so far as he risks extending to earthly princes (indeed to James I himself, whose love of hunting is unflatteringly alluded to) the reminder that they, too, are shadows all.

In a similar manner the poem's questions are arranged, with dazzling sleight-of-hand, to confound any normal reading response. In the context of pseudo-logic, 'Must to thy motions lovers seasons run?' looks like a rhetorical question expecting the answer 'no'; but can it be less than a real and tragic question for men in time? Lovers who ignore external pressures and realities must surely be conquered by them: such is the theme of the great romantic tragedies; such is the underlying cause of the sterility of so-called 'free-love'. Yet the poem's strange power is to cancel, or transcend, or mock the obvious – it is hard to say which – perhaps through its suggestions that the sun and the lovers have actually exchanged roles (the 'seasons' are controlled by the lovers, while the sun is linked with the 'motions' of physical love).

Such complexities continue through the second stanza:

> Thy beames, so reverend, and strong
> Why shouldst thou thinke?

> I could eclipse and cloud them with a winke,
> But that I would not lose her sight so long :
>   If her eyes have not blinded thine,
>   Looke, and to morrow late, tell mee,
> Whether both the'India's of spice and Myne
> Be where thou leftst them, or lie here with mee.
> Aske for those Kings whom thou saw'st yesterday,
> And thou shalt heare, All here in one bed lay.

The sun is accused of hollow boasts, but for dubious reasons; the poet could only 'eclipse and cloud' his 'beames' at a cost. If he closed his eyes, would a greater sun really light him, or would he merely be locked in a dream? Perhaps his love itself would disappear, along with all other values, as the uneasy excuse 'But that I would not lose her sight so long' more than half suggests. Once more, the poem's power pushes aside such doubts without wholly excluding them; the sun and the lovers again change roles, with the mistress for an instant becoming the sun, and her 'eye-beames' (cf. 'The Extasie', line 7) blinding the usurped lord of light.

The stanza ends with the claim that the countries and kings of the world have joined together in the lovers' bed. But, as the poem approaches its climax of supreme confidence, giddy with the richness of 'spice and Myne', it takes a further turn which is ultimately to undermine the warranty of that confidence. If love is indeed to be lifted up to the eternal world it must transcend the temporal; and such apotheosis requires something very different from the heavy sexual imagery of ruler and ruled and the basic language of the bedroom ('lie here with mee'; 'All here in one bed lay.'). The crowning irony, to which Donne would hardly have been oblivious, is that hierarchies sufficiently valid in spiritual contexts (cf. Book IV of *Paradise Lost*) become profoundly tainted when turned only to sexual ends.

In the third stanza the ideas hover explicitly between the exaggerated rhetoric of love, lost in lies or illusions, and the splendid platonic intimations of ultimate truth :

> She'is all States, and all Princes, I,
> Nothing else is.
> Princes doe but play us; compar'd to this,
> All honor's mimique; All wealth alchimie.
> Thou sunne art halfe as happy'as wee,
> In that the world's contracted thus;
> Thine age askes ease, and since thy duties bee
> To warme the world, that's done in warming us.
> Shine here to us, and thou art every where;
> This bed thy center is, these walls, thy spheare.

As we have suggested, the poet's declarations in the first four lines ring with the conviction of paradox apprehended as truth. But a taint of sexuality remains in the imagery, more dross to the poem (if another Donne image can be inverted) than allay. Such conviction could indeed be justified in some contexts, but not when love's 'contract' is 'contracted' along with the poem's world. If love is in truth to outlast 'seasons' it must be released from the shrinking and sexual connotations of 'contracted thus'; it requires a 'center' not in the bed, but in the soul.

Drawing together the complexities of 'The Sunne Rising', we immediately recognise their interdependence as they support, contradict and parallel each other, dictating in these tensions the poem's tone. Our sense that the poem allies love's psychology to the one metaphysic which ultimately validates it is strengthened by the fact that the mistress is always complimented, as it were, at one remove. There is no physical description of her beauty of the kind familiar in most Elizabethan love lyrics; the compliment exists wholly in what the poet feels. It is because she moves him to this dramatic urgency that we know her influence; in a manner wholly characteristic of Donne, it is the intensity of worship which guarantees worth. *Her* value is *his* veneration : and in as much as this does not leave her unbearably vulnerable to fickleness (a theme which Donne pursues in other, more cynical poems) we have to accept the superior truth of the spiritual world. Love is not a mere reflection of the lover's needs, subjective and transient; it is homage to beauty revealed and revered. Its habitat is a world where homage can be appropriate, and loyalty enduring; a world not yet caught in the egocentric snare. One could argue indeed that the outrageousness of the images goes hand in hand with their truth, even at the most literal level: if 'truth' is in their extreme of feeling, their exaggeration, this precisely attests the illusiveness and unimportance of the merely material world, and so of the sun, and of the great globe itself.

But the contempt for the sun which characterises the literal argument must undeniably affect our response to the poem in its own right (at least partially), and not simply as a signpost to the intensities of love. If so, it hints perhaps at a degree of unease surrounding the certainty, a residual anger as the poet makes statements which he feels should be true and even are true, but which must necessarily be dubious when made by mortal man. For so tormented a temperament, there must be a nagging fear that the sun might indeed shine on to mock lovers, as their intentions soil and their professions fade. And this poem is not in its essence serene and timeless; it is nothing like (say) Henry Vaughan's 'The Retreate' or T. S. Eliot's 'Little Gidding'. Rather it is violent, even in its unquestionable beauty, sweeping along moment by moment on currents of change.

It is at this point, no doubt, that we should take account of the poet's habitual cast of mind, which colours nearly everything he writes. Does the emotional charge of the poem relate after all more to the pseudo-argument, the rhetorical shadow-boxing, than to the still centre where the sun at last comes to rest? Donne is a poet who rushes into articulation, creating as he defines, initiating the reader into experience at its white heat. His soul seemingly knows itself in linguistic intensity – in this poem, in an extended conceit which is at once an elaborate game and an exploration, a supreme dramatisation of the whole man. On this aspect of Donne's poetry, T. S. Eliot's essay 'The Metaphysical Poets' is of course seminal,* and remains valid as a definition of

* Reprinted in T. S. Eliot, *Selected Essays* (1932; 3rd ed 1958).

one poet's peculiar sensibility, even if we reject its extension to quasi-historical theorising, as we surely must.

The effect in 'The Sunne Rising' is that statements and questions come alive with alternative meanings, none of which can be wholly suppressed. The poem thrives on extremes and quintessences, on paradoxes which look at one moment like intellectual scaffolding round simple emotions, at the next like internal complexities threatening the emotions themselves. We have to return in conclusion to the question of whether the ideas put forward in the poem are finally acceptable : or rather, to the question of what 'final acceptability', in such an instance, can be. If the poem's articulation is inseparable from the poet's experience, it must in an obvious sense be valid; yet the verbal construct remains, by any standards, bizarre. Few people would address the sun in this way seriously, or even fancifully; few would argue that human love can, in the manner asserted, defy time.

The problem turns on the relationship between erotic love and spiritual love; the poem yokes these two together, and apparently unites them, but are they fused, or confused, in the end? Human love naturally links with passionate needs for loyalty, which point, for a religious believer, to truths beyond time. The eternity demanded by love need not be mythic; the thoughts which dominate this poem can be directly and profoundly presented as truth :

Thou, Lord, in the beginning hast laid the foundation of the earth : and the heavens are the work of thy hands.
They shall perish, but thou shalt endure : they all shall wax old as doth a garment;
And as a vesture shalt thou change them, and they shall be changed : but thou art the same, and thy years shall not fail.

(Psalm 102, 25–7 : Coverdale translation)

When Donne wrote later in the religious poetry and sermons of his love for God, the extraordinary intensity and deviousness of his conceits remained, but they linked there with the more normal and inescapable paradoxes of Christian faith. The sonnet 'Death

be not proud' expresses one of those grand Christian doctrines
which separate believer from unbeliever irrevocably, in worlds
too disparate for any bridges to link :

> Death be not proud, though some have called thee
> Mighty and dreadfull, for, thou art not soe,
> For, those, whom thou think'st, thou dost overthrow,
> Die not, poore death, nor yet canst thou kill mee.
> From rest and sleepe, which but thy pictures bee,
> Much pleasure, then from thee, much more must flow,
> And soonest our best men with thee doe goe,
> Rest of their bones, and soules deliverie.

For the Christian, death has lost all power to hurt, except for the
deep and grievous, but temporary, anguish of bereavement. Such
a triumph can scarcely be portrayed without extravagance or be
seen as less than aggressive in its hope. In the most serious sense it
is shocking : St Paul rightly associates it with the 'scandal' of the
Cross, and celebrates it with famous verbal audacities of his own.

But such triumphs must belong, by their nature, to religion,
and to hopes which transcend, if they do not exclude, the flesh.
When Donne projects religious assurance into merely sensual
experience, he sets up tensions hard to resolve. Love's triumph
over time is convincingly asserted by Christian or Platonist only
when certain other factors intervene. It is the promise beyond 'till
death do us part' in the Christian marriage vows, the sacramental
bond only half anchored to the body and to the world of time. But
it must reach out beyond the bedroom if it is to carry conviction,
to clearer loyalties, stronger renunciations of erotic possessiveness,
than this poem affords.

It is because 'The Sunne Rising' celebrates Eros as a true
Immortal that it has a real, as well as rhetorical, nonsense at the
heart.

2 HERBERT'S 'REDEMPTION'

Having been tenant long to a rich Lord,
 Not thriving, I resolved to be bold,
 And made a suit unto him, to afford
A new small-rented lease, and cancell th'old.
In heaven at his manour I him sought :
 They told me there, that he was lately gone
 About some land, which he had dearly bought
Long since on earth, to take possession.
I straight return'd, and knowing his great birth,
 Sought him accordingly in great resorts;
 In cities, theatres, gardens, parks, and courts :
At length I heard a ragged noise and mirth
Of theeves and murderers : there I him espied,
 Who straight, *Your suit is granted,* said, and died.

Though this sonnet is quasi-Shakespearean in form,* it would be hard to imagine a greater contrast between Shakespeare's ornate images, exotic and hot-house themes, and Herbert's seeming homelincss. The simplicity is, of course, deceptive. In fourteen lines, Herbert traces a soul's journey from ignorance to knowledge, from sin to 'redemption', from death to life. The theme is a quest, and the treatment of time is highly sophisticated. The 'I' of the poem gathers his courage, sets out, seeks 'long', journeys to heaven, returns to earth, comes 'at length' to the place and person sought. All of this suggests an extended period, yet the

---

* It departs from the Shakespearean form by using the rhyming scheme 'effe' in the third quatrain instead of 'efef', and also by a layout on the page which 'looks' more Miltonic than Shakespearean. Note that the first and second pair of rhymes are further linked by assonance.

theme of journeying is linked with something resembling a continuous present. This is hinted at by the opening phrase, 'Having been', with its postulate of a past that was, a future that will be, and an action suspended between the two. The double perspective is reinforced linguistically in the tension between words and phrases such as 'long', 'the old', 'lately been', 'Long since', 'At length', with their suggestion of months or years of seeking, and the opposed hint of sudden action, total change in 'I resolved', 'bold', 'I him sought', 'I straight return'd', 'Who straight . . . said'. But in the deepest sense the action of the poem is perpetual and there is no contradiction; the place arrived at is always sought for and always available. It recedes in history, the deed once accomplished, 'Consummatum est', and it is always present 'This *is* my body, which is given for you' – the moment in and out of time; T. S. Eliot's 'still point of the turning world'. The title word, 'redemption', touches past, present and future in 'dearly bought' – the soul discovering its need of grace, and the grace freely given, in one insight.

We next observe that in the homely words and images, the simple diction and the almost leisurely syntax, there is tremendous compression, and of a recognisably 'metaphysical' kind. Even Donne, complexities worn on the sleeve, would be hard pressed to get more into a poem. Indeed, the central paradox of this poem is very close to Donne's 'Good Friday, 1613; Riding Westward'. But note the differences. Donne's effect is, as usual, to convey the white heat of intellectual striving and discovery, the mind's astonished perception of paradox :

> There I should see a Sunne, by rising set,
> And by that setting endlesse day beget;
> But that Christ on this Crosse, did rise and fall,
> Sinne had eternally benighted all.
> Yet dare I'almost be glad, I do not see.
> That spectacle of too much weight for mee.
> Who sees God's face, that is selfe life, must dye;
> What a death were it then to see God dye?

It made his owne Lieutenant Nature shrinke,
It made his footstoole crack, and the Sunne winke.
Could I behold those hands which span the Poles,
And turn all spheares at once, pierc'd with those holes?

In contrast, Herbert works through a simple *persona*, who does not himself grasp one half of the import his poem has for the reader, and who may not fully understand even its ending. If compression of the kind we become accustomed to in both of these poets is one generic mark of 'the metaphysical', we can add that compression so reticent about itself that the reader scarcely notices it is the particular and distinctive mark of Herbert. Again, just as Donne is famed for first lines that come with great power, driving straight to the heart of the poem, so Herbert is justly famed for his creation of last lines which convey immense surprise, and liberation, with a serene appearance of ease.

A further sign of 'the metaphysical' in 'Redemption' is its obliquity, centred here on the use of 'I'. The 'I' is characterised by a simplicity and directness of thought, relating to his own discovered unhappiness in life, which constantly stimulates the reader to run ahead of him in intellectual discovery. We gather that he is a man of simple common sense, setting out on a literal journey to find his landlord and to plead for a new lease, and with no awareness of allegory. His dissatisfaction is most basically stated, 'Not thriving', and he sets out on his travels, looking in wrong places, moving almost at random, coming at last to the right place, to his own great surprise. For him, the poem is clearly 'simple' in a manner it is not, and cannot be, for us. The reader, as Christian believer (Herbert would have expected), is led through his own stages of pilgrimage. The force of 'dearly bought' is apparent to him long before the 'I' of the poem understands it; the two leases conjure up the whole theology of Fall and Grace. 'Accordingly', which for the narrator is a word of simple common sense, brings into question, for the reader, that whole scale of values which associates greatness, and divinity, with the 'great resorts' of the rich. The narrator discovers in the last line (but the reader well knows from the first) that *this* 'great Lord' was born in poverty as a carpenter and died on a cross, yet is also the God who made all things, the Lord of Lords. There is, in this, something far more damatic than a challenge to snobbery; the basic effect, even, is of a different kind. God's descent is not cosmic levelling, but the meeting of man's sin with love's radical cure. Indeed, surely God *ought* to rule gloriously in heaven, not suffer on Calvary; and surely he will do so again, when the cure is complete? Nevertheless, 'accordingly' does question, and very sharply, a purely social view of greatness, reflecting, at the very least, Herbert's own preference for country life, wholesome values, over city and court.

Such implications direct attention to the extraordinary challenge implicit in the poem's tone. The poem's speaker is not aware of complexities, and perhaps only dimly aware, if at all, of the cost of his petition, or of its true nature; yet his very simplicity carries much of the poem's vision of grace. Christ did not come to save only those able to grasp difficult theology, complex art, with the intellect; he came for simple men aware of, and responding to, their need. If, then, as readers, we are tempted to congratulate ourselves upon our own intellectual superiority to the narrator, we have to note that it is he, in his simple quest, who is granted his suit. Our own ability to 'take the point' may run ahead of him, but this very skill, without humility, is of no effect. The poem's ease and serenity have the colour of *his* honesty; honesty which is a moral quality, single of purpose and transparent, and of a kind which notably eludes all but the simple (now in the best sense of that word) and the good. At the very least, it puts the reader back in his place if he is tempted to feel morally as well as intellectually superior – or, still worse, to imagine that the poem's intrinsic skill, and artifice, are meant as ends in themselves. This is especially salutary when we reach the poem's ending, where the language – suggesting a beautiful reversal of its literal meaning – is, so obviously, in its contrivance and strategy, a *tour-de-force*. Taken from the stand-point of the 'I', the final line is a piece of gratuitous good fortune. He arrives, more by luck than by judgement, just in time to receive the requested suit before the giver dies. But he does not need to ask : the suit is already known, and its granting, for all who seek, is the occasion of this death. Thus, 'said, and died' is the exact reversal of the theological ordering; the death is needed if the words are to be said. Moreover, the poem's triumph is to infuse into the word 'died' – the crowning desolation of Good Friday – the promise of resurrection and hope. Technically, the ease of the final line is reinforced by the metrical complexity which precedes it. In stress, the penultimate line is indeterminate. If one reads 'murderers' as three syllables, then 'there I' has to be compressed into the first (short) stress of an iambic foot, with a magnificent sense of speed and urgency; if one reads it as two syllables, 'there' comes with a heavy stress, and the last four words of the line seem long drawn out. Either way, the penultimate line plays with its stresses in a manner, for once, like Donne, and allows the conclusion an added peace in the contrast of its limpid flow.

Perhaps the poem's most interesting feature, however, and for a modern reader its most potentially disconcerting, is its imagery, rooted chiefly in money transactions and very basic capitalism. The title, 'Redemption', is an image from finance; so is 'tenant', 'rich', 'thriving', 'suit', 'afford', 'small-rented lease', 'dearly bought', 'take possession' and 'Your suit'. Again, the class images, 'rich Lord', 'manour', 'great birth' and 'great resorts' are closely related. Throughout the poem, the 'I' accepts as part of the immutable order of things the equation between greatness, and the possession of riches and comforts; and, for him, the main shock is to find this ordering wholly reversed in the event. He assumes that the 'great Lord' cannot possibly have anything in common with 'theeves and murderers', whether in their lives or in their deaths. What he discovers is that the 'great Lord' is not only a victim of 'theeves and murderers', but that he is put to death as one of them himself. Not only does this wholly confound the normal wisdom of men, and the canons of 'respectability', but it shows the Lord identified with men at their most abject and degraded point. Yet, if the Lord himself is to die as an alleged criminal, for this suit to be granted, this can only be because those whom he dies for – the whole of humanity – are criminal in fact. Christ takes on not only the true death but the true life of fallen man, and Herbert's short poem allows no evasion of this.

Here, then, is an adjustment of simple wealth and class judgements to St Paul's claim that Christianity abolishes – or, more accurately, reveals the total invalidity of – any value judgements not rooted in God. 'Lie not one to another, seeing that you have put off the old man with his deeds; and have put on the new man, which is renewed in knowledge after the image of him that created him : where there is neither Greek nor Jew, circumcision nor uncircumcision, Barbarian, Scythian, bond nor free : but Christ is all, and in all' (Colossians 3 :9–11). Clearly enough, 'Redemption' is a dramatisation of precisely this theology, with the old and new leases glossed in St Paul's words. It might even seem possible to suggest that the whole imagery is a devious, but effective, attempt to make the reader feel at home in a world of capitalist assumptions and simple class complacencies in order to shatter this framework in the end. But, though the poem includes such strategy, it does not rest in it; the secret is 'redemption', the poem's title, and its central effect. If experiences themselves are redeemable, so too are language and images drawn from experience, whatever sick parodies of both still remain in the world. The old hierarchy, where a Lord can appropriately be asked a favour, and grant it, is not mocked in the poem, though it is certainly modified. Herbert is no leveller or puritan democrat; the scandal of the Cross is not reduced (though it extends) to social terms.

We can recall usefully that St Paul did not identify 'the root of all evil' with money, but with the 'love of money', and that this, though undeniably radical, is a spiritual, not an economic, light upon sin. Again, we have to remember that the terrible corruptions of capitalism which produced the poverty and abuses of modern industrial and technological society were as unknown in Herbert's time (however much their roots might now be detected there) as they were in New Testament times. In

'Redemption', Herbert is using the language of everyday monetary transactions in the essentially homely manner of Christ himself. Christ used such imagery in many of his parables; and, in subsequent theology, 'redemption' has been one of the most normal words used to describe salvation, from its first appearances in St Luke, and St Paul.

The poem cannot then be read as an attack on capitalism, but it can, and must, be seen as an attack on 'the world'. Throughout the New Testament, the world's values of 'respectability' were challenged at every point by Christ, and not least in his own humble birth, and shameful death. The New Testament's message is not that God is undeserving of glory, and still less that he is not, in fact, glorious, but that glory is wholly different from anything usually understood in the fallen world. Perhaps the crowning subtlety of the poem is that the simple narrator, good though he is, remains blinded by a worldly scale of values, so that the full of cost of the paradox of redemption remains hidden from him right to the last. None the less, he demonstrates the quiet truth of the affirmation 'Seek, and ye shall find'; he has the essential humility of the suppliant; and the poem is a powerful reminder that the intellectual subtleties and surprises of Christianity are not the essence of salvation, even though they can, when allied to humility, greatly nourish the mind.

3 SERPENT IN EDEN: MARVELL'S 'THE PICTURE OF LITTLE T.C. IN A PROSPECT OF FLOWERS'

1 See with what simplicity
    This Nimph begins her golden daies!
    In the green Grass she loves to lie,
    And there with her fair Aspect tames
5 The Wilder flow'rs, and gives them names:
    But only with the Roses playes;
           And them does tell
    What Colour best becomes them, and what Smell.

    Who can foretel for what high cause
10 This Darling of the Gods was born!
    Yet this is She whose chaster Laws
    The wanton Love shall one day fear,
    And under her command severe,
    See his Bow broke and Ensigns torn.
15   Happy, who can
    Appease this virtuous Enemy of Man!

    O then let me in time compound,
    And parly with those conquering Eyes;
    Ere they have try'd their force to wound
20 Ere, with their glancing wheels, they drive
    In Triumph over Hearts that strive,
    And them that yield but more despise.
          Let me be laid,
    Where I may see thy Glories from some shade.

25 Mean time, whilst every verdant thing
    It self does at thy Beauty charm,
    Reform the errours of the Spring;
    Make that the Tulips may have share

>   Of sweetness, seeing they are fair;
> 30   And Roses of their thorns disarm :
>   But most procure
>   That Violets may a longer Age endure.
>
>   But O young beauty of the Woods,
>   Whom Nature courts with fruits and flow'rs,
> 35   Gather the Flow'rs, but spare the Buds;
>   Lest *Flora* angry at thy crime,
>   To kill her Infants in their prime,
>   Do quickly make th'Example Yours;
>   And, ere we see,
> 40   Nip in the blossome all our hopes and Thee.

The first two lines set the poem's tone :

>   See with what simplicity
>   This Nimph begins her golden daies!

'See', most gentle of imperatives, directs our attention straight to little T.C. and to her 'simplicity'. It is a word all the more striking for being so little insisted upon, suggesting wholeness and power. Our nearest modern equivalent is perhaps 'integration', but this defines its secret far less clearly. According to Aquinas, 'Simplicity' is a chief attribute of God, a concomitant of his unity and eternity. In men, it is not only the harmonious inner working of a consciousness, but the relationship, on which such harmony depends, between man and God.

The stanza continues with fresh and direct observation, which is also a first definition of 'simplicity' :

>   In the green Grass she loves to lie,
>   And there with her fair Aspect tames
>   The Wilder flow'rs, and gives them names

For Marvell, 'green' is always a healing colour, dissolving tensions, creating and uncreating in summer ease. Little T.C. is at home in the grass, an Eve in Paradise. She can both tame Nature and give things 'names' (a direct reference to the Creation story,

Genesis 2 : 19). As symbols of individuality, of the rights of beings
to exist as themselves, 'names' have an aura of magic about them,
the mystery of identity. (Just as it is the power of purity to give
names in Paradise, so the control of names has usually suggested
a taint of evil in our fallen world.) In the final lines of the stanza,
little T.C. can not only tame and name the flowers, but advise
them : 'tell' has total and beautiful authority :

> But only with the Roses playes;
>   And them does tell
> What Colour best becomes them, and what Smell.

There is no taint of power where love is perfect; yet all too soon,
the little girl's triumph will fade. Already, there are ironic undercurrents, so unobtrusive that one might miss them, lurking like
the serpent among flowers. 'Golden' hints at the world of Art in
its opposition to Nature, notably through association with that
seldom unambiguous word, 'Nimph'. The gentle wit of 'Wilder
Flow'rs' seems to take little T.C. as much as the roses as the
subject of its comparison, setting her apart from the other flowers.
Indeed, doesn't little T.C. appear a conscious artist as she strives,
like any child, to bring order out of chaos? – 'tames', 'Wilder',
'only', 'tell' are words of struggle and choice. Perhaps she is even
aware of the impact of her beauty, her 'fair Aspect', and
deliberately uses it as an instrument? (In his 'To a Young
Beauty', W. B. Yeats addresses the 'Young Beauty' as 'Dear
fellow-artist'.)

During the sixteenth and seventeenth centuries, many artists
believed that Art can move towards, as well as away from,
'reality',* yet unresolved tensions haunt the gardens, the golden
worlds and Edens of Art. When does 'native majesty' turn into
pride, cultivation into tyranny? When does freedom tip over into
rebellion and fall? In play, little T.C. risks exceeding the
prerogative of innocence, overriding the original designs of

---

* e.g. Sidney's 'Nature delivers only a brazen world, not a golden',
in *Defence of Poesie*.

Nature with designs of her own. And inescapably, the 'Roses' yoke together divine and erotic; the flower of love, above all, has its thorns.

Yet, if such undercurrents spell present ambiguity and future danger, the child's essential innocence is not in doubt. Her power, though she knows, and uses it, remains untainted; the poet's response witnesses – through its own ironies – to *this*. Only in the next two stanzas does the poem develop towards its larger pattern, starting with a journey into conjecture, and into time :

> Who can foretel for what high cause
> This Darling of the Gods was born !

The poet conjectures a 'high cause' for this 'Darling of the Gods', for surely the gods do not jest? But 'Who can foretel . . .' hints a doubt; and if on first reading the hint is too gentle to pause on, we may see it later as a turning point. Should the question be taken as rhetorical, an assertion of insight; or is it the shadow cast back on 'Glories' from a fallen world? We might see the 'high cause' as certain, but too splendid to visualise; we might find our stress falling on 'can'. The end of innocence is wrapped in mystery, this much is certain; and adult knowledge is all of paradise lost. T.C. may remain chaste, she may keep her virgin purity, but the quality of her love will change. This innocence, which enables the poet to parley with her eyes in the garden, is doomed to pass; the enchanted moment of the child's power must be caught 'in time'.

So the poet passes to the future and Eros enters the poem, with imagery of battle :

> Yet this is She whose chaster Laws
> The wanton Love shall one day fear,
> And under her command severe,
> See his Bow broke and Ensigns torn.
> Happy, who can
> Appease this virtuous Enemy of Man !

Little T.C.'s future 'command severe' of the 'wanton Love', and

her victory over him, at once parallel her authority over the roses
in the first stanza and fulfil the omens. She may defeat Eros, and
be a 'virtuous Enemy of Man', but she will not escape the pride of
conquest. The emphatic 'chaster' suggests a degree of unnatural-
ness, recalling the ambiguity which surrounds most of the great
chaste heroines of literature, Shakespeare's Isabella, the Lady in
Comus, Richardson's Clarissa. Do we understand by 'chaster'
that she will be 'chaster' than the 'Laws' of Eros; or that she will
be 'chaster' than any woman can, without severity, be? Whatever
her wishes, the chaste Lady triumphs over striving hearts, despises
the defeated, rejoices in victory; she cannot escape the puzzles of
love. Whether from excess of virtue or defects of pride, she cannot
evade enmity : the freedom of childhood is lost. And, such is man's
fallen lot, the adult T.C. will be wounding and alien even to her
admirers, in ravages inseparable from this conquest of love.

These ambiguities gain substance throughout the third stanza,
but their future victim – or his representative – enjoys a 'parly'
while time allows :

> O then let me in time compound,
> And parly with those conquering Eyes;
> Ere they have try'd their force to wound,
> Ere, with their glancing wheels, they drive
> In Triumph over Hearts that strive,
> And them that yield but more despise.
>   Let me be laid,
> Where I may see thy Glories from some shade.

And here, the imagery projects irony back on to the watching
poet; can he be wholly 'laid' aside as spectator, if he engages in
'parly'; can delight in beauty ever evade the sufferings of love?
'Conquering', 'wound', 'drive', 'despise' all belong to the future,
but 'compound', 'parly' and, inescapably, 'glancing' are here and
now. The 'parly' will be tender, playful, gently nostalgic for the
man and richly rewarding, but where and how 'in time' does it
really exist? The man knows the child's danger and suffers this
knowledge; on his side, 'in time' is not what it is for the child.

Naturally a man respects and delights in childish innocence, but adult perspectives transfuse the 'Glories' and infuse the 'Shade'. Indeed, a battle of kinds already exists, though the child may not know it; or – at least – she may not know the price of imposing, as princess, on a prince. In spite of the apparent insistence, through that accented and repeated 'Ere', that the soiling of little T.C.'s innocence is still in the future, her eyes are already 'conquering' in the shade. The poet is actually involved with her in a love battle, no less real for the innocence on his part as well as on hers. Isn't there an implication that the initiative is as much with the child as with the poet, a trial of her powers before their nature is known? Could there be a shade of falsehood on the child's side, or of exploitation on the poet's? If we catch a suggestion that innocence is precisely an attraction to the attentions that will destroy it, the poem's complexity takes a further turn.

The fourth stanza explores the actual moment of enchantment in the garden; and we do not need to invoke 'To his Coy Mistress' to assert that as much as any romantic, Marvell knew that certain intensities are in time, and for time, and for a short time only :

> Mean time, whilst every verdant thing
> It self does at thy Beauty charm,
> Reform the errours of the Spring;
> Make that the Tulips may have share
> Of sweetness, seeing they are fair;
> And Roses of their thorns disarm :
> But most procure
> That Violets may a longer Age endure.

Little T.C. here is a power of life. She is the microcosm healing and replenishing the macrocosm – a theme sufficiently familiar in metaphysical verse for the praise of a mistress, but turned now to archetypal celebration of innocence.

Yet here, in the charmed moment itself, is danger. In the gentle play of the flower symbols, we are made just to feel the presence of time. The roses have thorns; the violets are too short-lived.

Perhaps childhood really has the power which it seems to have at this moment. Perhaps it can disarm the flower of love perpetually; perhaps it can confer, on the flower of innocence, eternal spring. Yet recognition of doubt is an ironic undercurrent, in these dreamlike and ethereal imperatives addressed to the child. And the doubt is more than doubt : whatever the poet wishes, he knows the truth. The tone of the last two lines is already elegiac, a lament for violets which the little girl will not, after all, transplant out of time.

So the poet turns to address the child with a new immediacy; and this is a warning of danger and death :

> But O young beauty of the Woods,
> Whom Nature courts with fruits and flow'rs,
> Gather the Flow'rs, but spare the Buds;
> Lest *Flora* angry at thy crime,
> To kill her Infants in their prime,
> Do quickly make th'Example Yours;
>   And, ere we see,
> Nip in the blossome all our hopes and Thee.

Marvell is not resolving but exploring the tensions which become explicit, with the sudden introduction of sin. There are taboos to be observed, sanctities to be respected; there is a fitness, however stern, between acts and ends. By a *tour-de-force*, the poet transfers, to little T.C. in her innocence, responsibility for this danger that she cannot possibly understand. Nature is courting her, Nature is kindly, Nature is slave to her will as it once was to Eve's. If Flora does strike, there must be a false move first from the little girl's side; the harmony must be broken from there. But once the harmony *is* broken, vengeance comes 'quickly'; Nature will herself 'kill', forestalling little T.C.'s own future ruthlessness in courtship, in anger at the violation of an innocence still almost intact.

But how are inevitabilities so luminously foreseen to be avoided; how can innocence hope to evade its fall? In this immediate context, how can an innocent child at play even begin to perceive how she might avoid the common lot of man, the twin ways of experience and death? The poet's linking of little T.C.'s thoughtless gathering of buds with her own just death strikes one, at first, as almost superstitious. He seems to be dealing in vague fears and taboos, irrational speculations, beyond any logical defence. But he penetrates much deeper than superstition, adding to the traditional Jewish and Christian beliefs, which pervade the imagery of Eden, something more Greek, more Sophoclean in mood. There are cosmic rules and patterns not to be transgressed, moral laws as binding as gravitation, and as little to be appealed against. Ignorance can be no excuse: and if a wrong step is made, the gods will send punishment, out of all seeming proportion to the offence. One might understand these intimations as a kind of dark justice, a vindication of order just sensed to be right.

But it is a justice too inhuman to ease anguish, and too far outside human control for protest to reach. 'Even the gods bow to Necessity'; surely the wisdom of the Greeks must be invoked? Yet 'kill' and 'quickly' are shocking words, and clearly intentionally so, in the speed and urgency they acquire at the poem's close. 'Little T.C.' ends with the finality of death, to balance 'simplicity', reflecting death back on the glory that seemed so assured.

Up to this point, we have found our responses complementary, but now they diverge. So two endings are needed, differing in emphasis, though not amounting, perhaps, to a total divide.
A.E.D.: In Marvell's last stanza, the justice of the little girl's danger amounts to a sense of inevitability so far beyond the reach of reform, or of correction, that it seems beyond the effective reach of compassion as well. There is no human attitude to it possible except acceptance, since life is received, and must be honoured, on these terms.

But to put the matter in this manner may seem despairing, or merely stoical, and this is not the impression the poem finally makes. It is Marvell's Christianity – the Eden in his tone and diction as well as in his imagery – which recaptures such sombre insights for the green world. The poem holds in tension two poles of awareness : 'innocence', with its splendid simplicity (and with much Christian hope inalienably fused with this), and 'experience', with its tragic perspective of death. Marvell's gentle irony controls the poem – an irony grave and compassionate, for all its awareness of the limits of compassion; far removed from iconoclasm; too deeply religious to be called, in any social sense, 'urbane'. Irony does not destroy one pole at the expense of the other. Innocence is real, and so is experience; neither cancels the other out. But while experience knows the fragility of innocence, innocence cannot 'know' experience at all. Yet of the two, innocence is ultimately the more powerful : it impresses with the power to love, direct, replenish without taint. If it 'wins', this will not be in the world of time and mortality; but experience can salute it, however enigmatically, 'in time'. The poem is set in the tragic world of experience, but reaches in hope, beyond the stealing shadows of change.

J.L.: I am sure you are right to point to this note in the poem, and I would underline how the poem's total effect is, and (to be honest) must be achieved through a recognition of the anguish of fallen man (an anguish which lies at the centre of any deep religious feeling) rather than through a drowning or denial of such recognition in ironic negations.

But for me, there is still a residual fear that will not allow so confident a resolution as you imply. In the fourth stanza, we agreed that little T.C. has not the power that she seems to have, and that the poet knows this; but my own stress, even there, would return to the hint of some present taint. Little T.C. is already the artist glimpsed in the first stanza; there are ironic potentials in 'Reform', 'Make', 'disarm' and, surely, 'procure'. In the final stanza, I would lay greater stress on the irony of 'courts', which links the behaviour of Flora not only with that future capriciousness towards her suitors foreseen for an adult T.C., but even with the young child's 'parly' with the poet in the garden. The suddenness of 'kill', 'quickly', 'ere we see' and 'Nip in the blossome' is *too* shocking, and there is mockery as well as poignancy in the way they balance the 'glory' of the poem's opening lines.

Moreover, the invariable fitness between acts and ends, which we both find evident in all the poem's parallels, and which is made explicit in the final stanza (particularly in the literal hopelessness of the last line), does not seem to me easily reconciled to Christian belief. I agree that the tone reaches beyond social urbanity, and is profoundly religious, but the curious mingling of energy with ease, charm with impersonality, appears almost Olympian.

And just as little T.C.'s 'simplicity' may be more complex – more tainted, and ultimately impossible – than appears on the surface, so the poem's 'simplicity' is tainted as well. It never, to my mind, completely resolves its tensions, or finds a still centre, a refuge in the 'Shade'. In Marvell's luxurious and depressing Paradise, the serpent has triumphed even before the fall.

O much deceivèd, much failing, hapless Eve,
Of thy presumed return! Event perverse!
Thou never from that hour in Paradise
Found'st either sweet repast, or sound repose;
Such ambush hid among sweet flowers and shades
Waited with hellish rancour imminent
To intercept thy way, or send thee back
Despoiled of innocence, of faith, of bliss.
                                    (*Paradise Lost*, ix 404–11)

Eve has had her lovers' quarrel with Adam, that marvellous last
dialogue of innocence when Adam has encountered everything
that is feminine and much, if Tillyard is right, that is fallen,
before the Fall.* Now she goes off on her own to be tempted.

In many ways it is right that she should. The younger Milton,
as we know, could not 'praise a fugitive and cloistered virtue,
unexercised and unbreathed, that never sallies out and sees her
adversary, but slinks out of the race, where that immortal garland
is to be run for, not without dust and heat' (*Areopagitica*, 1644).
This militant optimism had found its apotheosis in *Comus*
(1634), where the Lady's virtue held against all assaults and
turned back the foe.

By the 1660s Milton was battered by life and familiar with
suffering, but his faith in freedom remained intact. In *Paradise
Lost* Eve's temptation is permitted both by God, who has created
her perfect and given her liberty ('Sufficient to have stood,
though free to fall', iii 99), and by Adam, who has received her
from God in trust. In Book ix Adam treats Eve as a free being
precisely in the manner of God's dealings with himself. He tries to

* E. M. W. Tillyard, *Studies in Milton* (1951).

dissuade her with lucid arguments, rational warnings, loving tenderness, but he does not constrain her against her will. In this he is surely right and acting wisely, even though Waldock* has hinted that his failure to restrain Eve forcibly may be the root cause of the Fall. The whole justification of God's ways to man turns on this issue, since the reality of freedom alone makes sense of exile and death. We have always to compare God's dealings with his creatures as they are actually imaged in the poem with the various charges evolved against him in the rhetoric of Hell. Is he indeed malign, tyrannical or inept, as is frequently asserted; is his omnipotence really cast in doubt by the fact of sin?

Milton's earliest plans for *Paradise Lost* (*circa* 1640) envisaged a tragic drama, and Alastair Fowler suggests in the Introduction to his recent edition of the poem that we 'should even, perhaps, consider it a tragical epic rather than a pure epic'.† This notion of a 'tragical epic' is a useful corrective to over-rigid *genre* criticism, but is not without dangers of its own. If we accept it, we should remember also that *Paradise Lost* is a specifically Christian epic, and tragic precisely in the manner and to the degree inherent in its theme. Milton's task is not now to sing the power of Virtue, as it had been in *Comus*, but to account for man's exile from Paradise in a mortal world. While there can be no evading the ironies – so close to tragedy – in this material there should be no overlooking the counterbalance of Christian Hope. All tragedy gravitates perhaps towards either hope or despair in its final suggestions, but only Christian tragedy is actually transformed by the assertion of hope. There is the hope of life after death, which most tragedy does not offer; more strikingly, there is the hope invested in a God who takes evil and turns it to good. So perhaps Christian 'tragedy' is more properly and accurately described as 'divine comedy', since it differs sufficiently from other tragedy in its resolution to need its own name.

* A. J. A. Waldock, *'Paradise Lost' and its Critics* (1947).
† Longman Annotated English Poets series (1968).

For present purposes 'divine comedy' points usefully, as a label, to that aspect of the poem's Christianity which most controls its ironic effects. It is a mark of *Paradise Lost* that it echoes throughout with double or even treble ironies, deriving from the presence in time of realities located outside. These 'realities' brood over every episode in Heaven, Hell or Paradise, operating irrespective of the 'before', 'after' or 'now' of the Fall. They can usefully be called 'original perfection', 'perfection lost', and 'perfection regained' – the triple perspectives haunting both angels and men. Since all three are perpetually present in God's consciousness, they are perpetually present in Milton's poetry from first to last. It follows also that they are perpetually present for Milton's readers, as the interplay of loss and hope, despair and joy in their lives. We read the poem not in alienation from its theme but through direct involvement, testing the fall and redemption of Adam in ourselves. If Milton's resonances chime in our hearts we can scarcely deny them; if we enact fall, judgement and redemption in our actual experience of reading, we go unusually far towards being convinced. Hence the key importance of Milton's relationship with his readers, which most modern critics fully acknowledge and stress. Stanley Fish has discerned Milton's formal 'intentions' in this area; Frank Kermode has testified to Milton's achieved and authentic effects.*

In what follows, it will be demonstrated that the poem witnesses to itself not only formally, as all art does, through beauty and structure, but with an added dimension implicit in its theme. 'Divine comedy' is a fluidity of overtone and suggestiveness, somewhere beyond tragedy, belonging to the simultaneous awareness of Paradise, Fall, Incarnation, Cross, Empty Tomb.

First then (with the lines quoted above in mind), we might take a hint from Fish, Kermode, and Milton's other recent critics, and try to catch the precise effect. '. . . much deceived' (we read of

* Stanley Fish, *Surprised by Sin: The Reader in 'Paradise Lost'* (1967); Frank Kermode, 'Adam Unparadised', in *The Living Milton: Essays by Various Hands*, ed. Frank Kermode (1960).

Eve); yes, but by whom? And when? How can we take our moral
bearings, or our bearings in time? Eve is not yet 'much deceived'
by Satan – who has indeed infected her dreams (IV 799–809),
but has not yet confused her waking judgement or her will
(V 28–128). And she is not yet 'much deceived' in the time-scale
of human experience (except perhaps in over-confidence?),
though in eternity, all is foreknown and foretold. Perhaps 'much
deceived' carries chiefly the sad foreknowledge of the poet,
lamenting from his own knowledge of good-through-evil as a son
of Eve? Perhaps it carries that general burden of bewildered
compassion, with which any tragic reversals of fortune may be
viewed.

The next phrase 'much failing' adds further ambiguities, since
'failing' is the word both of sin and of mortality. There is active
failing – failing God, failing oneself, failing (and falling from)
reality – but also passive failing : failing health, failing flesh; the
journey to death. And with 'hapless' we come to the possibility of
judgement : who is responsible, at this point in time? Is Eve
unlucky and unhappy, a victim of accident? Is she 'helpless'
even? – the resonance half pushes us towards these clearly false
views. Some readers blame God, some Satan, some Eve chiefly,
some even Adam; and these seeming ambiguities ('seeming'
because they are Satanic in origin) gather like clouds of the coming
storm. So 'presumed return' moves us further into the mystery :
'presumed' in the sense of 'expected' (and for readers expecting
no such thing, this is pure dramatic irony), but 'presumptuous'
hovers in the background as well. We have already seen the
possibility of over-reaching, suggested in that shade (so fatal!)
of feminine arrogance in Eve. But the poem is full of potentially
fallen attitudes in men and angels before they have fallen, as if to
suggest that some temptation to independence from God – to
nonsense – may be inseparable from freedom itself.

'Event perverse' : we come with this to the pivotal phrase of
the sentence, and again 'Event' is a floating word, raising more
possibilities than strict syntax permits. At first (seemingly) it
could refer either to this moment of parting (with 'perverse' a

direct judgement against Eve, or even arguably against Adam),
or it could refer to the fated outcome of the parting, the fall which
we know we are shortly to see. But as the structure unfolds, we
see rather that 'Event' is in fact the thing that did *not* happen,
the event that Eve has been anticipating just one moment before,
'To be returned by noon amid the bower,/And all things in best
order to invite/Noontide repast, or afternoon's repose'. So
'perverse' comes into its full root meaning of 'turned aside': *this*
is the event destined never – or not yet, for us as readers even –
to come about. It is the outcome of Eve's removal of herself, all
unknowingly but for ever, from the wished-for, the expected, the
taken-for-granted freedom of paradise. But 'perverse' must also
suggest – as it normally does – at least some degree of censure,
transferring itself (inevitably?) from the 'event' that never
happened to the act of Eve's which permanently stands in its way.
Certainly the poetic suggestions are all of freedom: Eve is to be
the responsible agent in this last act of pure human freedom, this
original perversity which will leave its permanent witness –
including empathy with Eve? – in ourselves.

So the poet continues his haunting lament, blaming now (as
surely a victim must blame?) the Enemy, who is already moving,
intent and powerful, towards his 'purposed prey'. It is natural
that a son of Eve should respond to her, and important that
Milton's response is closer to tragic pity than to hate. Nothing
could better suggest both the gravity of the sin, with its sequel in
permanent exile, yet also the survival of some virtue – much
virtue even – in man's fallen seed. 'Thou never from that hour in
Paradise' . . . this searing 'never' of loss echoes, but deepens, the
resonant 'No more . . .' at the start of Book ix. 'Such ambush
hid': and we are reminded again of secrecy, enmity, inner
torment – all those evils which Eve has been told about and
warned against, but which only initiation can make fully real for
her.

At this moment, the poetry glides, with the serpent, towards its
inevitable moment, which we have always known must come:

> For now, and since first break of dawn the fiend,
> Mere serpent in appearance, forth was come . . . (412–13)

'For now . . .'. First in Book II the idea was heard from
Beelzebub, 'devilish counsel, first devised/By Satan, and in part
proposed' (345–85). Then in Book III it was foretold by God,
as a moment in all eternity, 'so will fall/He and his faith-
less progeny' (80–96). It has been the chief heroic stage for the
testing of courage, first when Satan offers to attempt the hazardous
enterprise of destroying man and all Hell falls silent (II 430–66),
then when Christ offers to redeem man, as all Heaven waits (III
227–65). This moment was a datum in God's consciousness at
the time of creation, and it is the great and central paradox of the
Fortunate Fall. It is the point also on which the poem's central
and greatest polarity hinges. In Satan, we have the determination
to take good and turn it always to evil, 'Evil be thou my good'
(IV 110), and opposed to this, the divine power whose operation
is in the end the poem's triumph and truth :

> O goodness infinite, goodness immense!
> That all this good of evil shall produce,
> And evil turn to good; more wonderful
> Than that which by creation first brought forth
> Light out of darkness! (XII 469–73)

But in poetic terms, too, this moment is central, since everything depends upon the resonances working for, and in, us as we
read. *Are* we as mortals mere cosmic accidents, whose lives have
no meaning; or are we indeed betrayed and exiled sons of God? It
is Milton's chief distinction as a poet – and a distinction crucial
to the justification of God, which is his avowed purpose – that
he can make us respond not only to the truths of evil (a common
gift among writers) but also, and perhaps even more powerfully,
to the truths of good. The poem does not ask (indeed it discour-
ages) our literal belief in its images, whether of Heaven, Hell or
Paradise, but it does ask, and need, our recognition of spiritual

truths. And in this matter Milton habitually moves us at some level of consciousness deeper than reason, as in those moments when we remember childhood, experience sudden shafts of self-knowledge, peer into the dark backward and abysm of time. 'For now, and since first break of dawn the fiend . . .'. Yes, here it is : Evil, moving to confront the mighty opposite : not equal with God; not the eventual winner; but always there. Temporally, 'always there' for man, because the war in Heaven has been prior (as far as time counts) to the creation of Earth. But 'always there' too in our hearts and consciousnesses, at the place where we grasp our identity as men. Though God did not create evil, he created freedom; and perhaps the seeds of evil exist, perhaps they *are,* in freedom, by the nature of things ?

Critics such as Tillyard have worried away, interestingly, at the problem of how perfect beings can ever have come to have fallen into evil; and perhaps none of us can resist the metaphysical attempt. We know some problems elude us – did the universe have a beginning in time and space, or did it have no beginning ? – and it is hard to accept the limits which are set for human intellect (according to Raphael, they were set even for unfallen man, VIII 1–216). On the other hand, we know that we can and indeed normally do accept apparent contradictions when both sides are vividly present in universal human experience. 'The good that I would I do not,' said St Paul, 'the evil that I would not, that I do.' In just this manner, Milton sets about undercutting mere arguments, at moments when these would only confuse us, with images to which we cannot fail to respond. We recognise Satan's great rhetoric readily enough, with its denial of goodness; but we recognise equally – unless we are ourselves lost in evil – the vision which Satan himself, now, can never see. Milton will show us humanity holier, grander, more capable of joy than we normally dream of, and make us recognise realities to 'believe in' Eden than it is to believe in the serpent; yet in the in *these* images, with power in our souls. Naturally it is harder ruins of ourselves and our fellows have we never seen traces of Paradise, of the first Adam and Eve? Certainly there is something

unusually compelling to the imagination, in this fated arrival of
the serpent among the flowers :

> And on his quest, where likeliest he might find
> The only two of mankind, but in them
> The whole included race, his purposed prey.
> In bower and field he sought, where any tuft
> Of grove or garden-plot more pleasant lay,
> Their tendance or plantation for delight,
> By fountain or by shady rivulet
> He sought them both, but wished his hap might find
> Eve separate, he wished, but not with hope
> Of what so seldom chanced, when to his wish,
> Beyond his hope, Eve separate he spies. (IX 414–24)

Critics have worried, naturally enough, about how God lets this
happen. The epic apparatus and the nature of the sustained
allegory of war in Heaven undeniably make Gabriel, in particular, look less efficient as a guardian angel than one could wish.
But in fact it is made clear that the wolf has been allowed to
leap into the sheepfold by God's 'high sufferance' because freedom never is or will be violated from God's side. As the poetry
here beautifully mimes the serpent's progress, we have to remain
especially on our guard. It can seem – but subtly from Satan's
viewpoint – that a kind of dark providence is helping the work of
evil, or at least a devil's luck uncannily like the answer to
unoffered prayer. The effect is to underline, however, the inevitability of this encounter. By whatever means it has come about,
wherever in space or whenever in time, this moment manifestly
had to be. Among the poem's many extreme ironies is the fact
that at least once Satan – closely followed by most of the critics
who throw in their lot with him – actually blames God for letting
him get out of Hell to perform his task (IV 897–9). But God
never has been the arbitrary tyrant of Satan's rhetoric; Hell
never has been a maximum-security prison block. In Book III
(80 ff.) when God himself notes of Satan that 'no bounds/

Prescribed, nor bars of hell, nor all the chains/Heaped on him there, nor yet the main abyss/Wide interrupt can hold', he is neither confessing to inefficiency, nor being aloofly sardonic, but drawing attention to the uncancelled gift of freedom in his world. The poem takes care from the start to work through images which interact with, but in so sense constrain, its rational frame. At first Hell is flame and chains, and perpetual imprisonment; then it is a great debating chamber; then it is a gorgeous throne, where Satan sits exalted and adored. At times it is mediated through images of compulsive lust or of total vanity, with their torments that can be neither satisfied nor quenched. But Milton has always made clear that Hell exists in the mind and consciousness, and that it is no more to be identified with any one set of images than it is to be escaped by any mere shift of location in time or space. As we shortly see in Book ix, Satan carries Hell with him, though in mid-Heaven; potentially, any free being carries it in himself. The fact is that Hell is made by fallen angels and by fallen men after them; God merely permits it as an extension of freedom itself. The doors are locked from inside, not from outside; but they are indeed locked beyond any escape from within. The attendant irony is that because Hell is not created by God it is all negation and nonsense; but negation and nonsense with frightening power over *us*. So Hell is free to appear in Paradise, and at the appointed moment will appear there; it will come with its curious power of seeming wholly at home.

This brings us to another of the poem's two major polarities, which underlie its many shifts of imagery and tone. Created beings can respond to creation in numerous and varied ways locally, but in one of two ways only at the ground of response. Either they can celebrate and delight in it, in love and freedom; or they can reject and oppose it, in hatred and rage. The difficulty is that once the latter choice has been made it excludes the former, since the power to celebrate and to delight in celebration is then lost. Mammon's famous speech is, of course, the *locus classicus* (ii 237–57), but this theme haunts the poem from beginning to end. Milton is the last poet to imply that Heaven

or Hell are *merely* subjective, or to imply that they can in any
manner exist on the same plane. Heaven is made by God, and is
filled by him; Hell is the experience of whatever consciousness
is in exile from God. It follows that while Heaven and Hell are
eternally separate, they are eternally free to impinge on one
another, since the saved and the damned co-exist. The vision of
reality operative in each is of course different, with 'freedom',
'nature' and all other concepts pulled to opposite poles. We test
the realities only by looking beyond definitions to experiences:
are there fruits of peace and love, or of bitter despair? In this
aspect the moment in the garden again seems fated; Paradise
cannot know its fullest potential until the serpent appears.

The next section moves us to Milton's especially poignant vision
of Eve among the flowers, tending her Paradise for the last time:

> Veiled in a cloud of fragrance, where she stood,
> Half spied, so thick the roses bushing round
> About her glowed, oft stooping to support
> Each flower of slender stalk, whose head though gay
> Carnation, purple, azure, or specked with gold,
> Hung drooping unsustained, them she upstays
> Gently with myrtle band, mindless the while
> Her self, though fairest unsupported flower,
> From her best prop so far, and storm so nigh. (IX 425–33)

The phrase 'hung drooping unsustained' yokes together Eve's
concern for the flowers and her own predicament; does her own
tender care not deserve better than this? But if we ask again
whether it is God's fault, or Adam's, or Eve's that she is
'unsustained' at this moment, we divert ourselves from the text.
The rational answer of course is that it is Eve's fault; but Milton
is now concerned with the infinite pity of the fact. If Eve *is*
vulnerable (and this is not self-evident), perhaps this is partly
because she takes her own tender concern for the flowers more
for granted than she should? '. . . mindless the while/Her self'
beautifully fuses the supreme virtue of forgetting self in the service

of beauty with the supreme danger of being off guard. As Satan approaches, he is still exotic and majestic, 'not less than Archangel ruined' even now. He has indeed become a brute by his own choice and for his own bad ends, and this is ironic enough for one who aspired to be 'as a god'. But he comes freely, and in the innate beauty of the original serpent; he is not yet constrained to the brute form in punishment as he will be later (and Book x 504–47 is, even in this poem, one of the most astonishing images of Hell).

> Nearer he drew, and many a walk traversed
> Of stateliest covert, cedar, pine or palm,
> Then voluble and bold, now hid, now seen
> Among thick-woven arborets and flowers
> Embroidered on each bank, the hand of Eve :
> Spot more delicious than those gardens feigned
> Or of revived Adonis, or renowned
> Alcinous, host of old Laertes' son,
> Or that, not mystic, where the sapient king
> Held dalliance with his fair Egyptian spouse.
> Much he the place admired, the person more.
> As one who long in populous city pent,
> Where houses thick and sewers annoy the air,
> Forth issuing on a summer's morn to breathe
> Among the pleasant villages and farms
> Adjoined, from each thing met conceives delight,
> The smell of grain, or tedded grass, or kine,
> Or dairy, each rural sight, each rural sound;
> If chance with nymph-like step fair virgin pass,
> What pleasing seemed, for her now pleases more,
> She most, and in her look sums all delight.
> Such pleasure took the serpent to behold
> This flowery plat, the sweet recess of Eve
> Thus early, thus alone; her heavenly form
> Angelic, but more soft, and feminine,
> Her graceful innocence, her every air

Of gesture or least action overawed
His malice, and with rapine sweet bereaved
His fierceness of the fierce intent it brought :
That space the evil one abstracted stood
From his own evil, and for the time remained
Stupidly good, of enmity disarmed,
Of guile, of hate, of envy, of revenge;
But the hot hell that always in him burns,
Though in mid heaven, soon ended his delight,
And tortures him now more, the more he sees
Of pleasure not for him ordained . . . (IX 434–70)

And so we are returned to Satan, in these further poetic inversions
so deceptively simple that we can accustom ourselves to them
almost as readily as Eve accustoms herself, now, to a talking
worm. Already the serpent seems almost at home in Paradise, as
if the territory he hopes to win by desecration is already his. And
he admires it, at this moment, as it is with himself excluded : this
is one of those classic moments when evil has to pay its tribute
to good. So Iago has said of Cassio, 'He has a daily beauty in
his life/That makes me ugly' : he cannot deny the fact, though it
torments him. This is the factor in human experience – so deadly
for those who would see good as illusion and Paradise as fiction –
to which T. S. Eliot gave memorable utterance in a single line :
'The darkness declares the glory of light' (from the final chorus of
Murder in the Cathedral). Nowhere in our human exile perhaps
is there any insight more hopeful than this one, the warding off
of despair with the stuff of despair. But in *Paradise Lost,* at this
moment when evil stands lost for a moment in homage to goodness, the context gives to the hopefulness a further twist. Though
the glory of light impinges on its enemy, for this one telling
moment, it is now to be extinguished – at least in time – and death
ushered in.

The fuller insight into Satan is approached by way of the
simile, which is so reminiscent of a lot of later 'nature' poetry in
its theme of escape to the country from urban pollution that we

might overlook its novelty and subtlety in the context here. The situation depicted in the simile is by definition post-lapsarian, belonging to a world already despoiled. Satan's role for the moment is that of a simple peasant escaping from normal squalor into rural beauty, and enjoying the sight of a 'virgin' nymph as supreme delight. The simple image might remind us both that such nymphs are seldom symbols of innocence but, equally, that even seducers sometimes regret their success. In this setting, the description of Eve's 'heavenly form/Angelic' is beautifully poised between its inherent truth, as innocent and delighted appraisal, and its danger, as exaggeration and excess. Adam has already been warned by Raphael that true celebration can tip into idolatry, in the long passage (VIII 452 ff.) which is a key to Book IX. The notion 'Angelic' instantly shapes itself in Satan's mind towards the rhetoric of the coming temptation, but it is a genuine tribute while the moment lasts. The moment itself however transforms to Satan's sense of aberration; for him, it is a passing weakness, 'Stupidly good'. So the inverted tribute validates beauty at some level sensed by ouselves, as we read it, but it in no way eases Satan's evil – indeed the reverse. 'But the hot hell that always in him burns/Though in mid heaven, soon ended his delight,/And tortures him now more, the more he sees/ Of pleasure not for him ordained.' Since Satan's choice 'Evil be thou my good' has been granted, Paradise must after all torment him to the precise degree that he really sees it as it is.

Not the least of Milton's triumphs is his continual reminder that though God is omnipotent, the divine task of taking evil and bringing good from it is far harder than the satanic task of taking and despoiling good. To create (we are told) is greater than to destroy (VII 606–7): and certainly to re-create Paradise, as Christ will do later, is a more costly act than Satan's, in destroying it now ('So dearly to redeem what hellish hate/So easily destroyed' III 300–1). It is costly in a manner that Satan moreover can no longer conceive : which is no doubt why his rhetoric comes so very close to convincing himself. But as readers we are invited to see that, if freedom is real, love must be active, a continual fight to make its own nature prevail. This no doubt is the inner logic of the heroic images of war, even in Heaven (however incongruous, given God's love and omnipotence, these may sometimes seem). The suggestion is that there is energy, strife even, in the creation of freedom, just as there is energy and strife in remaining free.

The splendour of this particular poem is enhanced by its assertion of hedonism : Milton justifies the ways of God not by intellectual argument only but by celebrating all modes of happiness and delight. *Paradise Lost* is nothing if it is not a poem of love; and love is nothing in the poem if it is not a justification of creation in all of its parts. Books IV, V and VIII (in particular) have affirmed that one of God's supreme gifts to men is sexual happiness, surpassed in splendour only by the total mingling in love of the incorporeal angels themselves. The Fall disorders man's whole being, body, mind and spirit, but no images of its effect are more striking than those which depict the spoilation of sex. First, and obviously, there is the contrast between mutual love before the Fall, rooted in homage and ordered by ritual (IV 736–75), and compulsive eroticism after the Fall, culminating in shame and in mutual distaste (IX 1011–98). There is an explicit recognition that lust can be more intoxicating, in the act, than ordered sensuality, but also that it can never be the servant of dignity and love (e.g. 'Our wonted ornaments now soiled and stained,/And in our faces evident the signs/Of foul concupiscence' IX 1076–8). But Milton's clear intention is less to denounce the lustful than to celebrate the voluptuous, and to remind that the total union of love and sexuality still exists as a possibility, however difficult and elusive, for fallen man.

A further insight, less explicit but no less powerful, is the image of sexual pleasure arousing envy and hatred in those who are excluded from it, as a deeper, and spiritual, evil arising from sin. In one remarkable passage Adam has intuited that his sexual pleasure with Eve might be especially enraging to Satan (IX 261–4); and this is already known to us from Satan's famous outburst in Book IV 505–6 :

> Sight hateful, sight tormenting ! Thus these two
> Imparadised in one another's arms

Satan's essence is captured, again, in the powerful phrase in our present passage, 'And tortures him now more, the more he sees/ Of pleasure not for him ordained'. *This* is the kind of envy which will produce not only the sickness of sexual excess as an end in itself, as one response to it, but still worse excesses of malice and persecution from the sexually deprived. Satan takes on, as Kermode has noted, something of the character of a tormented voyeur, and his mentality is recognisably that which produces hatred of the attractive by the unattractive, of the young by the old, of the beautiful by the ugly, of the accepted by the rejected. It produces men like Angelo in *Measure For Measure,* the stoners of adulterers and of any who seem fair game to them. Milton sees, no doubt, that among the fallen hatred of sex itself will become more 'respectable' than its celebration, in that alienation from God leads naturally to dislike of his gifts.

But in Satan's approach to Eve, Milton manages to suggest also the centre of fallen relationship, with egocentric need or vanity replacing homage to people and things. It is no accident that the lovely word 'gratulating' which Adam has applied to Nature's delight in the first act of sexual love (vm 514) is used now, in darker parody, of Satan :

> then soon
> Fierce hate he recollects, and all his thoughts
> Of mischief, gratulating, thus excites (ix 470–2)

The whole temptation after this is in one aspect a dark seduction, as Fowler continually notes when commenting, in his edition, on the images of Book ix. Eve is literally to be seduced from Adam through the doubly inappropriate advances of a fallen angel disguised as a talking beast. Physically and powerfully phallic suggestions co-exist with the intellectual ones (e.g. 'so varied he, and of his tortuous train/Curled many a wanton wreath in sight of Eve,/To lure her eye' ix 516–18). Eve, moreover, is to be

seduced away from happiness and peace by a mixture of lies and
flattery prepared by the one creature in creation most experienced
in the desolation of Hell. Possibly the crowning irony, as so often
with Satan, is that he half deceives himself at such moments – an
archetypal seducer in this, as in all other ways. From the 'bondage'
of subjection to Adam and to reality, Eve is to be 'liberated' into
compulsion, need, envy and lies.

With this in mind, along with the terrible further reflections as
Satan turns to his work of temptation (ix 473–93), we can turn
to another passage central to our theme. Eve returns to Adam
after the Fall, elated and devious, offering him a share in her
newly gained knowledge and status, but (as C. S. Lewis pointed
out) harbouring something akin to murder in her heart. The
wreath of flowers which Adam had made for her falls faded; he
knows mortality in this form as he speaks :

> O fairest of creation, last and best
> Of all God's works, creature in whom excelled
> Whatever can to sight or thought be formed,
> Holy, divine, good, amiable or sweet !
> How art thou lost, how on a sudden lost,
> Defaced, deflowered, and now to death devote?
> Rather how hast thou yielded to transgress
> The strict forbiddance, how to violate
> The sacred fruit forbidden ! Some cursed fraud
> Of enemy hath beguiled thee, yet unknown,
> And me with thee hath ruined, for with thee
> Certain my resolution is to die;
> How can I live without thee, how forgo
> Thy sweet converse and love so dearly joined,
> To live again in these wild woods forlorn?
> Should God create another Eve, and I
> Another rib afford, yet loss of thee
> Would never from my heart; no, no, I feel
> The link of nature draw me : flesh of flesh,

Bone of my bone thou art, and from thy state
Mine never shall be parted, bliss or woe. (IX 896–916)

By any criterion, this is one of the great 'tragic' speeches of
literature; it is also the culmination of the poem's theme, the
'mortal sin original' which lost the race. Uniquely fused, we have
words expressing high and noble love as man now knows it, and
the root evil, cause of 'all our woe'. Even before he eats the fruit
Adam's decision is taken; he feels drawn by the link of 'nature'
and chooses death. His speech certainly demonstrates every
dangerous misunderstanding of hierarchy against which Raphael
has warned him. Does it also include much or, given the circumstances, everything which we feel to be good?

Adam begins with tragic grief at Eve's lot, not deceived by *her*
rhetoric : he knows, and laments, that all she was is now lost. He
is not deceived himself (if we take the comment at IX 998–9 at
face value), but he eats the fruit in the belief that Eve herself has
been deceived. And, of course, he is right in this : Satan has told
her nothing but lies. It is not only insidious flattery to which
she has been subjected; or the specious lure of divinity; or the
suggestion – so powerfully plausible, especially to readers coming
after the romantic revolution and the twentieth-century psychol-
ogists – that God may actually want her to disobey him, and so
come of age. Beyond these stratagems there has been the direct
lie, so important to the success of Satan's other obliquities, about
the crucial question of how a serpent can talk. Satan has claimed
to have eaten the fruit and come by speech in this manner :
hence the tree is a magic tree. It has proved its power to make a
beast rational; may it not also then make men divine? But the
tree is not magic; Satan has not eaten of it; his power of speech is
angelic, though disguised. The fact of this lie in no way justifies
Eve (of course), any more than *her* lie (IX 877–8) justifies Adam
now. But it is certainly true to see that she has been terribly
tricked; and, given this, Adam's anguished loyalty will naturally
seem the very essence of love. He echoes the marriage vow – 'flesh
of flesh', 'never shall be parted', 'bliss or woe', omitting only (but

how ironically) the notion 'till death do us part'. And who can fail to feel the terrible poignancy of this choice now hideously forced upon him, between human love at its finest, and the commands of God? Nothing could seem more natural than that God's law should appear at this moment harsh, cold or impossible; or that Adam's impassioned words should appear the quintessence of noble love. So the 'split' in the poem alleged by romantic critics again confronts us: *is* it 'natural' to respond as readers in this manner; and, if so, is it right? It is easy enough to conclude that while the analysis of Adam's 'uxoriousness' (as Tillyard calls it), his lack of proportion, his fatal disobedience, rings true intellectually, the tragic intensity transcends such analysis with truths of the heart. It is easy, again, to assume that when man's deepest love can earn only death, and God's cold anger, the 'ways of God' are not justified after all.

But if Satan is father of lies, and deceived Adam, is it not likely that the fallen sons of Adam will also be tricked? Indeed are we right to accept Milton's explicit assurance, already alluded to, that Adam himself is not deceived? The poetry *says* 'he scrupled not to eat/Against his better knowledge, not deceived/But fondly overcome with female charm'; but we have already heard Adam refer to God as 'threatening' (939), as inept creator (938–51), as 'fickle' (948), and we know by now where such perspectives originate and belong. Perhaps we also notice that even in his highest anguish Adam's stress has fallen even more on his own need for Eve than on her personal freedom and loveliness, as if the egocentric taint is already at work. He appears also to take for granted that his own love for Eve is much greater than God's love; and this assumption certainly strikes a new note. As C. S. Lewis pointed out we can never know now what God would have done if the unfallen Adam had presented himself to plead for her; but we do know that the future of humanity was vested in *him*. Adam's sense of Eve's uniqueness, her infinite preciousness and irreplaceability, is powerfully human; but have we any reason for thinking it less true of God? If individuals are in fact so precious that no one of them can ever replace another, then it is God's creative majesty not human need – however high and pure – that endorses this. Adam assumes that Eve must die for her sin, because God has said so; does he already doubt God's will and power to turn evil to good? It is arguable that if he does fail in authority in Book IX it is not, as Waldock assumes, when he allows Eve to go off on her own to be tempted, but when he fails, at this moment, to trust the mercy of God. And if we say: 'yes; this is coldly rational but has no warmth for the emotions', we should remember that Milton has not yet finished his tale. There is not only the moment of the Fall, but all the time after; there is the burden of consciousness to be continued, and resumed. At the end of Book IX, Adam and Eve have their second quarrel (1119–89): how unlike the first one; and how recognisably true? Later there is the terrible moment when Adam turns on Eve with a mixture of wounding savagery and relentless self-laceration, calling the 'bond of nature' which drew him to fall with her not a blessing, but a curse (X 867–908). To this the terrified Eve can now only plead 'Forsake me not thus, Adam, witness heaven/ What love sincere, and reverence in my heart/I bear thee' and, from the depth of her terror, beg Adam to honour the vow which he implied in the actual words, and images, and resonances of the Fall:

> bereave me not,
> Whereon I live, thy gentle looks, thy aid,
> Thy counsel in this uttermost distress,
> My only strength and stay : forlorn of thee,
> Whither shall I betake me, where subsist? (X 918–22)

It would be as dishonest to deny the sad familiarity of such passages, their truth to human emotions and relationships as almost any reader is likely to know them, as it would be to deny the goodness, however muddled, in Adam as he fell. Are we to assert indeed that the noble sentiments uttered by Adam in the elation and anguish of immediate sacrifice would, normally, sustain a lifetime's suffering endured, and on beliefs proved mistaken, for another's sake? Milton's poem forces on us that the antithesis between 'love' and 'law' remains a fallacy, a diabolical trick in the strictest sense, even when – and perhaps especially when – it is born of love and experienced in suffering. The satanic reading of the poem is indeed one-sided if it can enlist our dubious grasp on reality, our well-meaning but too indulgent and in the end ineffectual compassion, against a full experience and acknowledgement of life as it is. We must call to mind again the nature of Adam and Eve's love in the early books of the poem : not the sexual happiness only, beautiful though that is, but their serene delight in every moment of life. We have seen their pride in one another – touching and pleasing, whatever its dangers; their delight in each other's company; their daily ritual of celebration, in work, worship and loving; their dignity even when differing on the morning of the Fall. If these images, too, have their power; if they too (and this is the great test for the poem) strike us as possible, with a call on our allegiance : then we cannot afford, at any point, to simplify the poem's truths.

Frank Kermode points to Milton's subtle symbolic suggestiveness, reaching far beyond paraphrase, and to his sophisticated understanding of myth as 'fiction', at least in his art. (Kermode hints that Milton's understanding is close to his own, in *Sense Of An Ending*, 1969 : which in turn would make it possible to discuss *Paradise Lost,* as Stanley Fish comes close to doing,* in much the way that novelists are discussed in *The Rhetoric of Fiction* by Wayne Booth.) But Basil Willey has rightly reminded us that Milton believed the Bible narrative to be God-given (this is far more important than any belief or disbelief in its inspiration as 'literal'), and that his high poetic confidence rested chiefly on this.†

We can see these two views as complementary rather than as

* *Surprised by Sin.*
† Basil Willey, *The Seventeenth-Century Background* (1934). Note that the relevant material from this book, and much of the other criticism referred to here, can be found in the Macmillan Casebook on *Paradise Lost* edited by the present authors.

mutually exclusive, if we remember that while Kermode is right in his analysis of the actual effects of Milton's verse, he would be wrong to assimilate it, even if he wished to do this, to his own view of art. Milton was not offering the consolation of beautiful fiction in a world without meaning; he was raising echoes of lost, precious truths in our hearts. The essential insight is not that his truths are true because, and to the degree that, our hearts respond to them; but that our hearts respond to them, given grace and the proper occasion, because they are true.

The romantic tradition of criticism has witnessed to the fluidity of Milton's archetypes, whether by antinomianism, as in Blake and Shelley and modern critics such as Waldock and Empson, or through Jungian interpretations of Zwi Werblowsky's kind. But fluidity and ambivalence are not gods, demanding total homage; it is not Christian or Platonic – not Miltonic – to call all insights 'true'. We may believe that truth itself is relative, and conditioned by the needs and structures of believers; or we may believe that some insights correspond to reality and that others do not. The nature of Heaven and Hell, love and hate, salvation and damnation are clearly involved in this; and Milton's position cannot be in doubt. He did not believe that beauty, goodness and truth are relative and subjective; he believed that they are revealed in nature; in scripture; and supremely in Christ.

In *Paradise Lost,* the archetypal romantic is notoriously Satan, who ascribes power over reality itself wholly to the mind:

> The mind is its own place, and in itself
> Can make a heaven of hell, a hell of heaven. (1 254–5)

Like almost everything satanic, this is an important half-truth, perverted in its context into a lie. From the aspect of consciousness, Satan is entirely right, since it does lie within ourselves to celebrate God, or to reject. But God remains real and unchanged, whatever our attitude; we can alter our vision, our 'self', but not him.

On this matter, we confront one of the great and unbridgeable divides in human thinking, between those who understand the great verities as truths beyond themselves, received by revelation, and those whose final appeal is always to the court of the self. 'What I feel', 'what I think', 'what it means to me' become final criteria, offered from inside the imprisoned, and usually the contracted, heart.

Milton's place on this issue is with Christians and Platonists; for him Heaven is the supreme reality, made by God and inhabited by him; Hell is the reality of any consciousness alienated from God. Milton's readers may be on Milton's side here, or in the other camp; but they must recognise that if they take the satanic interpretation of events, as a whole, or even partly, they are shut with Satan, in Milton's understanding, away from the truth. Milton's method in his poem, however, is not to assert his great beliefs intellectually, in equal argument with Satan, but to demonstrate them by arousing echoes in ourselves of the divine.

Milton's view would be that art itself is a witness to the truths it celebrates, in that it incarnates the creative mind in union with the mind's chosen themes. Formally, *Paradise Lost* is among the symbols in time of timeless realities, the still point (to use T. S. Eliot's image) of the turning world. Throughout *Paradise Lost*, the time-scale is as shifting and fluid as the images, but at every point – as in the passages we have been examining – there are timeless resonances of Paradise, Paradise Lost, and Paradise Regained. The 'truth' is in the existence of these in art, and in their power over us; our denial of the poem, if we choose to deny it, must 'get round' them.

Since Milton is not staking his poem on anything quasi-historical or on anything merely literal, his scriptural fundamentalism is not, in this matter, to the point. We are no more forced to believe in the place and the occasion in Eden literally, than we are forced to believe literally in the fluctuating pictures and images of Heaven and Hell. We do not need to believe that Adam and Eve walked, in history, in a garden, as long as we are made to feel that they existed and still exist in us. The fallen Adam and Eve are doubtless easy to credit; it is the unfallen and the restored that we must also be persuaded to endorse. These images reach beyond their own powerful – and often inherently impressive – rational structures, to the place where great memories and promises haunt our lives. We have to feel again that these are not vain hopes; memories of the womb; desires for lost childhood; longings for escape, or bliss, or opium, or simple extinction; but that they are the spirit of God testifying within.

And in this Milton's theme unites with his form to help him, since both exist to salute glory from the heart of loss. *Paradise Lost* is the epic of exile; of greatness in ruins; of restoration possible and promised in the end. Beyond the 'event perverse' of the last morning in Paradise, and of our daily experience, there is another image that readers will always have in their minds. In balance with the moment when creatures tried to be as gods, and moved into exile, there is that other moment when God, made man, went to his death. Eve's noontide repast is still lost to our human experience, but there are words spoken to a criminal now triumphant in history : 'Truly, I tell you, today you will be with Me in Paradise.'

So, just as the shadow of coming loss falls over scenes in Paradise, the coming triumph of God holds, even in scenes of the Fall. Omnipotence is really itself, though it seems defeated; Satan's nonsense is still nonsense though it seems to win.

'O felix culpa' : in this cry is the heart of the poem, the testimony to an event 'turned aside' but still to come. As in *Samson Agonistes* Milton insists that since man is free, he is also guilty; and human guilt is the centre of hope. To blame God or Satan is to lock ourselves in Hell and to cast the key away; in Hell we rejoice in our 'freedom' and 'growth' as we wither away. Milton fully understood that the nonsense of Hell is also daily experience, and that if his poem were to be succeed it would have to dispel in us that particular enchantment of evil to which he had given marvellous expression in *Comus* :

> And they, so perfect is their misery,
> Not once perceive their foul disfigurement,
> But boast themselves more comely than before

Like Wordsworth he knew that most men pass gladly into 'the light of common day' at adolescence, making 'growing up' a permanent excuse for growing down. Fewer and fewer glances are cast back at the lost land, guarded by angels with swords against our re-entry; the lost land is forgotten or denied. Milton's triumph is to bring it back to us, so clearly and unmistakably, that we can forget or deny it only by forgetting or denying ourselves. If Keats's words can be adapted, *Paradise Lost* is indeed like Adam's dream for its readers; they awake, and find it true.

The balance of tensions in language and structure which have been explored here in particular passages can be traced in almost any of the parts. *Paradise Lost* is a poem where the whole to an extraordinary degree inhabits individual episodes, and individual episodes radiate out to the whole. Book by book Milton builds his verbal cathedral, so skilfully, that his main image can be released, with the whole poem in it, as the final touch. We note the conjunctions of 'providence their guide' with 'wandering', of 'hand in hand' with 'solitary'; we do not miss the ironies in 'all before', 'where to choose', 'place of rest'. But as Adam and Eve move away, God is justified. Love has power, the lines also testify, to bring *this* to good :

> The world was all before them, where to choose
> Their place of rest, and providence their guide :
> They hand in hand with wandering steps and slow
> Through Eden took their solitary way. (XII 646–9)

5 BEYOND THE POLEMICS: THE OPENING OF DRYDEN'S *ABSALOM AND ACHITOPHEL*

1 In pious times, e'r Priest-craft did begin,
    Before *Polygamy* was made a sin;
    When man, on many, multiply'd his kind,
    E'r one to one was, cursedly, confind:
5 When Nature prompted, and no law deny'd
    Promiscuous use of Concubine and Bride;
    Then, *Israel's* Monarch, after Heaven's own heart,
    His vigorous warmth did, variously, impart
    To Wives and Slaves: And, wide as his Command,
10 Scatter'd his Maker's Image through the Land.
    Michal, of Royal blood, the Crown did wear,
    A Soyl ungratefull to the Tiller's care:
    Not so the rest; for several Mothers bore
    To Godlike *David*, several Sons before.
15 But since like slaves his bed they did ascend,
    No True Succession could their seed attend.
    Of all this Numerous Progeny was none
    So Beautifull, so brave as *Absolon*:
    Whether, inspir'd by some diviner Lust,
20 His Father got him with a greater Gust;
    Or that his Conscious destiny made way
    By manly beauty to Imperiall sway.
    Early in Foreign fields he won Renown,
    With Kings and States ally'd to *Israel's* Crown:
25 In Peace the thoughts of War he coud remove,
    And seem'd as he were only born for love.
    What e'r he did was done with so much ease,
    In him alone, 'twas Natural to please.
    His motions all accompanied with grace;
30 And *Paradise* was open'd in his face.

With secret Joy, indulgent *David* view'd
His Youthfull Image in his Son renew'd :
To all his wishes Nothing he deny'd,
And made the Charming *Annabel* his Bride.
35 What faults he had (for who from faults is free?)
His Father coud not, or he woud not see.
Some warm excesses, which the Law forbore,
Were constru'd Youth that purg'd by boyling o'r :
And *Amnon*'s Murther, by a specious Name,
40 Was call'd a Just Revenge for injur'd Fame.
Thus Prais'd, and Lov'd, the Noble Youth remain'd,
While *David*, undisturb'd, in *Sion* raign'd.
But Life can never be sincerely blest :
Heaven punishes the bad, and proves the best.
45 The *Jews,* a Headstrong, Moody, Murmuring race,
As ever try'd th' extent and stretch of grace;
God's pamper'd people whom, debauch'd with ease,
No King could govern, nor no God could please;
(Gods they had tri'd of every shape and size
50 That God-smiths could produce, or Priests devise :)
These *Adam*-wits, too fortunately free,
Began to dream they wanted libertie;
And when no rule, no president was found
Of men, by Laws less circumscrib'd and bound,
55 They led their wild desires to Woods and Caves,
And thought that all but Savages were Slaves.
They who when *Saul* was dead, without a blow,
Made foolish *Ishbosheth* the Crown forgo;
Who banisht *David* did from *Hebron* bring,
60 And, with a Generall Shout, proclaim'd him King :
Those very *Jewes,* who, at their very best,
Their Humour more than Loyalty exprest,
Now, wondred why, so long, they had obey'd
An Idoll Monarch which their hands had made :
65 Thought they might ruine him they could create;
Or melt him to that Golden Calf, a State.

But these were randome bolts : No form'd Design,
Nor Interest made the Factious Croud to joyn :
The sober part of *Israel,* free from stain,
70 Well knew the value of a peacefull raign :
And, looking backward with a wise afright,
Saw Seames of wounds, dishonest to the sight;
In contemplation of whose ugly Scars,
They Curst the memory of Civil Wars.
75 The moderate sort of men, thus qualifi'd,
Inclin'd the Ballance to the better side :
And *David*'s mildness manag'd it so well,
The Bad found no occasion to Rebell.
But, when to Sin our byast Nature leans,
80 The carefull Devil is still at hand with means;
And providently Pimps for ill desires :
The Good old Cause reviv'd, a Plot requires.
Plots, true or false, are necessary things,
To raise up Common-wealths, and ruin Kings.

Our main emphasis in this chapter concerns the relationship between history and art. Is Dryden's *Absalom and Achitophel* chiefly a polemical work, with art at its service; or, beyond the polemics, is it chiefly a triumph of form ?

Obviously, *Absalom and Achitophel* is not as 'pure' as, say, Shakespeare's 'The Phoenix and the Turtle' or Yeats's 'Sailing to Byzantium', which may seem as independent of their age as any works made with words, by men, can hope to be. Dryden's poem relates to a particular situation which exerted more than usual pressures on its aesthetic form. No reader can expect to experience *Absalom and Achitophel* fully without some historical knowledge; though arguably, an attentive reader might deduce much of the data he needs from 'inside' the poem, rather than resorting at every stage to footnotes from outside. We shall discuss ways in which the historical pressures influenced the aesthetic structure, and ways in which the aesthetic structure uses and converts the historical pressures for larger ends.

First, a few facts. On 28 March 1681 Charles II dissolved the
Oxford Parliament, and on 8 April he published *His Majesties
Declaration To all His Loving Subjects Touching the Causes and
Reasons That moved Him to Dissolve the Two last Parliaments.*
These events threw the Whig opponents of his policy into con-
fusion, and began a hectic exchange of pamphlets, in which
Dryden took part. On 2 July the crisis took a new turn when the
Whig leader, the Earl of Shaftesbury, was charged by the Council
with high treason and committed to the Tower.

Shaftesbury's appearance before the Middlesex Grand Jury
(of presentment) was fixed for 24 November and during the
summer the King appeared to have regained the initiative which
he had all but lost since the Popish Plot erupted in August 1678.
Absalom and Achitophel was written, perhaps at the suggestion
of the King, and certainly with his approval, to arouse public
feeling against Shaftesbury, and to prejudice his trial. Shaftesbury's main offence had been his continued attempts to have the
King's brother, James, Duke of York, a Roman Catholic,
excluded from the succession in favour of the King's bastard son,
the Duke of Monmouth, a Protestant, on the grounds that
England was already threatened with the growing absolutism of
a corrupt Court and the possibility of a return to Roman
Catholicism as the national religion, and that these threats would
be much increased if the Duke of York ascended the throne. The
Commons was on record as believing that 'there has been and
still is a damnable and hellish plot, contrived and carried on by
Popish recusants, for the assassinating and murdering the King,
and for subverting the government and rooting out and destroying
the Protestant religion'. Fears of popery were played upon everywhere; indeed, Shaftesbury himself is reported as telling Charles,
in 1679, that if he were assured of Protestant succession and might
'enjoy the known rights and liberties of the subjects, he would
rather be under Kingly government, but if he could not be satisfied
of that he declared he was for a Common-wealth'. A full account of
the events which led up to Shaftesbury's trial, starting with the
Popish Plot, is to be found in *The First Whigs*, by J. R. Jones

(1961). For other aspects of the background, *England in the Reign of Charles II* by David Ogg (1968), and *The First Earl of Shaftesbury* by K. D. H. Haley (1968) are valuable. Readers of *Absalom and Achitophel* can now also consult the volume on Dryden in Routledge's *The Critical Heritage* series, edited by James and Helen Kinsley (1971). James Kinsley's text of the poem, in his four-volume Clarendon Press edition and in the one-volume Oxford Standard Authors version, is definitive.

Since his exile, Charles had often been compared with the Old Testament David, and in 1680 Monmouth had been compared publicly with Absalom, and Shaftesbury with Achitophel. It is this analogy between the Exclusion Crisis and the story of David which Dryden exploits and elaborates in *Absalom and Achitophel*. In the opening lines of the poem David is Charles, Michal is Charles's Queen, Catherine of Braganza; Absalom is Monmouth; Annabel is Anne, Countess of Buccleuch (a famous beauty, and Dryden's patron); Saul is Oliver Cromwell; Ishbosheth is Richard Cromwell; Israel is England; the Jews are the English people; Hebron is Scotland (of which Charles had been crowned King on 1 January 1651). '*Amnon*'s Murther' is an exaggerated allusion to the savage attack which had been made on Sir John Coventry in December 1670 at Monmouth's instigation, in revenge for insults directed by Coventry at the King. These facts are well-known; but to read the poem substituting the seventeenth-century faces and places for their biblical counterparts is naturally to oversimplify. Satire which exploits anachronism and glories in the frequent inappropriateness of seventeenth-century language to scriptural subjects must be two-edged; so must irony which potentially debunks the revered. To sense such discrepancies is to discover that beneath the apparent directness of language and simplicity of tone (qualities often noted in Dryden's verse) there are considerable complexities of direction, and of possible response.

Absalom and Achitophel is not a poem written in the study, but near the battlefield. The first reader Dryden would have had in

mind was the King rather than 'the general reader'. His intention
was to influence events and to avert civil war.

That the situation was potentially revolutionary seems clear,
though Shaftesbury would have denied it. From his point of view,
whether real or feigned, he was attempting to 'save' England.
He was advocating greater religious tolerance for dissenters, and
the removal of any threatened subjugation of England to the
Papacy. But in practical terms he was fighting for an extension of
the real political power of the most influential classes of his age,
including the prosperous merchants in the City of London, and
releasing again those forces which had led to civil war, and
regicide, in the recent past.

With hindsight, we might see this as the inevitable movement
of history, though such an argument raises issues on which
historians might disagree. In seventeenth-century Europe the drift
was in fact the other way, towards absolutism, and the toleration
of religious minorities posed problems for the virtual identity of
church and state of an immensely disruptive kind. Moreover,
Shaftesbury was a notoriously devious, though able, man, as all
his biographers agree. Arguably, any power politician who
survived the final years of Charles I, the Commonwealth, and the
Restoration would have had to adapt to circumstances in a
manner hard to distinguish from disloyalty. But Shaftesbury not
only survived, he flourished; and in the 1670s was himself the
chief architect of the chaos which, after feverish years of plot,
rumour, and political campaigning for Exclusion, culminated in
the three dissolutions of Parliament by the King, and in his own
arrest.*

* Though Shaftesbury used the Popish Plot as a pretext, he certainly no more believed in it than did the King. In December 1678
Charles is reported as saying to Burnet 'that the greatest part of the
evidence was a contrivance. But he suspected, some had set on *Oates*
and instructed him : And he named the Earl of Shaftesbury'. Shaftesbury, for his part, became the leading Parliamentary investigator
of the Plot, and is famous for the remark : 'I will not say who started
the Game, but I am sure I had the full Hunting of it.'

In *Absalom and Achitophel,* the case *for* Shaftesbury is naturally suppressed; or rather, it is handed over in its most damaging form to Achitophel, and represented as an exercise in deliberate temptation. Whereas Shaftesbury pointed to future possible dangers under a Roman Catholic monarch, Dryden stresses the danger of an immediate return to the confusion and bloodshed of the Commonwealth period. Whereas Shaftesbury tried to enlist the self-interest of the wealthy through fear of York, Dryden reminds them of the real and recently experienced horrors of anarchy. In the poem Shaftesbury is portrayed as a machiavel, though paradoxically a warped and even dwarfed machiavel (the mock-heroic allows both perspectives), intent on overthrowing order to exploit confusion :

> In Friendship False, Implacable in Hate :
> Resolv'd to Ruine or to Rule the State. (lines 173–4)

With this in mind, we must not forget that the Restoration of Charles II in May 1660 had come about largely for pragmatic reasons. The death of Oliver Cromwell left a power vacuum which nobody filled successfully, and the year 1659, with its total uncertainty in every area of national life and its virtual breakdown of government, must have been uniquely traumatic for everyone in England with wealth or power, and, indeed, for everyone with firm religious or political convictions. The killing of Charles I turned out also to have released 'levelling' tendencies which proved too powerful to be contained. The rich and influential people who helped to make or condone the Commonwealth discovered belatedly that the ideology and expectations of 'democracy' might pose a far greater threat to them – through extreme plans for redistributing wealth, for instance – than the former uneasy stability under a King. Charles II was restored by a motley alliance of people, including many of his former enemies, who saw him now as the lesser of two evils. But when he *was* restored, and had proved his general readiness to pardon and become reconciled to most men of power whatever their past, the instinct, of course, was to make restoration work. Dryden stresses also that Charles returned to great public acclaim ('And, with a Generall Shout, proclaim'd him King'), and that his continuing popularity in the country at large directly related to his power to keep destructive forces at bay. It was these practical factors which assured his real power, whatever the theory of 'divine right' might have been : and one has to admire Dryden's skill in basing his case ostensibly on the divine right, while taking advantage of all those practical fears and hopes vested on the King's side.

This brings us to a question which is central to both the period and the poem : where did real power lie? The Restoration period was necessarily very fluid, and there was no guarantee that the forces which unmade Charles I would not strike against his successor. In spite of the divine right, Charles I had been beheaded. And as the puritans demonstrated (Milton in his Tracts notably), divine precedents and sanctions could be effectively used either way. From 1670, in particular, the whole political climate and situation were in rapid transition, and the prospects changed every two or three years.

In this respect, it was rather like our present age – with different problems but similar uncertainties. There was a debate then, as now, about freedom. Is freedom the fruit of strong and unchallengeable political power; or is it the inalienable right of each individual to challenge his rulers? Hobbes believed that men are by nature competitive, and governed by fear and self-interest. Without strong law, their life is 'solitary, poore, nasty, brutish, and short'. In contrast Locke believed that men are by nature good and sociable and need social structures more to release these positive qualities than to contain evil (though as a realist he knew that containing evil was also necessary). These opposed concepts of freedom are clearly not 'academic'. They relate to civil order, and to civil war. For Dryden, the analysis of Hobbes was nearer the truth (though he did not, of course, subscribe to Hobbes's materialism) and Shaftesbury is represented as an essentially evil man, set on subverting order – a possible Cromwell.

It is also worth recalling that Marvell's 'An Horatian Ode

upon Cromwel's Return from Ireland', probably written in June 1650, depicts Cromwell's new and, at that time, supreme power as resting on naked might. The death of Charles I is described as 'that memorable Hour/Which first assur'd the forced Pow'r', and the moral drawn is that Cromwell

> Could by industrious Valour climbe
> To ruine the great Work of Time,
>> And cast the Kingdome old
>> Into another Mold.
> Though Justice against Fate complain,
> And plead the antient Rights in vain:
>> But those do hold or break
>> As men are strong or weak. (lines 33–40)

In 1681 this thought can never have been far from anyone's mind. And when Shaftesbury started to use the arguments which Milton had used earlier in *The Tenure of Kings and Magistrates* (that the King's power comes not from God but from the people; that the people who make the King can also unmake him; that true monarchy should be by popular election – a system under which Monmouth might have flourished – and not by birth) the danger of a return to 1649 must have been obvious. These arguments might colour themselves differently – with religious texts, or Lockeian principles, or references to the noble savage* –

* The myth of the noble savage was based on the idea that man in a 'natural' state is freer and nobler than man under a complex society. Law, custom, ceremony, are seen as repressive and destructive of man's free potential. The idea can be traced back a long way in European thinking, though its most dramatic developments have occurred since Rousseau and the romantics, who made it influential upon much political and educational theory. The argument is that man is naturally good, or at least perfectible, and that evil is chiefly the product of social values and environment. Clearly, this departs from both the Christian notion of Original Sin, and the more drastic notion of Hobbes of natural competitiveness. Its extraordinary

but in practice, they meant revolution. Later in *Absalom and Achitophel*, Dryden sees the democratic arguments for an elective monarchy playing into the hands of totalitarianism : it is almost startling to observe this lesson being learned from the English experience of revolution under Cromwell, so long before the events of the nineteenth century and our own :

> For who can be secure of private Right,
> If Sovereign sway may be dissolv'd by might? . . .
> But Government it self at length must fall
> To Natures state; where all have Right to all . . .
> The Tampering World is subject to this Curse,
> To Physick their Disease into a worse.
>
> (lines 779–80; 793–4; 809–10)

This leads us back to Dryden's main intention (and in a poem like *Absalom and Achitophel* it must be permissible to talk about intention, whatever some critics urge, whilst recognising, of course, that 'intention' isn't everything). Clearly, he wished to establish a new myth of political stability in a profoundly unstable period. On the one hand, he offered the immutable divine right and succession as a necessary foundation for stability (we know, of course, that the degree of stability actually achieved by the Whigs in the mid-eighteenth century was differently based, but it would be a fundamental error to see Dryden as a reactionary in his own time). On the other hand, he played on the very prevalent and justified fears of disorder to rally as many people as he could to this myth, coining phrases such as 'Drawn to the dregs of a Democracy' which must have had great polemical power.

But Dryden is an artist as well as a polemicist. In literary terms

---

power in a century like our own, which has been simultaneously influenced by evolutionary views of man, seems paradoxical. For a fuller treatment of the subject, see (for instance) Basil Willey's *Seventeenth Century Background* (1934) and Paul Hazard's *The European Mind* (1973).

he proves this by his choice of the literary mode most suited to his complex situation, so that the history serves the aesthetic structure of the poem, as well as the other way about, and the particular crisis of 1681 is universalised. The mock-heroic is one instance: it allows the use of historical analogies which can underline both the size of the danger and the smallness of man; in becoming Achitophel, Shaftesbury can be turned into a figure of genuine dread and simultaneously mocked. The Old Testament analogy is just the one needed to help Charles's cause. David was not only chosen by God; he was of the very line of the Messiah. But he was promiscuous too, and the begetter of a much loved though errant son. In a similar manner, Dryden exploits an analogy with *Paradise Lost.* By turning Monmouth into Adam (or, more precisely, Eve) and Satan into Shaftesbury, he makes the arguments advanced for freedom in the democratic cause the equivalent of the specious arguments which brought about the Fall. He implies that Shaftesbury is not mistaken but evil ('Resolv'd to Ruine or to Rule the State'); and in emphasising the idea of conspiracy, he generates in the poem that mood of fear which is most likely to persuade his readers into the mould of the new consensus presented to them. Moreover, he can leave open – very necessarily in the context – the ultimate fate of Monmouth. His own plea is that the King should see his son as the almost innocent victim of evil, and pardon him. But the King might have taken a sterner view. In much the same way, God could either have forgiven Adam (though not without cost), or exacted the full penalty of death. When Dryden wrote, there was no knowing what Charles would do. Dryden's mould allows him to suggest, without prejudging, a desired outcome.

Historically, if not aesthetically, Dryden's use of *Paradise Lost* is a great audacity. In Milton himself there had been a split – to some minds a glaring inconsistency – between his religious beliefs and his politics. In religion he had taught that disobedience is the prime and greatest sin, and stressed that there is no possible excuse, however apparently rational, for defying God. From Comus onwards his tempters specialise in 'reasons not unplausible', which have to be rejected resolutely by insight and will. But in politics Milton had denied the claim of English kings, bishops and magistrates to be God's chosen vehicles, and denounced them as impostors who should be swept away. In this he used as his model the Old Testament prophets who rose from time to time to denounce forms of authority thrown up by human error, and to call for a return to primitive simplicity. Politically, Milton was – in the 1640s anyway – a primitivist and revolutionary, pointing back to an ideal state of society which earthly rulers had destroyed, and teaching political revolution as obedience to the true will of God.

But Dryden, as a Conservative, sees the rule of the King and his established servants as an extension of God's rule on earth, and the hierarchy of human society as a reflection of divine hierarchy, not as its denial. His literary triumph is to turn Milton's theological arguments against disobedience in *Paradise Lost* into a political apologia for the *status quo*. It is also fascinating to notice how the understanding of freedom in a passage like the following is converted, by Dryden, from purely religious insight into a political doctrine wholly opposed to Milton's own (*Paradise Lost*, XII 82–90):

> yet know withal,
> Since thy original lapse, true liberty
> Is lost, which always with right reason dwells
> Twinned, and from her hath no dividual being;
> Reason in man obscured, or not obeyed,
> Immediately inordinate desires
> And upstart passions catch the government
> From reason, and to servitude reduce
> Man till then free.

For Dryden, the cult of the noble savage, and the revolutionary doctrines which have been inspired by it or have used it, were among the great human fallacies, and provide the scheme of ideas at the heart of *Absalom and Achitophel*. He believed that such fallacies stemmed from a basic misunderstanding of freedom.

True freedom is not the absolute right to do as you wish – to have
too many gods, too many rulers, too many women (in *Absalom
and Achitophel*, Charles's promiscuities link with this pattern of
false excess, whatever attempts Dryden makes, for reasons of
expediency, to disguise it). Rather, true freedom is the acceptance
of the law of restraint, written in the nature of things, without
which there can be no stability or inner peace for mankind or for
society.

So far, we have been concerned with the setting of *Absalom and
Achitophel,* if in general terms. We have been trying to deduce
from the poem the feel of the political situation; or the feel as
Dryden managed to convey it, with much contemporary success,
through his creation of a literary artefact with polemical ends.
The poem is anchored in 1681, and to overlook this is to miss the
raison d'être of its structure; but it is also anchored in a universal
habit of mind and debate. And this is where any difference of
emphasis between us exists, and where we therefore resort again
to dialogue. One reader may see the poem primarily as a
polemical piece, a wresting of literary form for political ends.
Another may see it as a literary achievement beyond the polemics,
a wresting of the circumstances (in this case historical, though
they need not have been) into the shape of organic art. But
wherever the stress falls, the effect is the same : Dryden is wedding
the stuff of his poem, its material in life, to appropriate form.
Once complete, the poem stands in its own right and universalises
its theme. It takes on relevances far beyond its moment of birth.
   We now move to more literary matters by tackling one of the
famous questions about the poem : why does it begin where it
does? If Dryden's most important reader was the King, why start
with his promiscuities and risk offending him? Of course,
Charles's way of life was well known, and he did not mind being
teased, especially when his virility was praised (though some, like
Rochester in a notorious poem, went too far). Even so, it does not
seem an ideal starting point. All the values of the poem move
against allegedly 'free' and 'natural' behaviour, like the King's.

Dryden is 'for' Christian order, 'against' anarchy, and that includes order in manners and morals, in every department of human living. He is among the late seventeenth-century writers who helped to form the ethos which was to be celebrated in *The Spectator* (1711–12) and is now usually, if loosely, called Augustan, in which the gentlemanly qualities, including courtesy and self-restraint, become central moral virtues. In this sense the gentleman became a natural antithesis to the noble savage : but Charles seems to be in the wrong camp. This was certainly noted by many early readers, including 'a Person of Honour', who, replying to the poem in 1681, commented : 'For how does he character the King, but as a broad figure of scandalous inclinations, or contrived into such irregularities, as renders him rather the property of parasites and vice, than suitable to the accomplishment of so excellent a prince. Nay, he forces on King David such a royal resemblance, that he darkens his sanctity, in spite of illuminations from Holy Writ.'

But the answer to the question 'Why start here?' is surely political, not aesthetic; 'No True Succession could their seed attend.' The one fact that Dryden must establish at the start is that Shaftesbury's ostensible candidate for the succession, Monmouth, is illegitimate, and has no claim. Given this, it appears a triumph of tactics that he plunges straight in, before he has established the values which must condemn the King, using a tone of robust geniality which the King can regard as a compliment, or at the very least as a necessary evil, but which more sober or perceptive readers can sense to be ironic, even before the direction of the irony becomes clear :

> In pious times, e'r Priest-craft did begin,
> Before *Polygamy* was made a sin;
> When man, on many, multiply'd his kind,
> E'r one to one was, cursedly, confind;
> When Nature prompted, and no law deny'd
> Promiscuous use of Concubine and Bride;
> Then, *Israel*'s Monarch, after Heaven's own heart,

> His vigorous warmth did, variously, impart
> To Wives and Slaves : And, wide as his Command,
> Scatter'd his Maker's Image through the Land.
> *Michal*, of Royal blood, the Crown did wear,
> A Soyl ungratefull to the Tiller's care :
> Not so the rest; for several Mothers bore
> To Godlike *David*, several sons before.

J.L. : These lines apparently celebrate the 'Pious times, e'r Priest-craft did begin' and, by implication, the King's behaviour. 'Piety' and priesthood are set in opposition to one another. 'Piety' is associated with 'Nature', with spontaneity and freedom. Priesthood is associated with the practising of a craft, like witches, with cursing, with the making of 'sin' and of 'law'. Yet such phrases as 'multiply'd his kind' and 'when Nature prompted' seem unfeeling and animal, and '*Polygamy*' and 'Promiscuous use of Concubine and Bride' are loaded terms. Isn't there a suggestion that the 'pious times' are not so pious after all ?

A.E.D. : The word 'Nature' seems discredited in its first appearance in line 5. Dryden's skill is in the geniality of tone which takes out some of the sting (if one misses its dangerousness), and even suggests a man-of-the-world bonhomie that might turn the moral irony back on itself. Not that this *can* be Dryden's view, or intention. But perhaps it helps him, as the King's advocate, to make the best of a bad job ?

J.L. : Or does it ? Don't you think that a sensitive reader is bound to get the implication ? David is depicted as vigorous and warm, but where is there any real sign of deep human emotion ? It is all words, not deeds. He is depicted as 'Godlike' ('after Heaven's own heart'; 'wide as his Command'; 'his Maker's Image'), and there is specific reference to the Parable of the Sower. But isn't the point so laboured that it mocks itself ? The words may praise, yet one notices the carelessness, the crudeness almost, which Charles displays when he discovers that his wife is barren ('did, variously, impart/To Wives and Slaves'; 'Scatter'd'; 'not so the rest'; 'several'; and, later, 'Numerous Progeny').

'*Michal,* of Royal blood, the Crown did wear' implies its
opposite, that, in spite of the show, David has taken other queens,
and there is a note of unpleasantness, of hurt pride, in 'A Soyl
ungratefull to the Tiller's care'. Typically, Dryden resolves the
moral ambiguities in a plain – and important – statement of
fact :

> But, since like slaves his bed they did ascend,
> No True Succession could their seed attend.

But this does nothing to alter the now inevitable moral placings
of the language. 'No True Succession could their seed attend' is
so qualified by the idea of unlawful usurpation (ascending his
bed), and so basically related to the theme of the poem –
Monmouth's inevitable exclusion from the succession – that it
must be taken as a moral and social truth, and not as a mere
sarcasm born of 'Priest-craft'. The qualification is reinforced by
the linking of 'attend' and 'ascend' through rhyme, when the
situation forces the words apart. The attitude of the poem, and
therefore our response to it, has shifted, or at least has been
defined. The apparent irony at the expense of 'law' is itself ironic :
the noble savage is no longer noble.

   A.E.D. : It would have been difficult, if not impossible, for
Dryden to justify the King's promiscuities, and we seem agreed
that he did not wish to. The sexual brutalities of the earlier
Restoration period already repelled him and it is worth remembering that in his *Ode to the Pious Memory of Mrs. Anne
Killigrew,* written in 1685, he blames not only other writers, but
also himself, for condoning that ethos to which the King himself
was central :

> O Gracious God! How far have we
> Prophan'd thy Heav'nly Gift of Poesy?
> Made prostitute and profligate the Muse,
> Debas'd to each obscene and impious use,
> Whose Harmony was first ordain'd Above
> For Tongues of Angels, and for Hymns of Love?

> O wretched We ! why were we hurry'd down
> This lubrique and adult'rate age,
> (Nay added fat Pollutions of our own)
> T'increase the steaming Ordures of the Stage ?

The linguistic energy recalls the opening of *Absalom and Achitophel,* but without irony, and one sees how a revulsion against the King's personal corruption would almost inevitably accompany any genuinely Christian vision of order. We are forced back on the sense that Dryden does not want to condone, but attempts instead the easier task (aesthetically if not morally easier) of explaining David's promiscuity at the beginning of the poem, before the parallel and attitudes of the poem have become fully established. David, because of his stature, could withstand attack better than Charles II. Indeed, an attack on David in this context seems perhaps less inherently comic than unthinkable – and this tempers the fierceness of the satire. But the *tone* is unmistakable : no reader of the opening lines will miss it.

J.L. : The poem remains on thin ice, however, as it directs its attention towards Absalom, who is in every sense an embarrassment as David's son :

> Of all this Numerous Progeny was none
> So Beautifull, so brave as *Absolon* :
> Whether, inspir'd by some diviner Lust,
> His Father got him with a greater Gust;
> Or that his Conscious destiny made way
> By manly beauty to Imperiall sway.

The forthright humour of David's begetting of Absalom is in sharp contrast to the vileness of Achitophel's begetting of a son (lines 171–2), but this does not rescue it from irony. We are perhaps reminded of Edmund's soliloquy in *King Lear,* one of the many celebrations of 'Nature' from a tainted source. The yoking together of 'diviner' and 'Lust' might pass muster in a purely Greek or Roman context, but not in the Jewish and Christian one. The alternative explanation of Absalom's 'Con-

scious destiny' takes us on to the actual ground of his offence –
pretence to succession – and reinforces the moral ambiguities of
his begetting. But the very praise of Absalom passes into
mockery, by pushing what could be heroic magnitude that one
step further than the real context permits, which, in satire of
this kind, is virtually a step into the abyss :

> Early in Foreign fields he won Renown,
> With Kings and States ally'd to *Israel*'s Crown :
> In Peace the thoughts of War he coud remove,
> And seem'd as he were only born for love.
> What e'r he did was done with so much ease,
> In his alone, 'twas Natural to please.
> His motions all accompanied with grace;
> And *Paradise* was open'd in his face.

This is a parody of the Whig Manifesto, and foreshadows the
excess of Achitophel's flattery of Absalom (lines 250–70), which
parallels Satan's flattery of Eve. The praise is further undermined
by the attribution to Absalom of the already discredited virtues
of 'pious times' : his manner is 'Natural', but this is surely 'our
byast Nature' of line 79; '*Paradise* was open'd in his face', but
this is Paradise with all the associations of primitive freedom
abused (Book x rather than Book iv of *Paradise Lost*). Then the
tone changes, as if assumed geniality has carried us as far as it
can, and, since the poet will shortly be leaving the thin ice,
almost as far as it need :

> With secret Joy, indulgent *David* view'd
> His Youthfull Image in his Son renew'd :
> To all his wishes Nothing he deny'd,
> And made the Charming *Annabel* his Bride.
> What faults he had (for who from faults is free?)
> His Father coud not, or he woud not see.
> Some warm excesses, which the Law forbore,
> Were constru'd Youth that purg'd by boyling o'r :
> And *Amnon*'s Murther, by a specious Name,
> Was call'd a Just Revenge for injur'd Fame.

The language is more direct and specific now, with a sharper edge
to the irony. 'Secret Joy' strangely contradicts David's openness
in the preceding lines, and casts doubt upon it. His 'indulgence',
which is expressed in his indiscriminate generosity to his son, and
which is an extension of sexual indulgence, renders him either
blind or obstinate: it is impossible to miss the scorn behind 'His
Father coud not, or he woud not see'. 'For who from faults is
free?': the answer, of course, is God: and the divine pedestal,
on which David and even Absalom have been placed, is shattered.
If anything, the lame excuse serves to emphasise Absalom's faults
instead of to gloss over them. Just as David's lechery goes under
the name of 'vigorous warmth', so Absalom's failings go under
the name of 'warm excesses'; the joke, however, is over. The
doubt cast by 'secret' is confirmed: paradoxically, the openness is
a cover for corruption, for 'Murther' even (the charge is filled
with anger, and bites); the openness is 'a specious Name' only.

> Thus Prais'd, and Lov'd, the Noble Youth remain'd,
> While *David*, undisturb'd, in *Sion* raign'd.

This couplet is the conclusion of an argument certainly, but
hardly of this argument? In such a context can 'Noble' Absalom
(the adjective is surely openly derogatory now) be 'Prais'd, and
Lov'd'? Should David reign 'undisturb'd'?

'But': the conjunction allows the poem to change direction,
and it moves on to firmer ground politically:

> But Life can never be sincerely blest:
> Heaven punishes the bad, and proves the best.
> The *Jews*, a Headstrong, Moody, Murmuring race,
> As ever try'd th' extent and stretch of grace;
> God's pamper'd people whom, debauch'd with ease,
> No King could govern, nor no God could please

Working through alliteration ('Moody, Murmuring' and
'pamper'd people'; and rhyme ('ease' and 'please'), it arouses
in the reader a contempt for 'The *Jews*'. But there is a complexity:
the reader is a Jew himself, and such an attitude is unlikely to win

his sympathy. Therefore the contempt is dressed in wit, sugared
with laughter. The notion of God-production as a national
industry – a jibe at those who use religion to achieve political or
commercial ends as well as at the proliferation of sects – is almost
too outrageous to be offensive (though its derivation from Psalm
106, which is taken up later in the equation between Republican
ideas of the State and the Golden Calf that was made in Horeb,
gives it great point; and one remembers such powerful and
pertinent verses from the Psalm as 14 and 15 : 'But lust came
upon them in the wilderness : and they tempted God in the desert.
And he gave them their desire : and sent leanness withal into their
soul') :

> Gods they had tri'd of every shape and size
> That God-smiths could produce, or Priests devise.

The six lines which follow consolidate, from a stronger position,
the attack which has already been gathering around the noble
savage. The image of the noble savage as a prehistoric man is
extraordinarily visual, a verbal cartoon :

> These *Adam*-wits, too fortunately free,
> Began to dream they wanted libertie;
> And when no rule, no president was found
> Of men, by Laws less circumscrib'd and bound,
> They led their wild desires to Woods and Caves,
> And thought that all but Savages were Slaves.

The distinction which is made between 'freedom' and 'libertie' –
the former means freedom within society, and the latter freedom
from society – is crucial to *Absalom and Achitophel*. '*Adam*-wits'
picks up the reference to *Paradise* and the Fall in the portrait of
Absalom, stripping it through 'wits' of its narrower associations,
and making tangible the implied link between the 'indulgent'
Court and the 'debauch'd' subjects. There is a real suggestion
that the King belongs, in his behaviour, among his enemies,
though his office – and its proper exercise – alone can save him
from them.

The precariousness of the King's position at the hands, literally, as well as figuratively, of a fickle people, is enlarged upon :

> They who when *Saul* was dead, without a blow,
> Made foolish *Ishbosheth* the Crown forgo;
> Who banisht *David* did from *Hebron* bring,
> And, with a Generall Shout, proclaim'd him King :
> Those very *Jewes,* who, at their very best,
> Their Humour more than Loyalty exprest,
> Now, wondred why, so long, they had obey'd
> An Idoll Monarch which their hands had made :
> Thought they might ruine him they could create;
> Or melt him to that Golden Calf, a State.
> But these were randome bolts : No form'd Design,
> Nor Interest made the Factious Croud to joyn.

'A Generall Shout', which combines tremendous power with ephemerality, is an instance of Dryden's ability to find the exact words in which to fuse the King's popularity and his power. 'An Idoll Monarch' affirms by irony, however, that Kings are, in the estimation of apostates, merely man-made : the image catches the suggestion that Oliver Cromwell was crowned posthumously, and so extends itself also to 'that Golden Calf, a State'. What the Jews do not realise, but Dryden does, is that a State is as much an 'Idoll' as a 'Monarch' (the same product in another 'shape' and 'size'), if one accepts purely pragmatic views of power. The very strength of 'No form'd Design/Nor Interest made the Factious Croud to joyn' – the metre throws the stress on 'No' and 'Nor' – acknowledges that there is a potential for 'form'd Design' or 'Interest'. In such ways, Dryden captures the tensions of the moment, which he will resolve by realigning the King's divine right with his actual popularity, and establishing behind both the people's real fears. Later in the poem, Achitophel will put the democratic case explicitly, but in a context of temptation (lines 230–490), and Dryden, defending the divine right, will consistently smuggle in Hobbesian arguments for absolutism drawn from expediency (lines 753–809 and 939–1031).

'The sober part of *Israel*', however, realises 'the value of a peacefull raign' :

> The sober part of *Israel*, free from stain,
> Well knew the value of a peacefull raign;
> And, looking backward with a wise afright,
> Saw Seames of wounds, dishonest to the sight;
> In contemplation of whose ugly Scars,
> They Curst the memory of Civil Wars.
> The moderate sort of Men, thus qualifi'd,
> Inclin'd the Ballance to the better side . . .

But who is 'the sober part of *Israel*'? As MacDonald Emslie has pointed out ('Dryden's Couplets: Imagery Vowed to Poverty', *Critical Quarterly*, vol. II, no. 1), the language describes the seventeenth-century merchants: 'value'; 'sober'; 'wise'; 'moderate'; 'qualifi'd'; 'Ballance'. Thus 'the value of a peacefull raign' is measured, by implication, in terms of pounds and pence; 'dishonest' means unprofitable as well as humiliating; the 'better side' is the 'better side' for trade. 'Inclin'd the Ballance' gives the impression of the merchants weighing up the situation as they would weigh up a transaction: politics strictly according to business. The irony is masterly, since though 'the sober part of *Israel*' may be only, or chiefly, 'free from stain' in this self-interested sense, Dryden hints that self-interest and sanity can co-operate in the cause of order. The alliance between virtue and capitalism which has often been associated with protestantism is one which he tries to bring over bodily into the King's camp.

David now returns, perhaps fittingly, to the poem

> And *David*'s mildness manag'd it so well,
> The Bad found no occasion to Rebell.

But this is not the coarse David of 'pious times' and sexual appetite; it is a responsible David, whose 'mildness' is to function from here on as his sole fault (and his crowning virtue). Lest the change seem too remarkable, we are allowed a mere glimpse of his new character. Dryden, who initially censured the King, now

takes his side, having disguised his shift of attitude by removing
David from the scene for forty lines, simultaneously modifying
the censure through an illustration of the utter vulnerability of
kings.

The passage ends:

> But, when to Sin our byast Nature leans,
> The carefull Devil is still at hand with means;
> And providently Pimps for ill desires:
> The Good old Cause reviv'd, a Plot requires.
> Plots, true or false, are necessary things,
> To raise up Common-wealths, and ruin Kings.

This conclusion – Man has a 'byast Nature' and is prey to a wily
Devil – is applicable universally, and indicates that the satire has
wider relevance than the Exclusion Crisis. The tension created in
the poem's opening is resolved with mock resignation: it is time
to push the 'Good old Cause' again, to ruin another King, to raise
another Commonwealth. It is time to go down to the 'Woods'
again. The Popish Plot is hatched.

A.E.D. : I agree with this analysis; but would add that it is a
linguistic and political triumph simultaneously. The very use of
language is in one aspect a confidence trick, an attempt to
assimilate to unassailably direct logic, syntax and imagery one
side of a very complex polemical debate. Dryden manages to
present his myth with the assurance of a man offering the
common-sense consensus, while tacitly underpinning it with a
skilful play on civic fears. He makes it as easy as possible for his
readers to hail the poem as sane and 'moderate' (the claim he
makes for it several times in the Preface), and thus to submit
themselves to the remarkable effectiveness of linguistic persuasion.

From the purely literary point of view, this is probably the
poem's most distinctive feature: the co-existence of apparent
linguistic directness with complex and devious irony. The complexities and deviousness were not altogether Dryden's wish: they
were forced upon him by events. The irreducible problem of a
King whose private life scandalously and openly failed to

conform to the general scheme of values for which he was being
made guardian could not be hushed up when his bastard son was
being used as a virtual Pretender. Nevertheless, Dryden is able
to keep the unwanted ironies from activating themselves in a
manner inimical to his design. Whereas a metaphysical or
symbolist poet might have rejoiced in the ironies as delights in
themselves, Dryden's whole aim is to tame them. Of all our major
poets, he is the one who could most plausibly echo Humpty
Dumpty's claim, 'When *I* use a word . . . it means just what I
choose it to mean – neither more nor less.' Take, for example, one
couplet :

> These *Adam*-wits, too fortunately free,
> Began to dream they wanted libertie

The astonishing thing is that Paradise and the Fall are referred
to explicitly, but not really evoked : our attention is focused
wholly on the precise meanings we are intended to take. These
are not, in themselves, simple; but they *are* simple if compared
with the overtones that might have been released if the poet
allowed. Dryden means '*Adam*-wits' literally : 'wits' are the
rational faculties, which are misled by the arguments of democrats
like Shaftesbury as surely as Adam was misled by Satan. The
error, as we have stressed, is primitivism : so 'dream' is a correct
antithesis to 'wit' – the mind asleep, and unguided by reason –
and 'too fortunately free' exactly describes the state which Adam
abused in his abortive quest for that one further freedom which
brings all freedom to an end. Dryden thus presents the traditional
Christian understanding of freedom with great economy, fuses it
unobtrusively but inextricably with political Toryism; and at the
same time excludes that whole range of further paradoxes (such
as the 'fortunate fall' theory; the romantic inversion of values;
and so on) which could complicate his effect.*

* Consider, for instance, as a comparison, the evocations of
Paradise (to keep within the same theme, and the same half
century) in Marvell's 'The Garden', or in Book IV of *Paradise Lost* :

It is remarkable that a poet can so totally annihilate unwanted meanings, and tame unwanted complexities. We are forced to wonder, with Matthew Arnold, whether this is a prosaic use of language? – and, in one sense, the answer has to be 'Yes'. It stands at a far remove from the kinds of 'wit' favoured by the metaphysicals, or from the kinds of resonance released by earlier poets like Shakespeare and Milton, and later poets like Pope, the Romantics and the Symbolists. We might even feel that the normal law of great poetry is its openness, its unresolved ambiguities – and its closeness, in this, to much of the life it imitates – while the use of language which imposes its author's intellectual understanding and rhetoric on events is more properly the sphere of discursive prose. Yet poetry has its ranges; and satire, the genre where polemical intention does and must count, is a kind of poetry where Dryden's distinctive gifts are most at home. It seems certain that Dryden makes a virtue of the necessary and striking limitations imposed upon him: and in this we may feel he actually demonstrates his thesis, that freedom is in fact a successful coming to terms with reality, a wedding of content to appropriate form.

So we can end by agreeing that *Absalom and Achitophel* is no

---

or, for a more exact comparison, the evocations in one couplet from Pope's *Windsor Forest*:

> The Groves of Eden, vanish'd now so long,
> Live in description, and look green in song.

Pope first calls up Eden, then banishes it, then restores it, but now in the world of art, not of nature. He does this in a couplet which, circling through powerful suggestions, enacts the process it describes. To read the couplet is almost uncannily to go through a complete circle, starting and ending with the unfading green, but passing downwards to 'vanish'd now so long', and then starting an ascent with that 'Live' which, placed at the beginning of the line, soars in such powerful counterpoint to the iambic beat. In Dryden, there is nothing analogous to this richness. His triumph is to exclude it.

exception to the general observation of W. K. Wimsatt in *The Verbal Icon* that 'Poetry is never altogether, or even mainly *poetry of statement.*' From one direction, it might be argued that harnessing topical fears to self-interest, and both to a new Tory myth of social stability, is the central strategy of the poem. From another, it might be urged that Dryden creates, from the events of the summer of 1681, a permanent and true fable concerning freedom. One argument appears to be 'historical', the other 'aesthetic', but ultimately the two are inseparable.

It is surprising that some critics have sought to excuse the censure of the King as a mere rhetorician's trick (or even worse, as a celebration of the King's humanity). It is patently neither of these things. The viciousness of tone, the introduction (or rather invention) of '*Amnon*'s Murther' and its hushing up, cannot be explained away so easily. If we let *Absalom and Achitophel* define Dryden's political position, instead of letting Dryden's presumed political position define *Absalom and Achitophel,* the problem resolves itself. In *Absalom and Achitophel* Dryden argues both the case of Charles II against Shaftesbury, and the case for a stable society. The two do not go hand in hand, as we might expect them to do. There is an inconsistency, certainly. But the inconsistency is in the Court, not in the poetry.

6 IN SPITE OF ALL HER ART: POPE'S *THE RAPE OF THE LOCK*

Some time in the summer of 1711 the young Lord Petre cut a lock from the head of Miss Arabella Fermor, the daughter of a wealthy Roman Catholic landowner. Whether he intended a joke or something more serious, Miss Fermor was outraged, and the long-standing friendship between the Petres and the Fermors was endangered. At the request of John Caryll, 'a common acquaintance and well-wisher to both', Pope wrote a poem to reconcile the two families. This was the first, Two Canto version of *The Rape of the Lock*, and was published in 1712.*

Initially, it was 'well received and had its effect in the two families', but later there were second thoughts. Perhaps the families turned critic, and began reading closely; perhaps Lord Petre's marriage to Catherine Warmsley, a fifteen-year-old heiress, turned the joke sour. One is forced to wonder indeed how far Pope realised the dangers, and deliberately sacrificed Miss Fermor's immediate prospects of happiness to his own, and her, future fame. Thalestris's speech might have been designed expressly to laugh Miss Fermor out of her vapours, but what young lady would wish to see it in print?

> Methinks already I your Tears survey,
> Already hear the horrid things they say,

* This Two Canto version, as well as the later text as we usually know it, is published in vol. II of the Twickenham Pope, from which all quotations are taken. Vol. II is edited by Geoffrey Tillotson. Vol. I (containing *Windsor Forest* and *An Essay on Criticism*) is edited by E. Audra and Aubrey Williams. Vol. III, *An Essay on Man*, is edited by Maynard Mack, and contains the excellent Introduction to which we refer later. Vol. 5, *The Dunciad*, is edited by J. R. Sutherland.

M.I.—D

> Already see you a degraded Toast,
> And all your Honour in a Whisper lost! (iv 107–10) .

The extravagance of 'Methinks already' merges into 'Tears' and
pathos; 'horrid things', a comically petty phrase, sharpens into
'degraded Toast'. Such lines have the air of self-fulfilling
prophecies, at least in the real social world where the heroine
lived. Later, Pope abandoned or transcended the occasion of his
poem, and allowed the inner genius of invention to have its way.
In 1714 the second, Five Canto version was published, with 'the
machinery' added, along with Belinda's toilet, the game of ombre,
and the Cave of Spleen. Miss Fermor was sufficiently flattered by
Pope's new Preface to regain her humour and agree to be
mentioned in it by name ('I have managed the dedication so
nicely that it can neither hurt the lady, nor the author'). But
perhaps she was still unable to pick up Pope's tone?

As to the following Canto's, all the Passages of them are as Fabulous,
as the Vision at the Beginning, or the Transformation at the End;
(except the Loss of your Hair, which I always mention with
Reverence.) The Human Persons are as Fictitious as the Airy ones;
and the Character of *Belinda*, as it is now manag'd, resembles You
in nothing but in Beauty.

In 1717, fearing that he had been misunderstood (or fearing the
reverse, a cynic might think), Pope added Clarissa's speech
(v 9–34). This certainly matched the surrounding lines in poetic
brilliance, and added a final touch to the poem, which then
existed in the form most familiar today.

Since *The Rape of the Lock* is all of a piece in everything,
including its elusiveness, the whole exists in the parts and the parts
in the whole. There is hardly one of the compulsively quotable
couplets which does not shed new gleams and radiances in shifting
lights. In theory Pope was always discriminating between the
'kinds' of verse and their appropriate decorum – the epic, the
moral, the pastoral, the satiric and so on; but in practice his own
verse has a chameleon quality which has seldom been matched.

This present discussion takes Belinda's toilet as its starting place and chief point of reference, but necessarily ranges through the poem as a whole. Its chief concern will be with the curious interactions of tone and imagery, which are central to the poem's effect.

I

> 121 And now, unveil'd, the *Toilet* stands display'd,
> Each Silver Vase in mystic Order laid.
> First, rob'd in White, the Nymph intent adores
> With Head uncover'd, the *Cosmetic* Pow'rs.
> 125 A heav'nly Image in the Glass appears,
> To that she bends, to that her Eyes she rears;
> Th'inferior Priestess, at her Altar's side,
> Trembling, begins the sacred Rites of Pride.
> Unnumber'd Treasures ope at once, and here
> 130 The various Off'rings of the World appear;
> From each she nicely culls with curious Toil,
> And decks the Goddess with the glitt'ring Spoil.
> This Casket *India's* glowing Gems unlocks,
> And all *Arabia* breathes from yonder Box.
> 135 The Tortoise here and Elephant unite,
> Transform'd to *Combs,* the speckled and the white.
> Here Files of Pins extend their shining Rows,
> Puffs, Powders, Patches, Bibles, Billet-doux.
> Now awful Beauty puts on all its Arms;
> 140 The Fair each moment rises in her Charms,
> Repairs her Smiles, awakens ev'ry Grace,
> And calls forth all the Wonders of her Face;
> Sees by Degrees a purer Blush arise,
> And keener Lightnings quicken in her Eyes.
> 145 The busy *Sylphs* surround their darling Care;
> These set the Head, and those divide the Hair,
> Some fold the Sleeve, whilst others plait the Gown;
> And *Betty's* prais'd for Labours not her own.

II

1 Not with more Glories, in th'Etherial Plain,
  The Sun first rises o'er the purpled Main,
  Than issuing forth, the Rival of his Beams
  Launch'd on the Bosom of the Silver *Thames*.
5 Fair Nymphs, and well-drest Youths around her shone,
  But ev'ry Eye was fix'd on her alone.
  On her white Breast a sparkling *Cross* she wore,
  Which *Jews* might kiss, and Infidels adore.
  Her lively Looks a sprightly Mind disclose,
10 Quick as her Eyes, and as unfix'd as those :
  Favours to none, to all she Smiles extends,
  Oft she rejects, but never once offends.
  Bright as the Sun, her Eyes the Gazers strike,
  And, like the Sun, they shine on all alike.
15 Yet graceful Ease, and Sweetness void of Pride,
  Might hide her Faults, if *Belles* had Faults to hide :
  If to her share some Female Errors fall,
  Look on her Face, and you'll forget 'em all.

J.L. : To begin with the images : lines 121–38 are a parody and inversion of the Catholic Mass, with its richly decorated altar, silver vessels and vestments, the opening of the tabernacle and the adoration of the Host. In place of cosmic powers are cosmetic powers; in place of the Host is a looking-glass. In her double role as priest and goddess, Belinda genuflects to the 'heav'nly Image' of self. For this ritual, the world's riches are plundered, with bibles trivialised into ornaments and living creatures 'Transform'd' to combs. Behind 'Transform'd' – a dazzling process – the word 'transubstantiate' clearly lurks. The irony appears to discredit Belinda's piety, along with her toilet.

From these uncompromising suggestions of blasphemy, we move to battle. Whatever claims may later be made for Belinda's innocence, her role here is active and aggressive. She is epic hero, preparing for battle ('Now awful Beauty puts on all its Arms');

she is Aphrodite rising from the sea. But, as Belinda 'rises in her Charms', she sinks into artifice; deftly, the image turns on itself. The scornful banter of 'puts on', 'Repairs', 'by Degrees' and 'purer' emphasises deception and artifice, working against the magic of 'awakens ev'ry Grace'. The description reaches its climax in 'And keener Lightnings quicken in her Eyes', a line which mingles, with the juice of belladonna, power, and danger, and beauty in spite of everything.

The picture has been of an experienced warrior in the sex-war donning the apparent innocence of a child. There is nothing allegorical here (as there is, say, in the Lady's moral 'armour' in *Comus*); real engagements are entered into, and real traps set. In our next section the preparations of this carefully contrived and deadly innocence culminate in the epiphany at Hampton Court. The 'sparkling *Cross*' again elevates ornament to the dignity of religion and debases religion to the deceptive sparkle of sex. Now, even beauty is qualified : 'white Breast' balances 'sparkling *Cross*'; the eyes are 'lively' but 'unfix'd'. Even the simple force of 'Bright as the Sun, her Eyes the Gazers strike' is weakened by 'And, like the Sun, they shine on all alike'. Behind 'Sweetness void of Pride' lurks 'the sacred Rites of Pride', with devastating suggestions of shallow emotion, flirtatiousness, and perhaps instability.

Such a simple observation of imagery could be pursued through much of the poem, and as Winifred Nowottney points out (*The Language Poets Use*, 1964), the impressions of moral severity are heightened by certain stylistic devices. In Canto II, lines 7–14, she points out that the caesura falls without exception after the fourth syllable, contributing an artificial rhythmic 'monotony', which is intensified by the inversion of the first foot in four consecutive lines (10–13). This brings us, then, to the critical problem apparent to all readers of the poem : why is its total effect so unlike that of its images? While imagery is a clue to the inner life of some works of literature, in this one, it is almost entirely confusing. The more deadly and apparently dismissive the allusions, the more a quality of radiance is felt :

Belinda smil'd, and all the World was gay. (II 52)

I cannot feel that this impression comes from careless reading, from sentimental indulgence (ironic though Pope is about this possibility), or even from original sin in the reader. The moral 'split', if there is one, is different in kind from the famous crux in *Paradise Lost*. Somehow the tone transmutes the imagery. If we can track down what happens, we shall be moving in the right direction.

A.E.D. : There will be no difference of opinion on this aspect : the poem 'feels' more like *A Midsummer Night's Dream* than like, say, *Measure for Measure*. Even the hard Restoration glitter becomes genuine sparkle; everything harsh is transformed.

Suppose that on reading the poem Belinda had cast off her finery and made for a convent; would Pope have been pleased? Suppose that she had changed very much in her inner nature; would he have welcomed even this? The poem's purpose is to reconcile her to Lord Petre; to marriage perhaps; to her own real fulfilment; indeed to the victory originally hoped from the ravished lock. If moral severity runs in excess of this aim it not only deflects itself, but may turn back, obliquely and powerfully, to the heroine's praise.

Perhaps one general point needs to be made before pursuing this : how often is straightforward panegyric ever really a success? While Dryden's Mrs Anne Killigrew remains obstinately unexciting (to me, anyway), Belinda's charm and gaiety never fail. Some degree of mockery seems an essential savour, in most purely human contexts, if praise is to make its way past the head to the heart.

It may be that Pope hits here on a quirk of human nature, but his precise effect is less easily explained. There appears to be a turning back of irony on itself in the poem, which operates consistently throughout. The transformation works as much, or almost as much, for Belinda's society, as it does for Belinda herself. Notoriously, we depend more upon *The Rape of the Lock* than

upon any other single work of literature for our delight in the
very ethos it sets out to mock. If we let our imagination loose on
the great Queen Anne houses, furnishing them with people, with
occasions, with the inner quality of their civilisation, where better
can we turn? Even the 'rape' conjures up the moral ethos it
violates, more completely than any incident one recalls. Could it
be that Pope's tone is itself the finest fruit of its culture and the
poem's true centre? – this combination of mockery with tenderness, judgement with compassionate wit?

J.L. : There is clearly an element of tone modifying content,
perhaps of tone being content to an unusual degree. There is the
possibility that the phenomenon is intrinsic to Pope's sense of
civilisation, and the certainty that it permeates his art.

To measure the extent of the transformation – before examining it further – two obvious comparisons lie to hand. First, the
opening speech of Volpone in Jonson's play (a speech which may
have influenced Pope). Volpone's worship of gold is a systematic
inversion of Christian worship, and the images are inseparable
from the poetic effect. Jonson is creating a world coldly savage
and single-minded, made in the image of Greed. The austere
substitution of gold for deity relates directly to the moral perception that one deadly sin can dominate and reduce humanity,
given its head. Jonson's sparkle is intellectual, not spiritual; any
radiance born of humanity is extinguished at source. The cold law
of Volpone extends to all the characters in the play to the precise
degree that they choose to be baptised in its name.

Second, there is the first section of Part II of *The Waste Land*,
where the description of Belinda's toilet clearly ran in Eliot's head.
This too presents a single-minded image of a world violated and
reduced. The Lady ('Belladonna') creates a cosmetic façade behind
which are loveless sex, sterility, emptiness, boredom and fear.
Eliot's evocation is heavy with drugged and deadly over-sweet-
ness, which even reaches back to involve Shakespeare's Cleopatra
on her barge.

The comparative straightforwardness of effect in both Jonson
and Eliot emphasises the essential and distinctive complexities in

Pope. While the treatment of Belinda and her society is certainly serious and astringent, its effect is curiously hard to pin down. Our reading experience of *The Rape of the Lock* is permeated by metamorphoses (and the centrality of metamorphosis has frequently been noted*) which somehow resolve the complexities towards enchantment and health.

A.E.D. : The dislocation between Art and Nature already touched upon is one of the poem's radical and persistent notes. But though the doctrines of Art and Nature as Pope presents them are often loosely called 'neo-classical', they are far from new, and far from 'classical' in a narrow sense. Their distinctive form, here, belongs to Pope and his ethos, but their roots are much further back. Whether we look at the Psalms, or at Plato, or at St Paul and the New Testament, we find Nature celebrated as the art of God, and the pursuit of beauty seen (with whatever reservations) as the fulfilled nature of man. These insights dominate medieval thinking, and remain, to some tastes in an over-ripe form, in most Renaissance works. Whatever tensions are perceived to exist between Nature and Art, as we know them, are traced to man's exile from reality, or to his fall from grace. The belief that radical dislocations originate in infected will, leading to moral blindness and mental confusion, is common to all three of the streams which fed Europe in the Christian years. Nature is God's art, visibly before us; man's art is Nature refined and disciplined to creative laws. While disharmony is the fruit, and image, of sinfulness, harmony is the older and recoverable law of creation itself.

An excellent exploration of Pope's universality as a thinker is offered by Maynard Mack in his Introduction to vol. III of the

---

* E.g. In *The Rape of the Lock*, Casebooks series, ed. John Dixon Hunt (1968), see articles by Cleanth Brooks, Martin Price, J. S. Cunningham and others. Future references to this work will be to *Casebook*. Cleanth Brooks's article, reprinted from *The Well-Wrought Urn*, is seminal, and all subsequent criticism of *The Rape of the Lock* is indebted to it.

Twickenham Pope, *The Essay On Man.** For present purposes, the concept can be simplified into this, that content and style (Nature and Art) are properly and divinely intended as partners, in a marriage of which civilisation is the fruit. To cross spontaneity with manners, intuition with common sense, instinct with structure, heart with head, passion with morality, is distinctively human because, in a prior and unalterable sense, it is divine. It is the law of real if difficult 'simplicity', as opposed to artful illusions of simplicity thrown up by the 'flesh' and the 'world'.

In Belinda's toilet, the relationship between Nature and Art is tainted, yet not vitiated; it exists somewhere between '*Nature* to Advantage drest'† and nature denied. Belinda is indeed a beautiful young woman, not Affectation (IV 31–6); her charm is real, if her childlikeness is a fraud. But the relationship, because tainted, is complex; cosmetics conceal as well as enhance. Pope's deadly 'purer' (I 143) follows the still more deadly 'Repairs' (I 141), yet Belinda's 'keener Lightnings' remain.

It is this ambiguous relationship between Nature and Art which qualifies our sense of Belinda as innocence despoiled (a view which she takes of herself after the outrage, and in which she is encouraged, of course, by Thalestris). Naturally, the view will not hold on reflection; how can any girl of this age be a child? But we then encounter a central paradox (or contradiction?) in the poem's strategy, that while its aim is to laugh Belinda out of taking the 'rape' tragically, many of the allusions point another way. There is a level at which the motives and attitudes of the Baron foretell an actual rape ('By Force to ravish, or by Fraud betray' II 32), and another at which a real rape might have been preferred by the heroine to the actual outrage, since it would (hopefully) have left a lesser mark. This view turns on Cleanth

---

* This is also the best introduction to any poem, or aspect, of Pope that we know.

† Cf. *True Wit* is *Nature* to Advantage drest,
   What oft was *Thought*, but ne'er so well *Exprest*.
                                            (*An Essay On Criticism*, 297–8).

Brooks's reading of IV 175-6 (*Casebook*), but once suggested, its plausibility is hard to evade. In this aspect, the poem's mockery of social values might suggest a perspective in which the heroine is indeed a quasi-innocent victim in her very sophistications : we are brought sharply up against the chaos of values in the beau-monde, where appearance counts for more than reality, reputation for more than virtue itself. The idea of 'honour' is a complex of falsities; small scandals that break are infinitely worse than large ones hushed-up.

We are forced to wonder how far Belinda really *knows* what she is doing, and how far she is still pure at heart. Might her cosmetics, her deadly lock even, be still a kind of child's play, an elaborate and only half-understood dressing-up? There are degrees of play and seriousness in flirtation, degrees of understanding in the sophistications of the young. Belinda fails to grasp the cynical wisdom of Clarissa's maturity (e.g. 'And she who scorns a Man, must die a Maid' v 28), as perhaps she failed to grasp the actual risks she ran.

In our toilet passage, there is such real warmth in, for instance, II 9-16, that the severity of implied censure surely to a degree mocks itself. There is something crabbed and harsh in it at the very least, whether it is directed at Belinda by puritan, by worldly sophisticate, or by prude. May not the extreme condemnation of Belinda as cynical flirt itself be a vicious instance of the World's long battle against the Flesh? To condemn so totally is to overlook Belinda's genuine loveliness, her capacity for happiness, which remain radiant even if she has made herself, by vicious imitation perhaps, 'fair game'. Possibly she deserves a delicate response of subtle impulses, generous respect, intimate courtship, of the kind which her sophisticated yet brutal society denies? There can be no doubting that worldlings and prudes both trample, if for different reasons, on the quicksilver charm of young love.

The references to childlikeness in the poem are always subtle, in their poise between reality and ironic pretence. In Belinda's dream-warning (I 37-40) Ariel says :

Some secret Truths from Learned Pride conceal'd,
To Maids alone and Children are reveal'd :
What tho' no Credit doubting Wits may give?
The Fair and Innocent shall still believe.

Though Ariel is trying to inspire Belinda with belligerent pride, and flatters to tempt her, there is a residual appeal to genuine charm. It haunts a line like 'They shift the moving Toyshop of their Heart' (I 100), where irony at worldly wiles again evokes something vulnerable and lovely. In the game of ombre, this characteristic effect of the poem is most marked. The 'game' foreshadows in parody battle the 'dire offence' impending, yet the imagery is oddly turned back on itself. In seeing the cards as if for the first time, with a child's eye, we are restored to the joys of conflict devoid of a sting. What remains strange is the manner in which early innocence can be conveyed through diction and syntax in the highest degree sophisticated, and attuned equally to severity of judgement and lightness of tone :

Behold, four *Kings* in Majesty rever'd,
With hoary Whiskers and a forky Beard;
And four fair *Queens* whose hands sustain a Flow'r,
Th'expressive Emblem of their softer Pow'r;
Four *Knaves* in Garbs succinct, a trusty Band,
Caps on their heads, and Halberds in their hand (III 37–42)

Such verse has the effect of restoring the triviality of Belinda and her surroundings – the trifling joys, the vicious personal encounters – to something almost paradisal. The vanity of the Sylphs is also assimilated to freshness :

Soon as she spreads her Hand, th'Aerial Guard
Descend, and sit on each important Card :
First *Ariel* perch'd upon a *Matadore*,*

---

* The three most important trumps are Matadors, and Ariel no doubt chooses Spadillo ('unconquerable Lord !'), the Ace of Spades. The rules of Ombre, which is now generally obsolete, are

Then each, according to the Rank they bore;
For *Sylphs,* yet mindful of their ancient Race,
Are, as when Women, wondrous fond of Place. (III 31–6)

Belinda's absorption in the game has a charm which infuses even
her shrieks of victory, and her 'livid paleness' (manufactured in
the Cave of Spleen – IV 70) at near defeat. Her abandon and
delight – supremely ambiguous aspects always, of the sensual and
sensuous – still survive their taint. The brewing of coffee after
the game furthers this mood, creating an image which for a
moment becomes the pure enchantment of high style and delicacy
(cf. the marvellous lines from Yeats's 'A Prayer for my Daughter' :
'How but in custom and in ceremony/Are innocence and Beauty
born?').

The effect of such ambivalence is to remind us that Belinda
may indeed be a warmly generous young girl, simply pulled out
of shape by social and sexual forces which she is influenced by,
but scarcely grasps. The lures and demands of her society, its
basic harshness and brutality under the polish, are undercut by
some lingering vision of what *might* be. If this derives from
Belinda herself – or from Pope's vision of her at its most tender;
or, as we shall suggest, from another powerful aspect of the poem
less often discussed in criticism, its tragic undercurrent – then
isn't the most savage indictment of Belinda itself tainted?
Perhaps true men should tease and compliment her with gentle
mockery (as Pope does in places), celebrating what is true,
nurturing the good? If she were treated with courtesy, let off
lightly, there might be real discoveries and rewards.

For readers then, there may be a special call to guard against
facile rejection, as the brutality at furthest remove from a fully
human response. What we necessarily return to, through Pope's

---

set out in Appendix C to the Twickenham Pope, vol. II, and explain
everything except whether the cards discarded are face up or face
down. We assume face down; and recommend the game, and the re-
constructed 'hand' from this poem, to students who have a few hours
to spare.

double vision of beauty deeply tainted yet radiant, is the much more jarring discord in Belinda's world. The ethos is still perceptibly that of the Restoration court; the literary conventions belong with the comedy of the half century before. We can see this in the treatment of the Baron; Sir Plume; the Sylphs; the Cave of Spleen; Thalestris; to some degree Clarissa. Arguably, this was the most brutal ethos in its attitudes to sexual relationships that has ever generally prevailed in articulate and influential English society, if we look back beyond the exceptional confusions of the present time. Every man a seducer; every husband a cuckold; every woman at heart a whore; every 'affair' a victory for sex, but rarely for love; every clap and pox a joke (they weren't); every man and woman a slave to lust. So ran the data : with kudos for every boast of conquest, however outrageous, and unremitting hostility for those actually exposed. Perverted ideals of 'honour' and 'reputation' were kept up in the squalor, it sometimes seems, chiefly to give added savour to seduction, added cruelty to exposure, added 'fun'. The endless boasts of lust by man to man and woman to woman are balanced by outright rejection when any boast is found to be true.

There is, of course, an element of stylisation in Restoration comedy – a farcical abstraction from 'reality' – which makes the plays hard to use in directly social terms. Each dramatist moreover has his own 'flavour', his own edge of farce playing over the sickening ethos of Charles's court. And the plays are also, of course, magnificently entertaining, an aspect that sterner critics are apt to forget.

For the present purpose, my suggestion is that Pope's treatment differs from the Restoration one, and that it differs in a direction of greater subtlety, greater purity and humanity of response. Belinda isn't a stock 'coquette', though she may look like one* : coquettes don't, by definition, discover earthly lovers

---

* The case for her as 'coquette' is argued by Hugo M. Reichard (Casebook) – an illuminating article, but in the last resort, to my mind, wrong.

lurking at the heart. What she needs at this moment above all is male delicacy, and privacy; the two qualities of which she is most notably deprived.

J.L. : You mention 'honour', and references to this, of course, abound. There is, for instance, the joking suggestion that 'honour' is not, as men think or pretend to think, human virtue, but the capricious and ambiguous intervention of 'sylphs' :

> What guards the Purity of melting Maids,
> In Courtly Balls, and Midnight Masquerades,
> Safe from the treach'rous Friend, the daring Spark,
> The Glance by Day, the Whisper in the Dark;
> When kind Occasion prompts their warm Desires,
> When Musick softens, and when Dancing fires?
> 'Tis but their *Sylph,* the wise Celestials know,
> Tho' *Honour* is the Word with Men below. (i 71–8)

It is because this so powerfully evokes the erotic and treacherous in combination that the last line is more than a simple mock heroic joke. The Baron later says that his 'Honour' will live by Belinda's dishonour, 'While Nymphs take Treats, or Assignations give' (iii 169); later again, Thalestris rubs in the brutality for Belinda 'And all your Honour in a Whisper lost !' (iv 110). Multiple meanings of 'honour' are played off against one another, for instance in the Baron's speech :

> But by this Lock, this sacred Lock I swear,
> (Which never more shall join its parted Hair,
> Which never more its Honours shall renew,
> Clipt from the lovely Head where late it grew
>
> (iv 133–6)

Here, 'Honours' points both to the natural beauty of Belinda's lock in its original setting and to its irrevocable separation (with 'sacred' again ironic) after the outrage. Both ideas are linked with social 'honour', and there are complexities throughout. The natural growth of the lock has been heightened by artifice, and the 'rape' is in a sense the intended culmination of growth. The process has been inherently painful to Belinda; and when Thalestris piles on reminders of all she has suffered (IV 97–102) the intention is to confuse, not to clarify, the emotions lying beneath. The phrase 'never more its Honours shall renew' under-lines the dishonour of Mortality : we recognise that while losing hair – even unnaturally – might be a fairly normal *memento mori,* the symbolism of rape adds a more sombre dimension. These aspects all interact with social reputation, and here we sense at least three strands. Belinda's natural dignity has certainly been violated, but in a way which ought, 'chagrin' apart, to be taken more lightly than this. Clarissa's good sense would have translated it into a public declaration, a preparation, acceptable to all parties, for ceremonies of marriage and a decorous conclusion to the affair. On the other hand, Belinda's vulner-ability has been exploited : and her reaction may in fact reveal her as still damagingly young. But there is also the matter of public reputation : and here, corruptions of 'honour' set the tone. The Baron initiates whisper and gossip (ironically perpetuated in Pope's poem), which indict a society ill-attuned to making its own 'style' work for good instead of for ill.

To bring this theme into focus, we might look at the central episode, the 'rape' itself, where Belinda's preparations for conquest end in defeat. The Baron takes the scissors from Clarissa :

> This just behind *Belinda*'s Neck he spread,
> As o'er the fragrant Steams she bends her Head :
> Swift to the Lock a thousand Sprights repair,
> A thousand Wings, by turns, blow back the Hair,
> And thrice they twitch'd the Diamond in her Ear,
> Thrice she look'd back, and thrice the Foe drew near.
>
> (III 133–8)

The sylph's warning of impending danger is both playful and exquisite. Belinda surely sees the Baron approaching ('Thrice she look'd back'), but makes no attempt to escape the attack; she

senses the nature of the intention, if not its form. Maybe she even
encourages it :

> Just in that instant, anxious *Ariel* sought
> The close Recesses of the Virgin's Thought;
> As on the Nosegay in her Breast reclin'd,
> He watch'd th'Ideas rising in her Mind,
> Sudden he view'd, in spite of all her Art,
> An Earthly Lover lurking at her Heart.
> Amaz'd, confus'd, he found his Pow'r expir'd,
> Resign'd to Fate, and with a Sigh retir'd. (III 139–46)

In tone this is serious, with the secrecy and calculation of 'close
Recesses' and 'th'Ideas rising in her Mind' contrasting sharply
with the openness and innocence of 'Virgin's Thought'. Belinda's
mask crumbles : beneath it she is a girl with ordinary emotions,
an 'Earthly Lover' as much as the Baron, though more vulnerable. '. . . in spite of all her Art' stresses in its powerful
monosyllables the unreality and impotence of art, yet also its
purity : this tension is echoed in the rhyme of 'Art' and 'Heart',
with the mind shifting uneasily between the two. Ariel retires, a
pathetic and comic figure, defeated not only in battle but also in
love (the sexual overtones are underlined in Pope's Preface : 'For
they say, any Mortals may enjoy the most intimate Familiarities
with these gentle Spirits, upon a Condition very easie to all true
Adepts, an inviolate Preservation of Chastity'). Deliberately,
under the strongest compulsions of nature without art, Belinda
breaks the 'Condition', and drives Ariel from 'her Breast'.

Again, the tone changes :

> The Peer now spreads the glitt'ring *Forfex* wide,
> T'inclose the Lock; now joins it, to divide.
> Ev'n then, before the fatal Engine clos'd,
> A wretched *Sylph* too fondly interpos'd;
> Fate urg'd the Sheers, and cut the *Sylph* in twain,
> (But Airy Substance soon unites again)
> The meeting Points the sacred Hair dissever
> From the fair Head for ever and for ever ! (III 147–54)

This account is in one way the culmination of the 'mock-heroic'. The 'glitt'ring *Forfex*' and 'the fatal Engine' raise the incident to absurd heights. The cutting of the Sylph, which alludes to the loss of Belinda's 'Honour' (cf. 1 77–8), is a lightly irreverent glance at the war in Heaven in *Paradise Lost:* but while the 'wretched *Sylph*' can be restored in a twinkling, like Milton's angels, with the heroine's severed lock it is otherwise. Here, the poem ceases to exaggerate, and 'for ever and for ever !' is undercut as humour (which derives both from Belinda's loss of proportion and from Pope's ironic perspective and apparatus) by irreducible fact. So the Fates cut their threads; so Troy fell; so all virtue, all life, have an end.

> Then flash'd the living Lightning from her Eyes,
> And Screams of Horror rend th'affrighted Skies.
> Not louder Shrieks to pitying Heav'n are cast,
> When Husbands or when Lap-dogs breathe their last,
> Or when rich *China* Vessels, fal'n from high,
> In glittring Dust and painted Fragments lie ! (iii 155–60)

Belinda's reaction is both violent and spontaneous. There is a hint of insincerity behind the excessive 'Screams', 'affrighted' and 'louder Shrieks', yet the critic who insists that Belinda is merely affecting anger here, as she certainly does later in the Cave of Spleen, is missing the complexity of her response.* The fact that she is a party to the attack does not prevent her from being horrified; once it has happened, her own complicity will surely sicken her most. If, in the beau-monde, the death of a lap-dog is mourned as much as the death of a husband, why not the loss of a lock also ? '*China* Vessels' shares the multiplicity of the '*China* Jar' of Ariel's warning (ii 106), and adds sexual implications (cf. 'Men prove with Child, as pow'rful Fancy works,/And Maids turn'd Bottles, call aloud for Corks', iv 53–4). 'Rich' and 'glittring' and 'painted' are again heavily ironic, but it must be

---

* Cf. the views of Aubrey Williams, *Casebook.*

an impassive reader who is not saddened by the passing of so
much beauty ('Dust', 'Fragments').

The third Canto ends, after a weakly dishonourable speech of
victory from the Baron, on an openly tragic note :

> What Time wou'd spare, from Steel receives its date,
> And Monuments, like Men, submit to Fate !
> Steel cou'd the Labour of the Gods destroy,
> And strike to Dust th'Imperial Tow'rs of *Troy*;
> Steel cou'd the Works of mortal Pride confound,
> And hew Triumphal Arches to the Ground.
> What Wonder then, fair Nymph ! thy Hairs shou'd feel
> The conqu'ring Force of unresisted Steel? (III 171–8)

When 'Monuments, like Men, submit to Fate', the satire probes
far beyond a social quarrel. Nothing is proof against the violence
of mankind. Twice the first foot of a line is inverted, throwing the
accent on to 'Steel', and emphasising its 'conqu'ring Force' :
man is the destroyer of himself and his heritage. Note how the
'Works of mortal Pride' are no less magnificent than the 'Labour
of the Gods'; note how 'unresisted' brilliantly combines Belinda's
vulnerability with her guilt; note the sexual reference implicit in
the last couplet (the most serious linking in the poem, perhaps,
between energy and destructiveness in man). The movement of
humour is through brutal clarity towards the tragic : for a
moment, we forget the mechanics of language; laughter is
muffled; there is a distant sound of mortality. The inner music
of the lines foreshadows that vision in the *Essay On Man,* of *homo
sapiens* floating, with no clear guide, in his passing world :

> Plac'd on this isthmus of a middle state,
> A being darkly wise, and rudely great :
> With too much knowledge for the Sceptic side,
> With too much weakness for the Stoic's pride,
> He hangs between; in doubt to act, or rest,
> In doubt to deem himself a God, or Beast;
> In doubt his Mind or Body to prefer,

Born but to die, and reas'ning but to err;
Alike in ignorance, his reason such,
Whether he thinks too little, or too much :
Chaos of Thought and Passion, all confus'd;
Still by himself abus'd, or disabus'd;
Created half to rise, and half to fall;
Great lord of all things, yet a prey to all;
Sole judge of Truth, in endless Error hurl'd :
The glory, jest, and riddle of the world !
                              (*Essay On Man,* II 3–18)

A.E.D. : This brings us to the tragic note in Pope. While this
has been less discussed than most aspects of his verse, we both
agree in finding it at the heart of *The Rape of the Lock.* Like
many satirists, Pope was deeply sensitive to beauty. T. S. Eliot
called him 'the great master of hatred', and this quality is seldom
more apparent than when he encounters violation – of reason,
by fools and dullards; and of life itself, by cruelty and cant. Consider these lines from an early poem :

See ! from the Brake the whirring Pheasant springs,
And mounts exulting on triumphant Wings;
Short is his Joy ! he feels the fiery Wound,
Flutters in Blood, and panting beats the Ground.
Ah ! what avail his glossie, varying Dyes,
His Purple Crest, and Scarlet-circled Eyes,
The vivid Green his shining Plumes unfold;
His painted Wings, and Breast that flames with Gold ?
                              (*Windsor Forest,* 111–18)

Though one explicit moral of the completed *Windsor Forest*
(almost certainly written several years after the above lines) is
that men should turn back from slaughtering one another in war
to hunting, the poem generates pity for all needless death. And
in the exquisite 'Elegy to the Memory of an Unfortunate Lady'
(1717), it is the violation of the Lady's youth and beauty – so

reminiscent in description of Belinda's – which leads to one of
Pope's astonishing outburts of vengeful hate :

> Cold is that breast which warm'd the world before,
> And those love-darting eyes must roll no more.
> Thus, if eternal justice rules the ball,
> Thus shall your wives, and thus your children fall :
> On all the line a sudden vengeance waits,
> And frequent herses shall besiege your gates.
> There passengers shall stand, and pointing say,
> (While the long fun'rals blacken all the way)
> Lo these were they, whose souls the Furies steel'd,
> And curs'd with hearts unknowing how to yield.
> Thus unlamented pass the proud away,
> The gaze of fools, and pageant of a day !
> So perish all, whose breast ne'er learn'd to glow
> For others' good, or melt at others' woe. ('Elegy', 33–46)

The first two lines may particularly recall the passage with which
the fifth and final Canto of *The Rape of the Lock* ends :

> Then cease, bright Nymph ! to mourn thy ravish'd Hair
> Which adds new Glory to the shining Sphere !
> Not all the Tresses that fair Head can boast
> Shall draw such Envy as the Lock you lost.
> For, after all the Murders of your Eye,
> When after Millions slain, your self shall die;
> When those fair Suns shall sett, as sett they must,
> And all those Tresses shall be laid in Dust;
> *This Lock*, the Muse shall consecrate to Fame,
> And mid'st the Stars inscribe *Belinda*'s Name ! (v 141–50)

The tragic groundswell here not so much transforms Belinda and
the poem as accounts for the transformations we have continually
felt. 'Millions slain' ceases to feel like mock-heroic exaggeration;
'die' ceases to look like yet one more tired pun about sex. The
music is much nearer to Shakespeare : 'Golden lads and lasses

must/Like chimney-sweepers come to dust.' It is a lament for the passing of youth.

This note of mortality sounds not only at the close of the poem, but to an attentive ear throughout. The poem's mood is so to mingle banter and tenderness, mockery and enchantment, that the mind moves elusively through many keys. What could be more beautiful that this image? – which in context, comes as one of Pope's more savage thrusts :

> Thus on *Meander*'s flow'ry Margin lies
> Th'expiring Swan, and as he sings he dies. (v 65–6)

And Clarissa's speech, though it culminates in a rather routine and stoical common sense, which certainly isn't the total 'moral' of the poem, offers a variety of tragic nuances. There is the realism of her direct advice to Belinda in the excerpt to be quoted overleaf (for Clarissa, what Belinda has lost, and indeed might lose in marriage, is not so very important); there is the compelling perspective of life's brevity; there is, too, the immense vitality of the rhythms, which tug against the iambic beat as powerfully as anything in Donne, though Pope naturally avoids the mimetic ruggedness of 'metaphysical' effect. The result (and I scan the lines as I would read them myself)* is to offer the very feel of the

* Individual readings of the poem will naturally differ, and one notable characteristic is that no two readings are likely to coincide. This seems true even with the same reader, since the quicksilver quality exists in rhythm as well as in tone. *The Rape of the Lock* is pre-eminently *worth* reading aloud, and even offering for experiment. If a group of people are involved, it might be worth tape-recording particular sections, with each reader performing before he hears the others, and comparing results. In my own scansion, offered here, only one line falls in the reading on its iambic norm – and this (28) comes almost with the effect of novelty : the 'norm', because it has become in context abnormal, seems to underline the detachable and proverbial quality of its content. So much for Keats's famous sneer at the 'rocking-horse couplet'! It seems certain that none of Pope's romantic detractors (and the romantics were not all, of course, in this category) ever *listened* to him.

dance that is rejected, and then the inner sadness of locks inevitably 'raped' by Time. In 1713 Lord Petre had died from smallpox, and when these lines were added, in 1717, Belinda was already six years exiled from her insulted youth :

> Oh ! if to dance all Night, and dress all Day,
> Charm'd the Small-pox, or chas'd old Age away;
> Who would not scorn what Huswife's Cares produce,
> Or who would learn one earthly Thing of Use ?
> To patch, nay ogle, might become a Saint,
> Nor could it sure be such a Sin to paint.
> But since, alas ! frail Beauty must decay,
> Curl'd or uncurl'd, since Locks will turn to grey,
> Since painted, or not painted, all shall fade,
> And she who scorns a Man, must die a Maid;
> What then remains, but well our Pow'r to use,
> And keep good Humour still whate'er we lose ? (v 19–30)

These tragic undercurrents to the comic vitality recall Shakespeare's most sparkling comedies, *As You Like It* as well as the more frequently cited *A Midsummer Night's Dream*. Though the effect is naturally different, and distinctive, there is a same flickering of wit and gaiety over unexplained treachery, near isolation, rebuffed love. Such notes certainly transform, in Pope, the Restoration harshness of ethos and imagery, ensuring a more complex and human, a purer, total response. Yet Pope – like Shakespeare – never topples over into softness; nor is there any of that descent into self-conscious 'sensibility', morbid self-indulgence and the like which we find later in the century when Cowper, Goldsmith and others adapted Pope's couplet form to melancholy themes.

The triumph of style is, of course, moral, as always in art of this magnitude. One cannot forget how exiled Pope was personally from Belinda's world. Nature had not framed him for the glamour and danger, the enchanted world of young lovers, 'The Glance by Day, the Whisper in the Dark'. He is a classic case of an artist exiled by personal ungainliness from the world of wit and polish, high 'style' in living and loving, of which he was one of the greatest masters in words. Pope was far too great an artist to sour his poetry : but the flickering dangerousness, the refusal of certainty, may be in part the language of exile. It helps of course to set the poem off, rounding it, paradoxically, to perfection.

J.L. : So we return to that matter where all discussion of this poem begins and ends : the curious and continuous interactions of imagery and tone. It is a matter of common experience that Pope's mood turns and changes from couplet to couplet, in a manner as different as possible from Dryden's normal accumulations and steady forward march. While Dryden excludes resonances, Pope glories in them : yet as much as Dryden, he is perfectly in control. The poem has scarcely started, before we encounter those sudden changes of direction, quick enough to deceive the ear and the mind :

> Say what strange Motive, Goddess ! cou'd compel
> A well-bred *Lord* t'assault a gentle *Belle?*
> Oh say what stranger Cause, yet unexplor'd,
> Cou'd make a gentle *Belle* reject a *Lord?* (i 7–10)

First, there is an assumption of gentle courtesy as the rule in society; then, the assumption of urbane cynicism as a general mood. These assumptions clash, with distinctive humour, dissolving any simple bearings at the outset. But their unity is a tone of mocking banter, which is one of the voices of friendship, even of love. It could be teasing; it could be mild flirtation; it could be tender intimacy; it could be intimacy made uneasy, or betrayed. Certainly this tone establishes itself before the more apparently savage images arrive; it is the ambiance of Belinda's dream, and the toilet scene.

If we move to a passage from Ariel's address to the sylphs on

the barge, we catch the poem's famous treacherous antitheses
arranging themselves in a similar way :

> This Day, black Omens threat the brightest Fair
> That e'er deserv'd a watchful Spirit's Care;
> Some dire Disaster, or by Force, or Slight,
> But what, or where, the Fates have wrapt in Night.
> Whether the Nymph shall break *Diana*'s Law,
> Or some frail *China* Jar receive a Flaw,
> Or stain her Honour, or her new Brocade,
> Forget her Pray'rs, or miss a Masquerade,
> Or lose her Heart, or Necklace at a Ball;
> Or whether Heav'n has doom'd that *Shock* must fall.
>
> (II 101–10)

Ariel's loftiness deflates itself, but the antitheses which follow are
serious as well as comic and deserve more than a passing smile.
When the breaking of '*Diana*'s Law' is set beside the breaking of
a '*China* Jar', implications reach several ways. The morality of
the beau-monde is mocked for equating the two (and there is
even the suggestion, already touched on, of reversed priorities, in
that fragments of *China* Jars can be less easily concealed than
fragments of virginity: cf. IV 175–6). But at the same time, the
two things are really equalised in very basic questions, not to be
solved by simple irony : does it really matter if either is broken?
Does it matter if both are? Does it matter, or not matter, in the
same, or in different degree? 'Important – unimportant', as the
King of Hearts said to himself, 'as if he were trying which word
sounded best'. We are thrown back on ourselves to ponder the
relationship between two very different things, which may both
be as really precious as they are practically useless, and may both
be rightly, or wrongly, valued in a society which assimilates them
to its own complex style. Can anything beautiful, anything good,
be lost beyond recovery, without causing sorrow? There is a sense
in which the beau-monde may, if not for its own reasons, be right.

In this and the other antitheses we are continually presented
with the ambiguous charm of this social morality, elusive to

judgement yet redolent of beauty; the poetry mocks and marvels at once. And, as in later such passages, we cannot say that there is a simple crescendo or diminuendo in the placings :

> Not youthful Kings in Battel seiz'd alive,
> Not scornful Virgins who their Charms survive,
> Not ardent Lovers robb'd of all their Bliss,
> Not ancient Ladies when refus'd a Kiss,
> Not Tyrants fierce that unrepenting die,
> Not *Cynthia* when her *Manteau*'s pinn'd awry,
> E'er felt such Rage, Resentment and Despair,
> As Thou, sad Virgin ! for thy ravish'd Hair. (IV 3–10)

The progress from 'youthful Kings' to '*Cynthia*' is more of a switchback ride than a straight descent, with the 'scornful virgins' anticipating Clarissa's moral, and the fury of scorned Ladies a proverbial power. If '*Cynthia*' is a dip in the ride, where is Belinda? The chagrins manufactured in the Cave of Spleen are not wholly a joke.

Such uncertainties lend power to the deeper transformations, such as the ambivalences in the Game of Ombre (already remarked upon) and the splendid apotheosis of the Lock towards which everything moves :

> But trust the Muse – she saw it upward rise,
> Tho' mark'd by none but quick Poetic Eyes :
> (So *Rome*'s great Founder to the Heav'ns withdrew,
> To *Proculus* alone confess'd in view.)
> A sudden Star, it shot thro' liquid Air,
> And drew behind a radiant *Trail of Hair*.
> Not *Berenice*'s Locks first rose so bright,
> The Heav'ns bespangling with dishevel'd Light.
> The *Sylphs* behold it kindling as it flies,
> And pleas'd pursue its Progress thro' the Skies. (v 123–32)

. . . and so on, through further exuberant fancies and exaggerations, to the beautiful closing lines. 'But trust the Muse' : perhaps Belinda pondered that ! Not the satiric Muse – pleased though she must have been – but the Muse of transformations now clearly evoked. This apotheosis of the Lock, which in mock-heroic terms is the poem's supreme extravagance, is artistically its moment of truth. 'Nor marble' wrote Shakespeare, 'nor the guilded monuments/Of Princes shall outlive this powerfull rime' (Sonnet 55). Even as Pope mocks, the magic happens. In the act of diminishing Belinda's lock with ridicule to a true social perspective, he transposes it, and her, beyond any girl's wildest dreams. As the tragic note sounds again – 'sett they must', 'laid in dust' – mockery is caught up in beauty, and both are simply lifted out of time. The 'fair suns', the ravished lock, pass into orbit, 'consecrate' beyond even Pope's humour, 'mid'st the Stars'.

It is the last and abiding note of *The Rape of the Lock* that Belinda's beauty is lost and won for ever. The many metamorphoses, including the continual transformation of ironic allusion by tone, culminate in the habitual miracle of art. We cannot fail to recall the end of *The Dunciad*, where an irony far more savage than any directed against Belinda climbs towards lines which affirm, in their triumphant artistry, the resilience they exist to deny : 'Art after Art goes out, and all is Night.'

In February 1714 Pope sent a copy of *The Rape of the Lock* to Mrs Marriott, and in a covering letter he wrote :

This whimsical piece of work, as I have now brought it up to my first design, is at once the most a satire, and the most inoffensive, of anything of mine. People who would rather it were let alone laugh at it, and seem heartily merry, at the same time that they are uneasy. 'Tis a sort of writing very like tickling.

The attempt here has been to examine some of the poem's 'tickling', as this shapes and dissolves and reshapes possible frames of response. But there comes a time with *The Rape of the Lock* as there does with all great literature when analysis is no longer satisfactory as criticism. A reader must then resign himself to mysteries, allowing the resonances to flow over him like a moody sea, feeling its calms and storms, its peace, its anger and laughter.

In *The Rape of the Lock* Pope satirises the chaos of values in the beau-monde, but he never ceases to marvel at its beauty. And what of his wayward *Belle*, goddess, warrior, flirt, lover, child?

If to her share some Female Errors fall,
Look on her Face, and you'll forget 'em all. (II 17–18)

Though the irony flickers over readers and poet, Pope is manifestly enchanted – 'in spite of all her Art'.

C. S. Lewis's *The Great Divorce* starts with a confession for which Blake's readers, and his critics especially, may be glad: 'Blake wrote of the Marriage of Heaven and Hell. If I have written of their Divorce, this is not because I think myself a fit antagonist for so great a genius, nor even because I feel at all sure that I know what he meant.' Blake's poetry certainly reflects his genius, in that it is usually immediately striking, and lingers in the mind. But although it often sounds aphoristic it remains baffling; readers are more apt to 'sense' lurking truths, than to explain what their Nature might be:

> Every night and every morn
> Some to misery are born.
> Every morn and every night,
> Some are born to sweet delight.
> Some are born to sweet delight,
> Some are born to endless night.

Such qualities guarantee perennial fascination and perennial discussion, while making any consensus hard to obtain. Blake, in one mood at least, would have welcomed this: 'I must create a system, or be enslaved by another man's.' What C. S. Lewis does is to make it easier for us to acknowledge something dangerous, as well as fascinating, in Blake's work, without feeling obliged to claim the fullest insight into it, and without being absolutely qualified even to judge. T. S. Eliot, of course, was somewhat sterner: in a notorious essay, he attributes Blake's obscurity to his lack of formal education, suggesting that mere muddle, not profundity, may sometimes lie at the heart.

In this chapter, we shall concentrate on two short songs, one

of innocence and one of experience, but first outlining, very
briefly, the fundamental ideas.

Anyone studying Blake soon discovers that the figures which
occur in his work usually belong, marriage notwithstanding, to
either Heaven or Hell. Since the groupings are unfamiliar one
needs the key – which, simply, is that any restraints on energy
originating from outside a man are, for Blake, bad. Thus Blake's
villains are all associated with law and repression; they include
Jehovah, Moses, Newton, Locke, priests, law-givers and, notably,
fathers. Jehovah and Moses belong with the 'Thou shalt not' of
moral commandment, which is the force that keeps men perpetually childish and perpetually unfulfilled. In an edict from Hell
Blake declares, 'I tell you, no virtue can exist without breaking
these ten commandments.' Newton and Locke, on the other hand,
guard the prison-house of empirical reason, locking men in the
dungeon of their five senses, and of the abstract and abstracting
life of the mind. In one of Blake's best-known pictures, Newton
is depicted as a maniac with a pair of compasses, drawing a small
circle in which men will be perpetually confined. Priests are
villains under both headings, creating restrictive rules to restrain
the body from its proper delight and intellectual systems of dogma
to enslave the mind. The first of these two evils of priestcraft is
suggested in the nightmare image which ends 'The Chapel on the
Green' :

> And priests in black gowns were walking their rounds,
> And binding with briars my joys and desires

The second of the evils is succinctly described in 'The Marriage
of Heaven and Hell', where an unidentified narrator finds
religion rooted in a misunderstanding or perversion of poetic
modes :

The ancient Poets animated all sensible objects with Gods or
Geniuses, calling them by the names and adorning them with the
properties of woods, rivers, mountains, lakes, cities, nations, and
whatever their enlarged and numerous senses could perceive.

And particularly they studied the genius of each city and country, placing it under its mental deity;

Till a system was formed, which some took advantage of and en- slav'd the vulgar by attempting to realise or abstract the mental deities from their objects : thus began Priesthood,

Choosing forms of worship from poetic tales.

And at length they pronounced that the Gods had order'd such things.

Thus men forgot that All deities reside in the human breast.

Judges likewise are evil : in 'A Little Boy Lost' the little boy who dares to tell the truth instead of coming out with simplistic hypocrisies is doomed by a judge, bound in chains, and burnt to death. Fathers, the archetypal authoritarians, become chief oppressors (and here we circle back to Jehovah, who is also Father in an ultimate sense). In one lyric the hero takes an axe and kills his father; but his own hairs are already grey, and he has waited too long. The father should have been killed earlier, while the hero still had youth and energy, and the will freely to accept his destiny for himself.

In contrast Blake's heroes are associated with the forces of joy and love, and include Israel, Isaiah, Ezekiel, Christ, and Satan (Satan's virtue is energy, certainly not joy or love). Israel is equated with 'the poetic Genius', most notably through the prophets Isaiah and Ezekiel, who dine with Blake, and confirm that this was indeed their purport. Isaiah glosses his prophecy as a discovery of something akin to Coleridge's Reason and Imagination (on which, see pp. 154–7 below), a faculty beyond the five senses, which directly perceives divinity and supersensuous truth :

Isaiah answered : 'I saw no God, nor heard any, in a finite organical perception; but my senses discovered the infinite in every thing . . .'.

Ezekiel also encompasses the exclusive claims of Hebraic religion in a romantic frame :

Then Ezekiel said : 'The philosophy of the east taught the first principles of human perception : some nations held one principle for

the origin and some another : we of Israel taught that the Poetic
Genius (as you now call it) was the first principle, and all others
merely derivative, which was the cause of our despising the Priests
and Philosophers of other countries, and prophesying that all Gods
would at last be proved to originate in ours and to be the tributaries
of the Poetic Genius . . .'.

This, it will be seen, neatly bypasses Jehovah and Moses, and
explains why, these famous lawgivers notwithstanding, Israel
comes out on the right side in Blake's equations :

>The Atoms of Democritus
>And Newton's particles of Light
>Are sands upon the Red Sea shore
>Where Israel's tents do shine so bright . . .

Christ is seen as the embodiment of love, and so the opposite of
the Father – not one with Jehovah, as in orthodox theology, but
the radical alternative and release. Satan is the voice which says
that energy is eternal delight and all energy is from the body.

What Blake appears to be asserting, somewhat in the face of
the evidence, is that *all* previous religions have been dualistic,
dividing man into body and soul, and equating evil with the
former and good with the latter. For him, this has been the great
error, the great divorce in man's integrity of being, which his own
proposed marriage of Heaven and Hell will mend. Near the start
of 'The Marriage of Heaven and Hell', Blake explains the
romantic doctrine of contraries : morality is not passive, not a state
to be attained and rested in, but active, the perpetual play of
opposites in energy and joy :

Without Contraries is no progression. Attraction and Repulsion,
Reason and Energy, Love and Hate, are necessary to Human
existence.

From these contraries spring what the religious call Good and
Evil. Good is the passive that obeys Reason. Evil is the active spring-
ing from Energy.

Good is Heaven, Evil is Hell.

This is immediately followed by a crucial passage ascribed to 'The Voice of the Devil'. Like the still more famous 'Proverbs of Hell', which come later, we are presumably meant to read this as half a truth – the half which 'the religious', according to Blake, have condemned as 'evil' but which properly married to its Heavenly opposite (*not* here enunciated) will give the true, because poetic, insight :

All Bibles or sacred codes have been the cause of the following Errors :
i. That Man has two real existing principles, Viz : a Body and a Soul.
ii. That Energy, call'd Evil, is alone from the Body, and that Reason, call'd Good, is alone from the Soul.
iii. That God will torment Man in Eternity for following his Energies.
But the following Contraries to these are true :
i. Man has no Body distinct from his Soul; for that call'd Body is a portion of Soul discern'd by the five Senses, the chief inlets of Soul in this age.
ii. Energy is the only life and is from the Body, and Reason is the bound or outward circumference of Energy.
iii. Energy is Eternal Delight.

The central argument is apparently that all moral systems putting restrictions on instinctual energy, and all religions sanctioning such systems, constitute a conspiracy of the weak and timid against the strong – a kind of revenge, or castration, used by 'normal', small men to tame or break those who are more alive, more truly divine. Certainly, many of the 'Proverbs of Hell' – again taken literally, and without the balance of their putative opposites – would seem to support this : 'The road of excess leads to the palace of wisdom'; 'The nakedness of woman is the work of God'; and, more striking and even dangerous, 'Sooner murder an Infant in its cradle than nurse unacted desires'. Undoubtedly, many later writers have followed such views to complete antinomianism; and the kind of primitivism which ascribes all human ills to repressive civilisation, advocating a return to unfettered energy and political anarchy as cure, rests heavily on ideas akin to Blake's.

Nevertheless, Blake is talking of a 'marriage', not of 'divorce'; his own vision of 'good' is not simply a reverse of the view it derides. Rather it anticipates a great deal of modern psychological thinking – in Jung particularly – and could be seen in some lights as a recovery of lost Christian truths. Equally, it would be possible to argue that Blake is attempting to recover Greek morality as, say, Euripides might have understood it, and that he has some right to be thought of as our most classical poet in this particular sense. For what he seems to mean is that when the 'giants' of energy have been released from their fetters of law, they will control one another, and a new balance, from *inside* freedom, will emerge. Thus the giant of sexuality will be controlled by the giants of tenderness and loyalty, the giant of anger by the giant of justice, the giant of reason by the giant of instinct. Whereas the morality of childhood is rooted in prohibition, the morality of adulthood will be rooted in love.

Hence it is an easy step to the terms of 'Innocence' and 'Experience' as Blake appears to develop them in his *Songs*. The world of 'Experience' is the social world as we know it, ruled by priests, lawgivers, fathers, and now especially scientists, and marked by cruelty and despair. It is a world where men are victimised by poverty, sexual repression, inequalities and privations of class, colour, and other human divisions, and where love is not only exiled, but persecuted when it truly appears. Black boys and chimney sweeps are victimised, the honest are burned, harlots (for Blake the product of sexual repression) disfigure the city. The world of 'Innocence', however, far from being the world of childhood and ignorance, is ruled by energies released and controlling themselves. It is in this sense that we suggest Greek thinking as a parallel, the notion that instead of giving your worship to one god, whether Artemis or Aphrodite, Apollo or Dionysus, you find wisdom by giving your worship to all of them in the measure due. One underlying insight is that all

powerful components of human nature are touched with divinity
and that sanity and health, civilisation and fulfilment, come from
the acceptance, not the denial of this.

Such a vision has real claims to acceptance : its logic, as we
have noted, has forebears in the tragic poetry of Greece, and
indeed in the paradoxes of Christ and St Paul. Yet the dangers
in Blake's particular formulations are manifest, not least in the
inflammatory zeal with which he appears to exult in paradox
itself. One could say that whereas 'Sooner murder an Infant in its
cradle than nurse unacted desires' could be a powerful and valid
protest against the wrong kinds of legalism, it could also, taken
literally, be the Moors Murderers' charter in its starkest form.
While it exemplifies that forceful onslaught on legalism which,
for example, characterises Christ's great battles with the Pharisees,
its verbal extravagance seems to betray an entertained hysteria,
the seeds of madness and hate. Blake, more than anyone, knew
that he walked a tightrope, which is why his best poems are the
only true vehicle of such potent ideas. If Eliot is right to suspect
a dangerous muddle in the ideas (is it really an uneducated
quality ?), then perhaps Blake's genius is his instinctive poetic tact.
He never abstracts his vision : it has a rich context, even in the
apparently simplest of verse.

This brings us to the two short songs which we wish briefly to
study. First, one of the *Songs of Innocence* :

'The Shepherd'

How sweet is the Shepherd's sweet lot !
From the morn to the evening he strays;
He shall follow his sheep all the day,
And his tongue shall be filled with praise.

For he hears the lambs' innocent call,
And he hears the ewes' tender reply;
He is watchful, while they are in peace
For they know when their Shepherd is nigh.

The poem begins with a straightforward declaration of the joy
of the Shepherd's way of life and of his good fortune in being able
to follow it. 'Sweet' appears twice in the opening line, and
though Blake handles the word as tactfully as George Herbert had
done before him, bringing out its most gentle and lilting qualities,
its repetition still just hints at a cloying excess, a warning, maybe,
that we should not take this delightful picture at face value only.
The second line emphasises the Shepherd's freedom both in time
('From the morn to the evening') and space ('he strays'), but the
freedom is immediately contradicted by his permanent commitment to his flock ('He shall follow his sheep all the day'). Or is
it a contradiction? In the economy of love, can the shepherd, in
doing his duty, still remain free? The note of exhilarating praise
on which the stanza ends (presented not as a religious ritual,
repressing energy, but as the spontaneous overflowing of delight)
suggests that he can indeed both 'stray' and 'follow' at the same
time, following his own will in the mutuality of joy. Nevertheless,
this 'Innocence' is no longer one which is blissfully unaware, but
one which teems with complexities and paradoxes that Blake
surely recognised, and even delighted to unloose.

Just as we have remarked above that the harlot was for Blake
the perfect symbol for a sexually sick society, so for him the most
perfect symbol for sex released into fulness was that of a mother
with baby : it is this fulness which opens the second stanza. In the
same way that the Shepherd has a commitment to his flock, so the
ewes have a commitment to their young, and the lambs a depend-
ence on their mothers; and though the paradoxes undoubtedly
remain, the constant 'call' and 'reply', the appeal and the
reassurance, sound more like the giving and taking of affection,
freely and willingly, than like an uneasy bondage. The crucial
word 'innocent' is used to describe the lambs' call, and opens up
another area of reverberation. To what extent is the 'innocent'
world of the new-born, of childhood, comparable to the adult
'Innocence' for which Blake makes such great claims? If adult
'Innocence' does share that freedom which comes from a lack
of knowledge of the real world and of fallen man, and this must

be an implication, then is it also rooted in a similar ignorance, a beautiful but impossible dream?

As the poem ends, the doubts continue, but so does the confidence of tone, the conviction that in spite of the complexities the Shepherd's watchfulness, though potentially inhibiting, is here comforting and releasing: the sheep's knowledge of his care for them (and how much trust there is in 'know') gives them 'peace', not captivity.

In 'The Shepherd', Blake shows that he was as aware as Coleridge or Wordsworth that he lived in a universe radiant with God: in common with these other great romantics, one of his main protests against the eighteenth-century tradition of empiricism was that it cut men off from the actual reception of divinity through beauty and love, through the supersensuous faculties of man. The fruit of the Spirit as understood by Christians – love, joy, peace – is linked with freedom from rules, yet with a mutual giving and taking of love between man and beast. (It is worth remarking here that one important aspect of romanticism is the link between creatures with one another as well as with Creator: in Coleridge's 'The Ancient Mariner', for instance, the ultimate community of all creatures in love, under man's natural lordship, is learned by the Mariner as wisdom born of suffering.) But the poem's apparent simplicity is deceptive. Questions arise at every turn, and cannot be answered. Or, if they can be answered, their solutions are so many as to provide no final resting place. There is so much difference, and of course so much likeness, between the unknowing innocence of the lambs' call and the larger 'Innocence' of the whole canvas, which has its being in the autonomy and responsibility God meant for man, and still is not as innocent as it seems.

In contrast, many of the *Songs of Experience* offer images of political and social persecution, a side of Blake's thinking which no total approach can overlook (for Bronowski, Blake was particularly important as radical and socialist – and, arguably, this element of his thinking went deeper than it did even in the early Wordsworth). However, we choose here another short but well-known song as example, since its simple appearance is again deceptive :

'The Sick Rose'

O Rose, thou art sick :
The invisible worm
That flies in the night
In the howling storm,

Has found out thy bed
Of crimson joy,
And his dark secret love
Does thy life destroy.

The first line is a direct, almost brutal, statement of fact : the 'Rose', flower of love, both spiritual and erotic (and already Blake is reconciling in this conventional image, the soul and the body, which the 'religious' would divide) is 'sick', cankered. The explanation follows : the canker 'worm', symbol of the devil and invested with all the sinister qualities of 'invisible', 'flies', 'night', and 'howling storm', has attacked it, infecting it with evil and devouring it from within. Is it perhaps Satan, disguised as serpent, arriving in Eden? (Milton's image lurks in the background) or is it the stuff of childhood nightmares, or the first encounter with sin?

The Rose is 'found out' – words which combine the inevitable discovery in nature of hunted by hunter with the idea of exposure. But is there real guilt which demands exposure and punishment? Or is it the false guilt which persecution hideously begets? The thing which is found out is surely sexual bliss ('bed/ Of crimson joy') : something, for Blake at least, to be celebrated, yet why, then, does the Rose try to hide it, as 'found out' must also imply, turning it into an undercover 'dark secret love' akin to the worm's? Does the worm perhaps stand for the pressures of repression, as 'dark' and 'secret', again in Blake's terms opposites of love, might suggest? And is it these pressures which implant an unfounded shame in the once proud and perfect

Rose? Why does the rhyme scheme link 'joy' and 'destroy' so inextricably, making the moment of delight the cause of death?

In a strange way, 'The Sick Rose' suggests a kind of gnostic dualism, two forces of energy equally matched and locked in mortal combat. But however well one knows the poem, it remains elusive: its resonances suggest many possibilities, and the very nature of its riddles (the ones we have posed, and many others) shift according to the reader's personal mood. The only certainty is that it rings unanswerably true. The vocabulary is as simple and basic as the situation; the threat touches all of us; perhaps Rose and worm meet in ourselves? At such times, Blake must know that when the deepest secrets of love, and evil, and good are probed, no simple marriage or divorce can serve as image. Perhaps his true power is not as a philosopher, but as an elemental poet, a poet of revelation. This, for the present authors anyway, is his strength, his weakness (if one's patience tires), and his mystery.

1805 text, Book II, 237–80
        Blest the infant Babe,
(For with my best conjectures I would trace
The progress of our being,) blest the Babe,
240 Nursed in his Mother's arms, the Babe who sleeps
Upon his Mother's breast; who, when his soul
Claims manifest kindred with an earthly soul,
Doth gather passion from his Mother's eye !
Such feelings pass into his torpid life
Like an awakening breeze, and hence his mind
Even [in the first trial of his powers]
Is prompt and watchful, eager to combine
In one appearance, all the elements
And parts of the same object, else detached
250 And loth to coalesce. Thus, day by day,
Subjected to the discipline of love,
His organs and recipient faculties
Are quickened, are more vigorous, his mind spreads,
Tenacious of the forms which it receives.
In one beloved Presence, nay and more,
In that most apprehensive habitude
And those sensations which have been derived
From this beloved Presence, there exists
A virtue which irradiates and exalts
260 All objects through all intercourse of sense.
No outcast he, bewildered and depressed :
Along his infant veins are interfused
The gravitation and the filial bond
Of Nature that connect him with the world.
Emphatically such a Being lives,

An inmate of this *active* universe;
From nature largely he receives; nor so
Is satisfied, but largely gives again,
For feeling has to him imparted strength,
270 And powerful in all sentiments of grief,
Of exultation, fear, and joy, his mind,
Even as an agent of the one great Mind,
Creates, creator and receiver both,
Working but in alliance with the works
Which it beholds. – Such, verily, is the first
Poetic spirit of our human life,
By uniform control of after years,
In most, abated and suppressed; in some,
Through every change of growth or of decay,
280 Pre-eminent till death.

★

1850 text, Book II, 232–65
232   Blest the infant Babe,
(For with my best conjecture I would trace
Our Being's earthly progress,) blest the Babe,
Nursed in his Mother's arms, who sinks to sleep,
Rocked on his Mother's breast; who with his soul
Drinks in the feelings of his Mother's eye !
For him, in one dear Presence, there exists
A virtue which irradiates and exalts
240 Objects through widest intercourse of sense.
No outcast he, bewildered and depressed :
Along his infant veins are interfused
The gravitation and the filial bond
Of Nature that connect him with the world.
Is there a flower, to which he points with hand
Too weak to gather it, already love
Drawn from love's purest earthly fount for him
Hath beautified that flower; already shades
Of pity cast from inward tenderness

250 Do fall around him upon aught that bears
     Unsightly marks of violence or harm.
     Emphatically such a Being lives,
     Frail creature as he is, helpless as frail,
     An inmate of this active universe :
     For feeling has to him imparted power
     That through the growing faculties of sense
     Doth like an agent of the one great Mind
     Create, creator and receiver both,
     Working but in alliance with the works
260 Which it beholds. – Such, verily, is the first
     Poetic spirit of our human life,
     By uniform control of after years,
     In most, abated or suppressed; in some,
     Through every change of growth and of decay,
     Pre-eminent till death.

It is easy to see why one of Wordsworth's critics gravitated to the phrase 'the egotistical sublime' for a book title,* and why few of his other critics leave it entirely alone. Since epic is the literary form especially attuned to celebrate man as hero, what greater epic theme than 'the self' can there logically be?

> Of genius, power,
> Creation and divinity itself
> I have been speaking, for my theme has been
> What passed within me. (III 171–4)†

Yet traditionally most epic writers have remained aware of the tragic element in human destiny, and of the shadow of mortality, holding pride in check. Neither Marlowe's Tamburlaine nor Milton's Satan are genuine epic heroes, but are instances, rather, of insanely self-destructive pride. Milton's *Paradise Lost,* taking

---

* John Jones, *The Egotistical Sublime* (1954).

† Quotations are from the Penguin Parallel text of *The Prelude,* edited by J. C. Maxwell (1971). All references, except when otherwise stated, are to the 1805 version.

its leave of Adam and Eve with the marvellous phrase 'The world was all before them, where to choose . . .' crystallises the irony, as well as the hope, of its great theme.

It was left to the European romantics to propose, for a heady moment, that if a man really has the courage to be himself, and to rise to his freedom, then he may enter into his fullness as a divine being in this earthly existence, here and now. Can it be an accident that Wordsworth's *Prelude* opens with lines in which human freedom and joy are asserted so independently of irony that the very phrase used by Milton at the expulsion from Paradise, becomes a paean of hope?

> *Now I am free, enfranchised and at large,*
> *May fix my habitation where I will.*
> What dwelling shall receive me? In what vale
> Shall be my harbour? Underneath what grove
> Shall I take up my home? and what sweet stream
> Shall with its murmurs lull me to my rest?
> *The earth is all before me.* With a heart
> Joyous, *nor scared at its own liberty,*
> I look about. . . . (1 9–17) [Our italics]

The poet's 'freedom' seems as joyful and simple as a natural element, his very choosing a search among blessings. If this is not hubris, then must it not be sublime conviction? – the 'all shall be well and all manner of things shall be well' of ultimate faith.

Yet, as most critics agree, the political euphoria of 1789 is an important ingredient in the young Wordsworth's exuberance, co-operating as it did with his mystical temperament and with his continuous experience of natural beauty and peace. The rejection of old tyranny for new innocence: we are immediately reminded that for a brief moment in the 1640s, this had been Milton's dream too. But, whereas both poets suffered political disillusionment, Wordsworth's basic optimism was less permanently touched than Milton's. The hopes of 1789 dissolved in tragic complexity, as those of the 1640s had done earlier, but the final effect on the two poets was far from the same. Wordsworth's

political disappointment is recorded in later books of *The Prelude,*
and as we know, he came close for a moment to despair :

> Thus I fared,
> Dragging all passions, notions, shapes of faith,
> Like culprits to the bar; suspiciously
> Calling the mind to establish in plain day
> Her titles and her honours; now believing,
> Now disbelieving; endlessly perplexed
> With impulse, motive, right and wrong, the ground
> Of moral obligation, what the rule
> And what the sanction, till, demanding *proof,*
> And seeking it in every thing, I lost
> All feeling of conviction, and, in fine,
> Sick, wearied out with contrarieties,
> Yielded up moral questions in despair. (x 889–901)

This experience was Wordsworth's in the mid-1790s, and his
rescue was effected as much through his friendship with
Coleridge, and his contact with Coleridge's mode of thinking, as
through any other source. The opening of *The Prelude,* which
followed this rescue, records the moment in 1799 when
Wordsworth eventually settled at Grasmere; and we can legit-
imately infer that the experience of 'freedom' which it celebrates
had survived the perplexities and doubts of his bitterest years.
It seems clear, therefore, that Wordsworth's real hope had never
been *contained* in political naïveté, and so had never been
doomed to total questioning and eclipse. The political hopes had
been attracted, rather, to a nature already deeply and mystically
attuned to freedom at some far deeper level; so that, when they
collapsed, they could come to be seen by him eventually as an
aberration from his highest hopes and idealisms, rather than as
the soil in which hope and idealism had grown. By the time,
therefore, that Wordsworth came to record the false elation of
his earlier self ('Bliss was it in that dawn to be alive/But to be
young was very Heaven!' x 693–4) he could undercut the
ensuing awareness of political frustration with a newer, and

sweeter, possession of deep, inner hope. The promise of youth
pointed after all not only to political folly, but to a far more
enduring truth, beyond time itself. For this reason, again, *The
Prelude* was designed expressly to test Wordsworth's powers to
write an epic, rather than to be, with 'self' as sole hero, the epic
itself.

But before this is pursued further, Wordsworth's basic understanding of Nature must be touched on. For Wordsworth, the
entire external world of rocks, trees, sea and sky is Nature, and so
also is the world of thoughts and feelings, a man's 'inner self'.
Again, Nature is the living and creating fount of blessings behind
and through all things, the power to which men have more
normally given the name 'God'. In various poems, Wordsworth
discerns different stages of our human experience of Nature. The
'glad animal movements' of boyhood give place to the deeper
raptures of early manhood, and later to a profound humanism,
not unmixed with stoic endurance, in adult life. Profound
changes come to a man, at about the time of puberty, both
physical and spiritual. Much depends upon the sense of 'wonder',
which is either forfeited at this period, as it is in those who resign
themselves to a low view of man, or further nurtured, as it is by
poets and mystics. The supreme awareness of Nature is given and
secured at moments of transcendental openness, when a man is
caught up in the mystical energy and unity behind appearances,
and in a sense possesses, and is, all things, beyond space and time.
Such moments initiate us to the deepest truth of ourselves, from
which we are normally exiled, and give grounds for a faith strong
enough to see us through all life's less exalted moments, and all
its trials :

> Enough, if something from our hands have power
> To live, and act, and serve the future hour;
> And if, as towards the silent tomb we go,
> Through love, through hope, and faith's transcendent dower,
> We feel that we are greater than we know.
>
> ('River Duddon', Sonnet 34)

The distinctive feature of Wordsworth's sensibility is, clearly, its mysticism. This links him with a seventeenth-century poet such as Vaughan, and a modern such as T. S. Eliot, as well as with the long tradition of mystical experience from many men and traditions. In his own period it unites him with Blake and Coleridge, and possibly with Shelley, and can be seen as romantic in this popular, and usefully limited, use of the term.

At the same time, however, Wordsworth can be regarded as a poet whose witness to Nature is primarily through the emotions rather than through the intellect, and this aspect of his work is perhaps romantic in a much wider sense. Most readers recognise, also, that the eighteenth-century Nature poets prepared the way for him, and that he fulfils, as well as challenges, that older tradition, in certain crucial ways.

Throughout the eighteenth century indeed, as Basil Willey traced in *Eighteenth-Century Background* (1946), a process that can be called 'the divinisation' of Nature had been taking place, Wild nature – nature untamed by man, uncreated by him, and owing little or nothing to him in the way of cultivation – was increasingly invested with the reverence due to a god. This process was never without its complexities, since the rediscovery of 'wildness' occurred inside an intellectual, and usually empirical, frame. Nature had come more and more to be thought of in terms coloured by Newton's physics and Locke's epistemology, as a great machine working to mechanical laws. Because men discovered these laws through discursive intellect working upon sense data, they came to value observation and logic chief among human powers. 'God' was more and more thought of as a being to be known through a rational deduction made from his universe – as the great Intellect who first created, and then revealed himself to mind *as* Mind. 'The laws of Nature', wrote Locke, 'everywhere sufficiently evidence a deity' – by which he meant that, wherever we look, order is to be observed, and a first, great cause of order is to be deduced. The whole creation, from the turning of the stars to the fall of an apple, proclaims purpose, not chaos, as its ultimate truth.

But, since God was in this manner intellectualised, and purged of mystery, the result was a reduction, as well as a confirmation, of religious belief. Man's confidence in his own rational power and destiny was boosted, but poetry and mystery, the two older witnesses to divinity, were pushed out of sight. For many they fell into disgrace, along with medieval metaphysics and scholastic philosophising, as possible causes of priestcraft, superstition, even dissension and war. In this manner, science and religion came together again in alliance, after their sixteenth-century battles, but very much on science's terms. Human instincts and passions tended to be regarded askance, whether in matters of conduct, where they were suspected of being ungentlemanly, or in matters of worship, where they featured as relics from an irrational past.

The eighteenth-century divinisation of Nature was to a high degree therefore its scientificisation also, at a time when God seemed a sure, but wholly rational fact. Yet the eighteenth-century poets, caught in complexities they only half understood, though understanding was their passion, were already straining to break the rigidly logical frame. As Nature became the epic hero of Thomson, and to some degree of Young, Akenside and many other mid-eighteenth-century poets, it yearned towards sanctions unfettered by Locke. The Cambridge Platonists and the Third Earl of Shaftesbury were invoked,* as platonic rather than empirical thinkers, to do justice to the *felt* delight and sublimity of Nature in its untamed forms. While the eighteenth-century poets seldom 'evoked' the divine mystery in any manner comparable to Wordsworth, they none the less strove, in Miltonic blank verse, towards just this effect. Their humanist optimism, though still in essence rational and scientific, strained to capture celebration and delight. Very occasionally, the effect anticipates Wordsworth – as if by accident, yet still remarkably, as this brief extract from Akenside's *Pleasures of the Imagination* shows :

* For a lucid account, see R. L. Brett, *The Third Earl of Shaftesbury.*

O ye Northumbrian shades, which overlook
The rocky pavement and the mossy falls
Of solitary Wensbeck's limpid stream;
How gladly I recall your well-known seats,
Belov'd of old, and that delightful time
When, all alone, for many a summer's day,
I wander'd through your calm recesses, led
In silence by some powerful hand unseen.

What, then, is the distinctive contribution of Wordsworth, and of certain other romantics, to the divinisation of Nature? If we leave aside again, for the moment, the most important aspect in Wordsworth himself – his religious mysticism – we can identify, as a very important ingredient, the decisive romantic rejection of Lockean thought. The 'abstracting intellect' comes to be seen as cold and reductive, when measured against experience felt on the pulses and known in the blood. Instead of the 'Great First Cause' we encounter, now, the 'Wisdom and Spirit of the Universe', as Wordsworth returns to older, and richer, language, and modes of thought.

O there is a blessing in this gentle breeze,
A visitant that while he fans my cheek
Doth seem half-conscious of the joy he brings
                              (1 1–3 1850 version)

These opening lines of *The Prelude* suggest a creative and healing play of nature, notably in this later version, where Wordsworth uses 'he' instead of 'it' to describe the breeze, thereby pushing the word 'half-conscious' away from metaphor, and correspondingly nearer to a direct suggestion of the presence of God. From the first, there is a constant mystery of mutuality. Nature inspires revelations which, when creatively received, pass into and transform the inner man. One of the Lucy poems develops this theme in a manner akin to the Christian doctrine of sanctifying grace. Nature chooses Lucy, sets her apart as worshipper, and gradually moulds her :

> The stars of midnight shall be dear
> To her; and she shall lean her ear
> In many a secret place
> Where rivulets dance their wayward round,
> And beauty born of murmuring sound
> Shall pass into her face. (1799)

Even in this comparatively slight lyric we find Nature guarding her chosen one jealously against merely human competitors, and fulfilling her in the mystery of death. It is interesting to notice that in the lines 'There was a boy', written in 1798–9 and later incorporated into *The Prelude,* a very similar, and unexplained, transition also links election with death :

> Then sometimes, in that silence while he hung
> Listening, a gentle shock of mild surprise
> Has carried far into his heart the voice
> Of mountain torrents; or the visible scene
> Would enter unawares into his mind,
> With all its solemn imagery, its rocks,
> Its woods, and that uncertain heaven, received
> Into the bosom of the steady lake.
>
> This boy was taken from his mates, and died
> In childhood . . . (v 406–15)

Most readers sense that Wordsworth was thinking of himself in these lines, and that the paradox of life through death, linked with election and divine indwelling, is very close to the Christian mystery. Like all mystics, Wordsworth catches the speechless language of the universe, making human speech an echo of unutterable truths, 'the nourishment that came unsought' (II 7). His 'spots of time' testified, inside mortality, to transcendental realities, and remained as a witness to these, despite all the deadening influences of normal experience :

> This efficacious spirit chiefly lurks
> Among those passages of life in which

> We have had deepest feeling that the mind
> Is lord and master, and that outward sense
> Is but the obedient servant of her will. (xi 269–73)

Here, 'mind' is platonic mind, superior alike to sense and to mere reasoning, directly intuiting the supersensuous truths, and itself creative. At such moments, 'mind' provides inestimable blessings to soul :

> Thence did I drink the visionary power.
> I deem not profitless those fleeting moods
> Of shadowy exultation : not for this,
> That they are kindred to our purer mind
> And intellectual life ; but that the soul,
> Remembering how she felt, but what she felt
> Remembeing not, retains an obscure sense
> Of possible sublimity. (ii 330–7)

Wordsworth's receptivity to blessings is his *raison d'être* as a poet; he stores them, in words, against the days when they seem lost, or unreal. At ii 291 he records a time when 'a trouble came into my mind/From unknown causes. I was left alone/Seeking the visible world, nor knowing why'. But the context is one in which 'my mind lay open', still drinking in the impressions of youth and sustained by an inner working of grace. In the 'Tintern Abbey' lines, composed on 13 July 1798, Wordsworth had already expressed, in what remains perhaps the most remarkable passage of its kind in his work, his deep rapport with Nature. Beyond any psychological probings, he conveys the numinous feeling of timeless communion :

> And I have felt
> A Presence that disturbs me with the joy
> Of elevated thoughts; a sense sublime
> Of something far more deeply interfused,
> Whose dwelling is the light of setting suns,
> And the round ocean, and the living air,
> And the blue sky, and in the mind of man :

> A motion and a spirit, that impels
> All thinking things, all objects of all thought,
> And rolls through all things.

Such experiences must be described as prophetic; certainly they make Wordsworth, like Milton, a poet with a missionary view of his art. To a degree that at first might surprise us, both poets share a Christian language, for the truths of their heart. Wordsworth is elect:

> I was a chosen son.
> For hither I had come with holy powers
> And faculties ...
> I was a Freeman; in the purest sense
> Was free, and to majestic ends was strong. (III 82–4; 89–90)

The word 'free' receives here a Christian gloss; there is nothing in it of vagueness or mere primitivism, but a direct testimony to purification from gross sensuality by the discipline of love. Wordsworth records the moment when he became conscious of his election, almost as a conversion experience, and with something approaching the special monastic vocation lurking as well:

> Ah, need I say, dear Friend, that to the brim
> My heart was full; I made no vows, but vows
> Were there made for me; bond unknown to me
> Was given, that I should be, else sinning greatly,
> A dedicated spirit. (IV 340–4)

Such dedication seems needful to balance the assertion of almost unqualified freedom at the start of *The Prelude*; indeed, it makes such freedom a real possibility, rather than a childish dream. The precise choice of words – priest, prophet, holy – very clearly defines Wordsworth's role, as a man standing between God and other men, mediating sacraments of grace:

> to the open fields I told
> A prophecy: poetic numbers came
> Spontaneously, and clothed in priestly robe

> My spirit, thus singled out, as it might seem,
> For holy services. (1 59–63)

Not surprisingly, Wordsworth shares with Milton a quality that sets him apart from his fellows. In passages such as the famous winter skating (1 452–89), we watch the boy move into solitude. The numinous mood overtakes him and, 'retired/Into a silent bay' he holds communion, alone among the 'solitary cliffs', with deep mysteries. In its nature this is akin to prayer – to the pattern of prayer set by Christ himself, among the mountains. The experience of the purgation of the senses, of all that might sully, all that is sensual and gross, again links this apparent nature-worship to mysticism. Finally, Wordsworth shares with Milton a sense of prophetic destiny for his own generation. In both poets this essentially religious impulse became allied to revolutionary politics, and in both, the sequel to revolution produced bitter disillusionment. Yet of the two, Wordsworth was the least basically shaken, no doubt because his religious thinking was never as wholly integrated with his political as Milton's had been. The experiences of Milton in the 1650s and 1660s changed the basic nature of his proposed epic, perhaps by bringing home to him, in practice, the doctrine of original sin. Wordsworth's epic, in contrast, was unchanged in its major insights, since his view of man's divinity could always transcend the merely social world :

> Dearest Friend!
> Forgive me if I say that I, who long
> Had harboured reverentially a thought
> That Poets, even as Prophets, each with each
> Connected in a mighty scheme of truth,
> Have each for his peculiar dower, a sense
> By which he is enabled to perceive
> Something unseen before; forgive me, Friend,
> If I, the meanest of this band, had hope
> That unto me had also been vouchsafed
> An influx, that in some sort I possessed

> A privilege; and that a work of mine,
> Proceeding from that depth of untaught things,
> Enduring and creative, might become
> A power like one of Nature's. (XII 299–312)

It was this majestic and assured consciousness which sustained Wordsworth through his darkest perplexities, and which his friendship with Coleridge not only rekindled but united, at last, with insights into its own true nature and deepest needs. The passages in Book x when Wordsworth describes his debts to his sister Dorothy and to Coleridge are moving not only as a record of the reopening of 'a saving intercourse/With my true self' (x 915–16) but as a testimony to the quality of human love which is, after all, the crown, and not the denial of such felt sublimity in the self :

> And, lastly, Nature's self, by human love
> Assisted, through the weary labyrinth
> Conducted me again to open day. (x 922–4)

We should notice, while considering this profound link between Wordsworth's own poetry and his consciousness of destiny, that he recognises a quality of revelation in all great art. The following passage in Book v deserves more attention than it usually receives, as a tribute to the influence upon him of other poets. His personal training as a child of nature fuses with his reading, to make a further authentic, if not readily definable, experience of 'visionary power' :

> Here must I pause : this only will I add,
> From heart-experience, and in humblest sense
> Of modesty, that he, who in his youth
> A wanderer among the woods and fields
> With living Nature hath been intimate,
> Not only in that raw unpractised time
> Is stirred to ecstasy, as others are,
> By glittering verse; but he doth furthermore,

In measure only dealt out to himself,
Receive enduring touches of deep joy
From the great Nature that exists in works
Of mighty Poets. Visionary power
Attends upon the motions of the winds,
Embodied in the mystery of words :
There, darkness makes abode, and all the host
Of shadowy things do work their changes there,
As in a mansion like their proper home.
Even forms and substances are circumfused
By that transparent veil with light divine,
And, through the turnings intricate of verse,
Present themselves as objects recognised,
In flashes, and with a glory scarce their own. (v 608–29)

If we were to describe this whole aspect of Wordsworth in a literary manner, we might, adapting one of his own phrases, say that he either discovers in, or transfers to, Nature concepts which Christians have habitually found in their relationship with God. The use of Christian language goes deeper than metaphor, reaching to the heart of experience itself. Wordsworth is neither shedding dogma nor paganising worship, but striving to evoke his particular, and mystical, sense of personal destiny. His intention, as a young man especially, was to celebrate an entirely individual discovery. In this we may recognise the perpetual charm and right of youth, as one ingredient; yet Wordsworth felt 'set apart' in an altogether higher way. His inner resonances are always of incarnation, revelation, death and resurrection, all nearly experienced, whether in the 'nature' outside, or within. Later, the Christian language became explicit, and Wordsworth moved towards the religion where they first belonged. But it would be a shallow reader who imagined that his acceptance of formal Christianity was the result merely of political disillusionment, or of encroaching respectability, or that the changes in this direction in the later version of *The Prelude* were in any way a denial of the experiences originally explored.

When we look at Wordsworth's philosophising (as opposed to his thought; a somewhat different matter) we find that he returns often to the problem of perception. In common with Coleridge, and with many romantic and modern writers, his attempts to link subject and object loom large. How does our consciousness relate, in fact, to the external world which stimulates it? How do our inner perceptions, received by the five senses and conveyed by the nervous system to the brain, where they appear as images, relate to whatever realities 'cause' them in the world outside?

The existence of a gulf between 'our' words and concepts, and the objective world which these reach towards, has, of course, always been perceived. Plato's elegant mythologising takes conscious account of it, and most Greek and Jewish writings implicitly do the same. The notion that a particular formula of words, images, moralisings and teachings can be definitive and sacrosanct has been reserved for dogmatists of the narrower kinds. But, also, men have most usually felt that their perceptions, along with the structures of thought and feeling based upon these in social discourse, reach outwards towards, and to some degree reflect, 'reality', in however tentative a mode. Thus, in formulating ideas and feelings, as we are urgently pressed to do by their joy and their burden, most men assume that truths outside, as well as within, themselves are under account. In the simplest form this is the belief that the external world existed prior to ourselves and in some manner produced us, rather than that it is an autonomous and unverifiable concept in our own minds. Behind our gropings towards him, God is really present, the supreme truth beyond all partial guesses and intuitions of merely human minds. This basic insight has never been better expressed in its religious form than by the psalmist : 'It is he that has made us, and not we ourselves; we are his people, and the sheep of his pasture.' In contrast, only the solipsists have travelled the whole way to subjectivism, and asserted that since external realities are wholly unknowable, we are irrevocably locked in the 'self'.

Readers of *The Prelude* have to bear in mind those eighteenth-century debates which were always in the foreground of

Wordsworth's thought. Locke had believed that the 'primary' characteristics of things – their size, shape and magnitude – are objective, while their 'secondary' characteristics – smell, taste and so forth – relate to the perceptions of human sense. On this basis, he accepted that Newton's law of gravitation was deducible from the observation of primary realities, and that a further logical deduction from the existence of order in creation to the existence of the first Great Cause of order was demonstrable truth. It was left to Berkeley to modify this, and to Hume to suggest that primary characteristics might be as subjective as secondary – thereby mutating empiricism towards solipsism from inside. Indeed, Hume's thinking drew attention to the inner needs and structures which modify our very perceptions, and so to the relativism which has proved congenial to many modern minds.

What is certain is that most religious men, and artists, have never been at home with empiricism, and least of all in its solipsist form. Unless religion and art touch 'reality' outside, as well as inside, the human psyche, how are they to make for themselves any very high claims? They might pass as self-expression, self-indulgence, communication, or even as therapy, but not as guides to sublime and transcendental truths. For Wordsworth, certainly, a diminished view of man, and nature, would not be enough. If the God within us is not also and ante-cedently the God without, how safe from vicissitude can any man hope to be? Time might dull or hopelessly diminish even the poet. Our whole vision might decay, with the body's own energies, and be lost in death.

From the first, moreover, Wordsworth rejected the notion that we receive impressions from the external world merely in passiveness. (The 'wise passiveness' of 'Expostulation and Reply' is surely related to religious and mystical openness, not to uncreative perception; and his choice of the 'self' as hero was the reverse of solipsist in intent.) In the 'Tintern Abbey' lines, his famous phrase 'all the mighty world/Of eye, and ear, both what they half create/And what perceive' clearly hints at a more

dynamic and Coleridgean view (even though Wordsworth himself later acknowledged a forgotten echo from Young). It is true,
of course, that the young Wordsworth's belief in the importance
of environment and education, and so in the efficacy of political
revolution, was indeed indebted to Locke's theory that we come
into the world with minds like blank sheets of paper, and are
shaped by whatever influences surround our minds and lives.
Certain critics have taken pains to point out the evidences of
associationism in various of his poems, and no one can deny that
this was a strand in his thought. But Wordsworth's temperament
always pressed him towards more mystical views, and so towards
the very different system which he later embraced. He was
Coleridgean in temper long before he knew Coleridge – so that
Coleridge's ideas came to him not only as a personal form of
salvation, but as a clarification of insights already half understood.

Coleridge's distinctive contribution, at least as far as it touches
our reading of *The Prelude,* was to allow Wordsworth to adopt
an essentially Platonic view of Reason and creation, and to link
this with a theory of perception itself. Coleridge's beliefs set out
from the view that man's purely analytical powers ought not to
be called Reason, as they had been in the Locke tradition, but
that they should be given some other, less exalted, name. His own
word for them was 'understanding', which covered all processes
whereby we observe, judge similarities and dissimilarities, build
complex ideas from simple ideas, and thereby come to a reliable
knowledge of the external world. 'Understanding' therefore
includes the whole of Locke's Reason, and the whole scope of the
logical and discursive mind. Coleridge accepted, of course, the
importance and validity of 'understanding', but asserted that
men have higher faculties of insight than any which are acknowledged by Locke. For these, he reserved the word Reason – a
term describing now that divine spark which the Cambridge
Platonists had called 'the candle of the Lord' and seen as the very
image of God, planted in us at creation, and sealing us men.
Reason is no less than our intuitive perception of beauty, goodness
and truth not, essentially, as qualities existing in objects sensibly

(though they are this too, and as such come within 'understanding's' province), but as direct, supersensuous revelations of the divine. Reason is our awareness of a divine creation and destiny, a play between God and the self using, but always transcending, the material world.

Coleridge went on to attach to this view of Reason a precise psychology, tracing the growth of our inner consciousness to the interactions of primary and secondary imagination (attributes of our nature which create, as well as perceive, the external world). Thus, he insisted that the act of perception is *in itself* active, and not the merely passive receipt and reassemblage of data that Locke had seemed to suppose. In a sense, this may seem almost obvious, when we recall the strange complexities which link us with the world outside. A summer garden may seem simple and unified, as we lazily enjoy it, yet sounds, scents, tastes, smells and sights all reach us by different paths. They enter the appropriate organs, become transmitted as nervous energy, yet arrive in the mind as a clear, and apparently unified, view of the garden itself. We are aware that if one or more of our senses is defective, or wholly missing, then our awareness of the garden is to that degree impaired. Yet the whole picture, as it comes to us, is taken for granted, and we make no conscious effort to bring disparate data into one seeming whole.

Simple perception therefore involves (Coleridge decided) something in us akin to the original creative I AM. In every moment of perception, whether the moment seems exalted, or merely humdrum, or indeed depraved or degraded, a miracle of creation is in fact going on. This process is, Coleridge pointed out, involuntary, in that it happens with no conscious effort on our part. Yet it is also in his view an active and pre-eminently a divine manifestation – a miracle, which ensures that the continuous assault on our nervous system made by sights, sounds, tastes, smells and feelings arrives in the consciousness not in the form of piecemeal chaos, but with the distinct impression of an ordered and organic and non-disparate whole.

But, in addition to this 'primary imagination', which contin-

ually creates order out of potential inner chaos, we have also a
faculty which is specifically associated with creative thinking, and
with art. This 'secondary' imagination, unlike the primary, is of
the will, and so voluntary; only artists and trained creators
employ it to the full. The secondary imagination 'dissolves,
diffuses, dissipates, in order to recreate' the original sense
impressions, and, if it turns into art, issues in entirely new
works of its own. Coleridge made a sharp distinction between
'fancy', which is the mere rearrangement of impressions received
through the understanding, and 'imagination', which is new
creation in its own right. So a man takes some substance from the
natural world – whether sounds, or words, or canvas, or stone or
plastic – and impresses on it his own unique, creative forms. The
work of art comes into being as objective reality, taking its place
for other men alongside trees, sea and sky, the whole creation of
Nature itself.

Here, then, is the great analogy, between man as creator, and
the Creator himself. God takes (after first creating it) the raw
material of Matter, and, imprinting his creative power further
upon it, makes the whole world of Nature, including man. Man,
in turn, takes certain materials from God's world, and, imprinting
his own creativity on them, makes the whole world of art. The
revelation in both cases is complex and teasing, with the creating
mind concealed, as well as revealed, in its own works. Man's art,
like God's Nature, is elusive, mysterious and complex – yet in
both the grand imprint of beauty, goodness and truth may be truly
discerned. Since the 'creative' in man is itself divine, and made
in God's image, all works of art witness, in their formal existence,
as symbols, to God.

This creative process cannot, on any showing, be merely subjective, any more than Nature itself can be thought to be so.
Nature is not a system of fixed and frozen objects (still less of
such concepts), but a loving dance between matter and soul. As
Coleridge also put it, there is 'a bond between nature in the
higher sense and the soul of man'. Creative man therefore
demonstrates, as well as exercises, his divinity; in its primal

reality, all art is revelation. Great poems, we might also say, are prophetic signs and symbols – a truth that Wordsworth surely felt from his earliest years.

Coleridge's insights are poised between the religious and the psychological. Their common ground is the God who exists both outside us as Creator, and within, in the kingdom of the inner self. Divinity, which is present in a man from his instant of creation, testifies to itself in his consciousness, his love, and in the works that he makes.

Is Wordsworth himself a philosopher or a psychologist chiefly, when he writes on these themes? Though he appears often to be discussing ideas, in eighteenth-century fashion, we are always struck first by his emotional power. The experience of reading him is characteristically one of deliquescence, as John F. Danby pointed out in his brilliant book, *The Simple Wordsworth* (1960). The lines seem to dance together behind us, rather like the sea in play. One result is that *The Prelude* is unusually hard to remember correctly; with rare exceptions, the phrases do not stay clear in the mind. Even the argument becomes elusive if we try to paraphrase; it is not unlike the egg in *Through the Looking Glass,* which rose shelf by shelf as Alice tried to focus on it and finally passed out of sight through the roof. The difficulty is not precisely that syntax and symbol are baffling, as in (say) Shakespeare's 'The Phoenix and the Turtle' or Yeats's 'Byzantium', but that the literal meaning is not so much an end as a means to an end. What appears to be thought is in fact evocation, and the effect is more memorable, more unanswerable certainly, than the arguments *per se.* As we read on, we are characteristically aware of a process that leads from point to point satisfyingly, and with continual increments of refinement, yet which defies us to recall exactly what was said thirty, or even ten lines before. When we go back, it can often seem that Wordsworth has been repeating himself, or that under the guise of clear argument – still there to be discerned and analysed, if we are determined on this – he has been weaving an incantation or a

spell. To sort out the ideas intellectually is not only difficult, but
is almost certain to lead us away from the poetry – away from the
real meaning, embodied in power. In terms of seminar discussion
or formal criticism it may be a recipe for disaster – a melancholy
fulfilment of Wordsworth's own famous warning :

> Sweet is the lore which nature brings;
> Our meddling intellect
> Mis-shapes the beauteous forms of things;
> We murder to dissect. ('Expostulation and Reply')

Perhaps then it is no accident that among the best comment on
The Prelude extant we must still include Coleridge's lines written
on first hearing parts of the poem recited by its author. When
looked at closely, these lines seem less like comment than contin-
uation – pastiche almost (yet Coleridge, of all men, had earned
this right).

It is clear, on any objective showing, that Wordsworth's verse
does not have the density of texture, the concrete richness of
imagery, or the complex play of irony that we find in Milton,
even though Milton's influence, mediated through the eighteenth-
century Nature poets, is to be clearly discerned. Wordsworth's
syntax is deliberately less ornate, less latinate and, in grammatical
structure, less unEnglish, than Milton's; in his own account of it,
the ambition is to move closer to prose. Yet it is not really like
prose, except through illusion; it is altogether too fluid and
baffling in the manner described. Its peculiar strength seems
bound up rather with a self-imposed poverty, a deliberate
avoidance of rich imagery, of clear structures of metaphor or
myth. This leaves it free to move through mysterious formulations near the unknown, strangely familiar terrain of the inner
self. When inspiration fails, the penalty is immediately obvious,
since the most threadbare travesty seems all that is left. The reader
arriving at (say) III 459–91, or VII 244–309 is bound to feel
this – the extraordinary barrenness of style when the magic
departs. But, while the visionary light shines, so too does the

poetry, with its haunting resonance of consciousness raised to levels exalted and sublime.

Wordsworth's peculiar power is to evoke numinous and mystical experience more powerfully than perhaps any other poet in any tongue (T. S. Eliot is the one obvious exception) has ever ever done. Again, he can remind us that these experiences are after all familiar, and immensely refreshing, and quite central to our humanity, even if we normally neglect them, or even make them *tabu*. His evocations require content, require (too) images, and the appearance of reasoning, since numinous experience is the fullness, not the absence, of normal human powers. We apprehend that the whole self, mind and senses as well as spirit, have been lifted to intensity, in an experience which cannot none the less be *communicated,* even to our own reasoning minds. For once we possess the fullness too completely to need the props of 'understanding', yet 'understanding' is satisfied, or seems to be, in the moment itself. Ever afterwards, 'understanding' may be baffled to know *what* satisfied it; and this, the successful evocations of art (or religion) alone can recall. 'Recall', not 'explain': the difference is crucial, as Wordsworth, of all men, well knew. Even for himself, the purpose of verse was largely 'enshrinement' – a concept most exactly defined in the famous passage (XI 338–43) to which we shall return.

In reading Wordsworth, we require then a kind of honesty which breaks through the academic barriers of 'Eng. lit.' in an immediate way. While it is true, of course, that all writers must be personally recreated in the reader's imaginative experience, there are few others who depend so crucially upon this. Just as reading Lawrence (say) requires an openness, a vulnerability in the reader, to his personal experience of sexuality, so Wordsworth requires an openness, a vulnerability, to his religious self. Any such demand is to some degree confessional, so that critical discussion can seem embarrassing, if consent is withdrawn.

But again, the critic may be embarrassed by his own apparent simplicity; many of Wordsworth's most famous passages invite

simple, not complex, comment, as the way to their heart. The
well-known episodes of the stolen boat, followed by winter skating
(I 371–504) are, for instance, incredibly pictorial. The setting
of darkness among hoary mountains, moon and shadow, silence,
mingles with the stealthy taking of the boat, the exhilarating
skating, and, in the slightly hectic tone which develops, with
the suggestion of lost innocence – 'troubled' pleasure when
'untroubled' might be expected, leading to the most graphic, yet
subtle, coming alive of the mountains. The boat leaves 'small
circles' – stillness and gentleness here – and melts to 'sparkling
light'. This is pure enchantment; it is as though the boat had laid
the track which sparkles behind it (and a similar effect comes later
when the boy cuts across the image of a star, glancing sideways –
one's own small game, turned into enchantment). Wordsworth
captures first the boy's childish pride in being captain, and
then the collision of pride with those elemental powers which
diminish him to a guilty figure, stealing home, pursued by
'a dim and undetermin'd sense/Of unknown modes of being'.
Throughout, there is tension between the boy's sense of closeness
to nature – identity with it almost, in its mysterious grandeur –
and the alienation, even violence, in phrases such as 'struck and
struck again' as he senses, profoundly threatening to himself, the
terror and judgement. To simplify this, as Empson does, into
the psychology of guilt – the using of mountains as a father-figure,
and so on – is manifestly to miss the profoundly complex, yet
recognisable, rhythm of religious awakening. We surely notice
that the description of the child's total exile from everything
secure and childlike is at once nightmarish (indeed akin to
mystical descriptions of 'the dark night' of the senses and the
soul), yet also coexistent with apprehended divinity. A little
earlier Wordsworth has testified that 'The mind of man is framed
even like the breath/And harmony of music. There is a dark/
Invisible workmanship that reconciles/Discordant elements'
(I 351–4). Now, he embodies the boy's dereliction in words of
unforgettable immediacy :

                        in my thoughts
There was a darkness, call it solitude
Or blank desertion. No familiar shapes
Of hourly objects, images of trees,
Of sea or sky, no colours of green fields;
But huge and mighty forms, that do not live
Like living men, moved slowly through the mind
By day, and were a trouble to my dreams. (1 420–7)

and yet is able to move straight from the passage of which this is a
part (a formulation speaking very directly also to much modern
breakdown and alienation, as seminar discussion is apt to show)
to an exalted address to God, with no sense of contradiction, or
even transition :

Wisdom and Spirit of the universe !
Thou Soul that art the eternity of thought,
That giv'st to forms and images a breath
And everlasting motion, not in vain
By day or star-light thus from my first dawn
Of childhood didst thou intertwine for me
The passions that build up our human soul;
Not with the mean and vulgar works of man,
But with high objects, with enduring things –
With life and nature, purifying thus
The elements of feeling and of thought,
And sanctifying, by such discipline,
Both pain and fear, until we recognise
A grandeur in the beatings of the heart. (1 428–41)

'Not in vain': God as prime mover, maker of forms and images,
building man as he builds nature, and making souls: the poet
fuses his awareness of this in both grandeur and terror. 'The
passions that build up our human soul' : is this all the soul is;
accumulated passions? The passions are included certainly, yet
so is that added dimension implicit in this as in all Wordsworth;
the passions come from looking on *high* objects, on enduring

things, in life and nature. A key word is 'purifying' : an activity
captured, here, in this crucial phase of the young Wordsworth's
moral education, and linking it with that 'purification' of art
which converts the works of man also from 'mean and vulgar'
things to divine grandeur.

The following passage, the skating, again links rapture with a
certain 'alien' intimation, as the boy encounters the God who is
within and without his heart in both darkness and light. Few
poets have better captured a meeting with God in autumn gloom,
in mist, in every scene of nature – not as an idea, or system of
thought, but as a true experience, which words can, beyond
argument, recall :

> In November days,
> When vapours rolling down the valleys made
> A lonely scene more lonesome, among woods
> At noon, and 'mid the calm of summer nights,
> When, by the margin of the trembling lake,
> Beneath the gloomy hills I homeward went
> In solitude, such intercourse was mine. (1 443–9)

Looking at the whole passage, one is struck by the recurrence of
the original image of mountains coming alive, and taking on their
own energy and power. The 'voice/Of mountain echoes' seems
to transcend its origin, in the boat's movements, and become a
greater, answering voice of its own. This prefigures the moment
of terror when the rising of the mountains behind the boat ceases
to be a normal, natural phenomenon – as at one level the boy
clearly knew it was – and declares itself as a pursuit, which he
wards off with answering violence, yet with no hope of escape :

> a huge cliff,
> As if with voluntary power instinct
> Upreared its head. I struck and struck again,
> And growing still in stature the huge cliff
> Rose up between me and the stars, and still,
> With measured motion, like a living thing,
> Strode after me. (1 406–12)

In the skating episode, a similar pattern is repeated; the 'precipices rang aloud', taking up the echoes of human merriment, but then, it is as if the hills return not echoes only, but their own sound – alien and therefore vaguely menacing, yet at some deeper level, part too of the boy's delight in nature, and his own inner power :

> Meanwhile, the precipices rang aloud;
> The leafless trees and every icy crag
> Tinkled like iron; while the distant hills
> Into the tumult sent an alien sound
> Of melancholy not unnoticed, while the stars
> Eastward were sparkling clear, and in the west
> The orange sky of evening died away. (1 467–73)

When he retires apart, it is to move into a loneliness which is, rather, tumult and exhilaration. The incredibly physical phrase 'When we had given our bodies to the wind' introduces an image in which the alternations of human energy and surrender seem not only to set in motion, but to be overtaken by, energies waiting to be released through the whole natural world :

> and oftentimes,
> When we had given our bodies to the wind,
> And all the shadowy banks on either side
> Came sweeping through the darkness, spinning still
> The rapid line of motion, then at once
> Have I, reclining back upon my heels,
> Stopped short; yet still the solitary cliffs
> Wheeled by me, even as if the earth had rolled
> With visible motion her diurnal round !
> Behind me did they stretch in solemn train
> Feebler and feebler, and I stood and watched
> Till all was tranquil as a dreamless sleep. (1 478–89)

This time, the passage ends with silence, but no fear; the exhilaration has culminated not in terror, but in seemingly timeless communion. For the reader, as for Wordsworth, the effect is of initiation – which is no doubt why Wordsworth remains, for many, a 'personal' poet, in a manner that no exact verbal analysis could ever probe.

To ask, in fact, if Wordsworth's thinking is 'about' philosophy, or psychology, or religion, is to miss the fusion (not confusion) in the experience itself. As an error, it is perhaps akin to taking Donne's arguments in his love poems 'literally' (though these two errors are entirely different from each other in kind). In practical terms it means that a reader will be worried about Wordsworth's intellectual 'vagueness' only if he asks the wrong questions, which he will do, in turn, only if he fails to respond. For, in writing of Wordsworth, one must sooner or later admit to a scandal. It is that readers, if any, who have never had – or who will never admit memories of having had – mystical experiences will never, whatever their intelligence and sensitivity, make head or tail of his work.

But, after admitting this scandal, we do not want to take refuge in it; some attempt at precision – intellectual as well as verbal – must be made. For this purpose, we return to the passage from Book II about the baby, in illustration, as far as possible, of its exact effects. In themselves these lines are not finer than many other passages in *The Prelude*, but possibly their theme lends itself to this method more than most.

'Blest be the infant Babe': by and large, the eighteenth century would not have echoed this sentiment, or seen its point. The child is a 'little lady' or a 'little gentleman', with the emphasis on 'little'; any interest it has will come later, when manners, morals, polish have been drafted in. Locke had said that we each come into the world with minds like blank sheets of paper, on which environment and education can write what they will. Throughout the eighteenth century, 'individuality' tended to be seen as a fruit of experience, not as an original datum; and it was our general humanity, not our uniqueness, that was habitually stressed.

To the romantics, it was precisely these aspects of the eighteenth-century tradition that seemed most abhorrent, in their apparent denial of the individual and instinctual life of a man. As we see, Wordsworth's attention is drawn to love and creativity, linked in the first moments of existence; like Blake in 'The Little Black Boy', he offers the baby at his mother's breast as the prime image for both. Is there, implicit in this, a belief in pre-existence? There may be, but the answer is not wholly clear. In the Ode 'Intimations of Immortality from Recollections of Earliest Childhood' (published in 1807, and written in the three or four years before) Wordsworth seems, in section 5, to state the doctrine of pre-existence in a classic form:

> Our birth is but a sleep and a forgetting:
> The Soul that rises with us, our life's star,
>   Hath had elsewhere its setting,
>   And cometh from afar.
> Not in entire forgetfulness,
> And not in utter nakedness,
> But trailing clouds of glory do we come
>   From God, who is our home:
> Heaven lies about us in our infancy!

If this means that the child is born with some memory of his 'true' self, and of the home from which all earthly experience is exile, then the loss of a sense of wonder which Wordsworth notes in most men at adolescence might indeed be a loss of the *memory* of reality; and the poet, who retains his wonder, remains closest to the child's forgotten truth. On the other hand, some critics take the references to pre-existence in the Ode as metaphor, and it seems unlikely that Wordsworth's literal belief in it was ever as strong as, say, Vaughan's. In *The Prelude* there is a passage in which pre-existence is explicitly relegated to the sphere of agnosticism, as if to emphasise that it is not the chief point of concern:

> Our simple childhood sits upon a throne
> That hath more power than all the elements.

I guess not what this tells of Being past.
Nor what it augurs of the life to come;
But so it is. (v 532–6)

The more important aspect in all major references to childhood appears to be that in exalting children – as, elsewhere, he exalts unsophisticated shepherds and peasants – Wordsworth is recovering Christian insights which the Western cultural tradition had mislaid, or perhaps never fully taken to heart. On many occasions, Christ called children 'blessed', and held them up as examples of qualities that adults must be reborn into if they are ever to inherit the kingdom of heaven. This was in no sense sentimentality, or the mere mistaking of ignorance for innocence, but an assertion of certain kinds of spontaneity, honesty, delight as truly divine. Again, Christ chose simple working men, like himself, for his first disciples, and it was in these that the qualities of the kingdom most readily took root. It is hard for the rich and sophisticated to enter the kingdom of heaven, hard indeed for the educated, if their sense of wonder is lost. When noting Wordsworth's attitude to children as revolutionary in its immediate context, we must not forget that it was the earlier tradition which had come adrift from Christianity in this respect. Again, in place of the idealised and flagrantly unreal shepherds of pastoral tradition, Wordsworth made his Michael a real, and recognisably wise and valuable, man. It needs to be noted that romantic insights of this kind are not mere primitivism, nor mere rejection of classicism, but the recovery of important, lost wisdom, rooted in love.

Equally important however, and some readers will think still more so, is Wordsworth's insight into the development of personality through infant love. In this he was seminal, alike to much in the Victorian novel and much in modern psychology, and so to our distinctive 'modern' understanding of man. As we would expect, Wordsworth seems divided between associationism and a more Coleridgean attitude, but in the passage before us his main intentions are fairly easy to see. It is noteworthy that the lines in the 1805 version which point more directly to associationism (244–54) are cut, in the 1850 revision, in favour of a new image (245–51) which emphasises the creative inspiration rather than the 'discipline' of love. The picture of the baby at the breast, first protected and sleeping, then learning to give and take in loving mutuality, is strikingly 'modern' in tone. All the stress falls on the *active* nature of love. First there is kinship : the baby is 'no outcast', even at the start of life, but 'kin' with his mother, and so with human kind. Long before he can understand, he experiences : this is the life of imagination, of Reason in Coleridge's sense, which belongs with love. The active 'drinks in' of 1850 is far more powerful than the passive 'gather' of 1805; and whereas in 1805 Wordsworth traces the stages of initiation by which the infant faculties are quickened, in 1850 we have a phrase much more suggestive of mystical experience and of 'spots of time'. The 1850 lines 232–40 recall indeed the central passage from the Tintern Abbey lines, through their hint that love, incarnate in the mother, both springs from and perpetuates the highest consciousness :

> For him, in one dear Presence, there exists
> A virtue which irradiates and exalts
> Objects through widest intercourse of sense.

In contrast, the 1805 wording is very much closer to the Locke tradition, suggesting a process of cause and effect almost mechanical :

> Such feelings pass into his *torpid* life
> Like an awakening breeze, and hence his *mind*
> Even in the first *trial of its powers*
> *Is prompt and watchful, eager to combine*
> *In one appearance, all the elements*
> *And parts of the same object, else detached*
> *And loath to coalesce.*

Though our italics point the comparison between the two versions, it is fair to note, however, that the phrase 'Like an

awakening breeze' creates organic suggestions even in 1805.
Wordsworth presumably made his revision not because he
renounced an interest in the psychological workings of growth,
but because he wanted to make still clearer his awareness of a
divine mystery. From here, both versions proceed to the famous
lines :

> Along his infant veins are interfused
> The gravitation and the filial bond
> Of Nature that connect him with the world.

The Newtonian concept of gravitation as the divine power
linking all the material operations of nature is most interestingly
yoked together with 'filial bond', the divine law operative through
all relationships of love. Body and soul literally 'interfuse', with
the result that the baby 'belongs'. 'No outcast he' refers both to
the baby's eternal destiny, his ultimate status as son of God, and
to the process which will make him a secure rather than neurotic
personality in adult life – in fact, at home in *this* visible world.
The mother's love confirms the baby's individuality and self-
hood, in a manner laying up future happiness, so that the child
is indeed father of the man.

Wordsworth, however, would surely not have regarded this
psychological process as a total guarantee of happiness, unless the
divinity hedging all men about were also perceived. The happiness built up in a child through maternal affection might still
dissolve in the 'light of common day' at adolescence, unless his
sense of wonder were preserved, and the communion with Nature
confirmed, and strengthened through daily choice. The 1850
version inserts, before the powerful phrase 'Emphatically such a
Being lives', a new image, which reinforces the baby's power as
an agent of blessing. These exquisite new lines (1850, 245–51)
suggest that before the baby is strong enough, physically, to
'gather' a flower (and, surely, before he is strong enough,
mentally, to 'understand'), he can still point, and thereby
beautify. Something of the paradisal associations of Marvell's
Little T.C. are invoked, but unlike Marvell, Wordsworth is not

consciously employing conceits and metaphors. He asserts rather
that the infant is a real fount of pity and healing – a perception
that has nothing to do with associationism and is likely, therefore,
unless religiously understood, to appear sentimental. The Child,
celebrating beauty, however inarticulately, sets up a dance of
love, between creator and creation, thereby demonstrating,
indeed being, the 'active' world. So, in both versions, the poet
goes on to his all-important vision of mutuality :

> From nature largely he receives; nor so
> Is satisfied, but largely gives again.

All laws of calculation, whether brutally Hobbesian, or whether
more prudently rooted in the competition of money, class, status,
sensual gratification, or even sensitivity and high culture, yield,
through this early experience, to higher laws of love. To give and
to receive are both blessed, both indeed complementary; both
inseparable even, since when a man is in love, who is to say where
giving and receiving begin and end? Wordsworth goes on to
proclaim that the baby is already 'Even as an agent of the one
great Mind' – a phrase which once more connects the psychology
of consciousness with something akin to the distinctive activity of
prayer. The reference must be to an indwelling and outflowing
of divine activity, whether this is glossed as a neo-platonic dance
of Anima Mundi in the whole cosmos or as the presence of the
Holy Spirit in the temple of man. In the lines immediately
following, Wordsworth is able to see the baby's mind as potential
father of the artist and the prophet as well as the man, as it

> Create[s], creator and receiver both,
> Working but in alliance with the works
> Which it beholds.

The 'status' of our perceptions is neither subjective nor objective,
but exists in this dance. 'Primary imagination' is at work in the
child long before he is able to understand it, and certainly long
before he is capable of 'secondary imagination' and the making
of art. Yet, paradoxically, the child is purer in his perception

through his very inarticulateness, purer through the absence of whatever elements of experience might dry up the springs. Since love and blessing belong naturally to the child he is indeed the 'hiding place' of man's greatness, the arcane mystery most suited to Wordsworth's prophetic art.

Inmate of an *active* universe : but this, too, brings us to the sting. We remarked at the start that Wordsworth seems more at home than most religious poets do in *this* world, finding blessings almost as though Paradise had never been lost. And isn't even his baby a trifle unusual, in the apparent absence of cross-currents in his pristine world? Most babies seem to sense that they are already partly in exile, if only in the strong alternations of laughter and tears. The book of *Genesis* captures this beautifully in its two accounts of creation, with the original image of lost bliss, the once-upon-a-time of all our days. Exile lurks, too, in the earliest nursery rhymes and the simplest fairy-tales, just as it haunts all the literature, all the religion and thought, of adult man. As J. R. R. Tolkien put it, in his brilliant essay 'On Fairy-Stories' : *

'Thou shalt not' – or else thou shalt depart begarred into endless regret. The gentlest 'nursery-tales' knew it. Even Peter Rabbit was forbidden a garden, lost his blue coat, and took sick. The Locked Door stands as as eternal Temptation.

And indeed Wordsworth had known and come to terms with this experience before *The Prelude* was started, even though it seemed terribly at odds with his dearest truths. The loss of youth and vision, the coming of exhaustion; how is even a poet to survive unscathed?

> Thou little Child, yet glorious in the might
> Of heaven-born freedom on thy being's height,
> Why with such earnest pains dost thou provoke
> The years to bring the individual yoke,

* First published in *Essays Presented to Charles Williams* (1947); now available in the paperback *Tree and Leaf* (1964).

> Thus blindly with thy blessedness at strife?
> Full soon thy Soul shall have her earthly freight,
> And custom lie upon thee with a weight,
> Heavy as frost, and deep almost as life!

In the Immortality Ode, these lines, addressed to the child, are followed by an expression of that deep foreboding which haunts much of *The Prelude*:

> those obstinate questionings
> Of sense and outward things,
> Fallings from us, vanishings;
> Blank misgivings of a Creature
> Moving about in worlds not realised

And, in the mysteriously dark passages of 'Resolution and Independence', composed mainly in the late spring of 1802, similar forebodings reach out to the poetic vocation itself:

> By our own spirits are we deified:
> We Poets in our youth begin in gladness;
> But thereof come in the end despondency and madness.

This is the sting not only in the 'creator and receiver both' of our present passage, but in the phrase embedded in the marvellously visionary Tintern Abbey lines themselves:

> all the mighty world
> Of eye, and ear – both what they half-create,
> And what perceive

It is in moments of exhaustion, when vision wanes, that we most strain, as if to breaking point and, at such moments, the romantic visionary is exposed to a very special cross. Suppose that the creative power really does reside within him; may it not be as vulnerable to destruction, then, as he is himself? The classic expression of this fear is in Coleridge's 'Dejection: An Ode', written on 4 April 1802:

O Lady ! we receive but what we give,
And in our life alone does Nature live :
Ours is her wedding garment, ours her shroud !
    And would we aught behold, of higher worth,
Than that inanimate cold world allowed
To the poor loveless ever-anxious crowd,
    Ah ! from the soul itself must issue forth
A light, a glory, a fair luminous cloud
    Enveloping the Earth –
And from the soul itself must there be sent
    A sweet and potent voice, of its own birth,
Of all sweet sounds the life and element !

After all is said, the main danger for the romantic will *be* solipsism : that danger which lies in wait whenever the intensity of personal experience, the egotistical sublime, claims final authority over all other experience, so that the God within is more effectually real than the God without. In Wordsworth himself the balance between revelation and creation is usually kept more finely, so that 'dejection' could seldom be a description of his own lonelier moods. It would be as oversimple – he seems always to sense – to claim that moments of heightened conscious-ness are 'merely' given by God and as received by man in wise passiveness, as it would be to claim that they are 'merely' gener-ated by exuberant and answering energy within. The former view might lead simply to mystical detachment, the latter might tempt towards a search for short-cuts to ecstasy, perhaps through the use of drugs. Yet in the last resort, the objective and prior existence of God must be attested, the God who 'is', whether or not he is present to a man's consciousness. It should be no surprise that Wordsworth and Coleridge both moved to a more orthodox Christian faith not merely as a result of disillusionment with political events, and not merely as a result of lost youth, but as the ultimate logic of their religious quest. In Wordsworth a final 'belief' in God is everywhere apparent, along with thanks-giving for a bonus, an unearned grace, in the visionary moments themselves. In Book VII even the greeting of redbreasts touches him, with the thought of allies given, and not 'of' himself :

> A delight
> At this unthought of greeting, unawares
> Smote me, a sweetness of the coming time,
> And listening, I half whispered, 'We will be
> Ye heartsome Choristers, ye and I will be
> Brethren, and in the hearing of bleak winds
> Will chant together'. (VII 31–7)

Perhaps the most perfect balance in *The Prelude* is to be found in the lines in Book XI when the insights contained in our passage about the baby are revisited, but with the emphasis now thrown upon our need to 'give', as a willed response :

> O ! mystery of man, from what a depth
> Proceed thy honours. I am lost, but see
> In simple childhood something of the base
> On which thy greatness stands; but this I feel,
> That from thyself it is that thou must give,
> Else never can receive. The days gone by
> Come back upon me from the dawn almost
> Of life : the hiding-places of my power
> Seem open; I approach, and then they close;
> I see by glimpses now; when age comes on,
> May scarcely see at all, and I would give,
> While yet we may, as far as words can give,
> A substance and a life to what I feel :
> I would enshrine the spirit of the past
> For future restoration. (XI 329–43)

Surely the Christian sense of duty – of 'giving' as a response to creation more fundamental than receiving, or even than feeling, yet in God's economy also inextricably linked with both – is the inner logic, also, of much of *The Prelude* ? Only by building a life, by making and giving, do we fulfil ourselves; and Wordsworth's Nature has, after all, strained always towards 'God'. It was with this insight also that Wordsworth defined his art in these healing terms; as a boon not only to other men, in whose hearts it might awaken precious, lost echoes, but also and not least to his own older self, when energy wanes and the end of exile draws near.

'Masterful images': in the end, Wordsworth is a religious poet, like Milton; both 'enshrine' images of God. Both proclaim the kingdom of heaven on earth, waiting to be occupied; both accept the discipline of moral purity to fit them for the high calling of art

> I never, in the quest of right and wrong,
> Did tamper with myself from private aims;
> Nor was in any of my hopes the dupe
> Of selfish passions; nor did wilfully
> Yield ever to mean cares and low pursuits,
> But rather did with jealousy shrink back
> From every combination that might aid
> The tendency, too potent in itself,
> Of habit to enslave the mind, I mean
> Oppress it by the laws of vulgar sense,
> And substitute a universe of death,
> The falsest of all worlds, in place of that
> Which is divine and true. (XIII 131–43)

> It is an ancient Mariner,
> And he stoppeth one of three.
> 'By thy long grey beard and glittering eye,
> Now wherefore stop'st thou me?'

'It is' . . . Coleridge's poem starts from the present tense, active, and, as it turns out, irresistible; the tense of absorbed narrative and compulsive confession. It is as if the whole poem is here in embryo: narrative vividness, fixed and immediate; human encounter, intense yet trancelike; questions, asked in terror or nightmare, needing answers but getting none, for whatever 'answer' there is comes obliquely. It is as if the story comes loose from time, gravitating towards that somehow eternal quality which haunts all its parts – the dramatic violence of sudden storms and appearances, sudden actions. 'By thy long grey beard and glittering eye' – strange invocation, as if feared and hypnotic qualities could be somehow besought! From the start, there is curious double vision; everything is fated and necessary, everything startling and dreadful. Whether 'it is' an ancient Mariner, or an albatross, or a ship of death or a hermit, we encounter the object and it encounters us as in a dream. Everything seems perfectly alive, perfectly unexplained, perfectly inescapable, terribly intense. The poem is full of elementals. Its setting, perhaps the only one possible, is the sea. Its images are calm and storm, sun and moon, life and death; its values are loyalty and betrayal, fear and hope, guilt and deliverance. Everything is extravagant – the extreme case, the ultimate possible image:

> With throats unslaked, with black lips baked,
> We could not laugh nor wail;
> Through utter drought all dumb we stood!

> I bit my arm, I sucked the blood,
> And cried, A sail ! a sail !

Is such poetry allegory? Certainly not, in any systematic
fashion. Yet it is full of ideas. Is it a dream? Art so highly wrought
must originate chiefly in the waking consciousness, radically
heightened; yet it has the feel of a dream. Perhaps our best word
for it is 'fantasy' – a form of literature which creates a world with
its own rules and laws, depending wholly on inner consistency, yet
which, at its best, continually draws strength from the 'real' world
of human psychology, human intuition and spirituality, and
continually feeds its own insights back into that world.

In terms of immediate influence, of course, Coleridge is directly
indebted to the ballad form, which had been revived, along with
much general feeling for the 'medieval', in the mid-eighteenth
century, and which became a highly stylised and consciously
'literary' cult among many later romantics. The ballad is one of
the most elemental and powerful forms of poetry. Like its near
neighbour, the nursery rhyme, it is strongly rhythmic in form,
basic and often brutal in theme, austere in diction, stark and
archetypal in imagery, hypnotically repetitive in effect. Its total
experience is caught up often in a refrain – some burden, grim
or gay, returning with insistence, with precision, with mounting
and complex irony, to intensify primitive feelings. For these
reasons, the ballad is adapted to that kind of strong narrative
line which demonstrates, rather than describes, human hopes,
fears and sufferings, approximating to ritual re-enactment in its
effect. Most of the best ballads have openings very similar to 'The
Ancient Mariner' in their power to arrest attention, to sketch in a
situation that bypasses particulars such as names, places, dates,
by drawing very immediately on the reader's own intensities :

> The twelve-month and a day being up,
> The dead began to speak :
> 'O who sits weeping on my grave,
> And will not let me sleep ?'

Such poetry stimulates personal echoes, personal resonances, much as the symbolists later consciously set out to do.

> He was a braw gallant,
> And he rid' by the ring;
> And the Bonny Earl of Murray,
> O he might have been a king.

Again, such poetry moves us beyond discussion and argument, as Coleridge believed creative imagination always should. In Coleridge's own categories 'The Ancient Mariner' is poetry of 'imagination', not of 'fancy'; of 'Reason', not of 'understanding'. Perhaps the function of great art is, nearly always, to probe beyond those arguments and reasonings which continually, and rightly, attend man's attempt to make sense of himself, seeking to initiate us rather, intuitively and directly, into psychic and spiritual realities of evil and good. We recognise such an achievement in Sophocles and Euripides, Shakespeare and Milton, Dickens and Dostoievsky, indeed in most literature and drama of high excellence. At a purely speculative level, we will wonder why Iago acts so (as he does himself), we will ponder Oedipus and Satan, Tulkinghorn and Raskolnikov, searching for clues. But, while motives are baffling, the truth is self-evident; no one can doubt the realism of their sufferings and deeds.

Coleridge recognised 'imagination' as the realm of revelation through recreation, the realm where beauty and goodness, and their mighty opposites, are known. Philosophers might then discuss the phenomena almost indefinitely (might so bemuse themselves, as often happens, that they become lost in words, and forget the experiences to which their words strive). But the artist, like the saint or the sinner, offers an image: a particular and tangible embodiment of complex truth. You can no more doubt Lady Macbeth, or Joe Gargery, than you can doubt Hitler, or Mother Teresa; you can no more hope to 'explain' the fictions, analytically and definitively, than you can the historical men. Coleridge recognised this great realm of 'reality' as the artist's province, just as, in his role of philosopher, he recognised it as the region of 'truth'. His poem is, therefore, in essence realistic, at this profound level, even though fantasy, not social realism, is its artistic mode.

The *Biographia Literaria* outlines the conscious plan which Coleridge and Wordsworth decided upon for *Lyrical Ballads*, and their decision to approach 'reality' in their art by two opposite paths. Since the passage is both justly famous and, by Coleridge's standards, readily accessible, it is best left to speak for itself :

During the first year that Mr. Wordsworth and I were neighbours, our conversations turned frequently on the two cardinal points of poetry, the power of exciting the sympathy of the reader by a faithful adherence to the truth of nature, and the power of giving the interest of novelty by the modifying colours of imagination. . . .

In this idea originated the plan of the 'Lyrical Ballads'; in which it was agreed, that my endeavours should be directed to persons and characters supernatural, or at least romantic; yet so as to transfer from our inward nature a human interest and a semblance of truth sufficient to procure for these shadows of imagination that willing suspension of disbelief for the moment, which constitutes poetic faith.

Mr. Wordsworth, on the other hand, was to propose to himself as his object, to give the charm of novelty to things of everyday, and to excite a feeling analogous to the supernatural, by awakening the loveliness and the wonders of the world before us; an inexhaustible treasure, but for which, in consequence of the film of familiarity and selfish solicitude we have eyes, yet see not, ears that hear not, and hearts that neither feel nor understand.

Of course, this begs many questions; and Coleridge's phrase 'that willing suspension of disbelief for the moment, which constitutes poetic faith' has been much discussed. For our present purpose, the important point is that Coleridge is 'to transfer from our inner nature a human interest and a semblance of truth sufficient' for his intended effect. Many times, he recognises that effects akin to those he produces in 'The Ancient Mariner' are known through various 'delusions' – through dreams, drugs, or delirium for instance, none of which we finally think of as 'real'. Yet he also recognises that 'the supernatural' is not always allied to phantom experiences but, rather, that its intensities link with good and evil, joy and dereliction, wholeness and damnation, in the inner life.

What then is the best way to start reading 'The Ancient Mariner'? To our minds, it is best first to release the visual imagination, allowing this to roam through the images. Everything is striking and extraordinary. The visual play suggests a near meeting of dream psychology and conscious image-making, a world close to modern imagism or modern cinema. Something like Walt Disney's *Fantasia* might suggest itself for comparison. If so, could we attempt to match the poem with appropriate music, thereby creating a *Fantasia* in reverse? An approach of this kind has the advantage of directing our attention immediately towards the archetypal image, where the poem's power surely chiefly lives: a solitary man, caught up in a drama of mortal personal guilt and divine deliverance, doomed to roam the world, telling his tale when its moment comes. The affinity is with the wandering Jew, the Flying Dutchman (a possible source for music?), with the exiled Cain even – stories linked only tangentially with religion in its orthodox forms. Perhaps we all have something of the Ancient Mariner in us (as Coleridge himself alleged of Hamlet)? – though if so, mercifully most of us keep him in check.

A legend of this kind attracts material from various sources like a powerful magnet, yet Coleridge's organisation excludes any systematic interpretation of one, definite, kind. From the literary point of view, his poem works a little like Eliot's *Waste Land* – to which, indeed, it is also spiritually akin. We are helped in our exploration if we know something of Coleridge personally, as modern scholarship has generously ensured that we may. *The Road to Xanadu*** is a round-up of Coleridge's own extensive reading, looking for every possible source of his inspiration in other art. Coleridge's ideas have also been intensively studied,

---

* John Livingston Lowes, *The Road to Xanadu* (1966).

often by critics wishing to clarify, as well as to expound. Yet, in the end, Coleridge's poetic imagination had unusual licence, even apart from the conscious plan as he described it himself. He was familiar with opium visions, with their strange dislocation of consciousness, and their apparent heightening of consciousness in a fantasy world. The passage from *Biographia Literaria* already quoted includes the following puzzling words, again in connection with Coleridge's own part in the proposed scheme :

the incidents and agents were to be, in part at least, supernatural; and the excellence aimed at was to consist in the interesting of the affections by the dramatic truths of such emotions, as would naturally accompany such situations, supposing them real. And real in *this* sense they have been to every human being who, from whatever source of delusion, has at any time believed himself under supernatural agency.

Such formulations leave the gap (the mystery?) between perception and objective reality notably yawning, and the emphasis on '*this*' (Coleridge's italics) scarcely helps to make '*this*' clear. Again, anyone reading Coleridge's poetry, and grappling (as we certainly should) with its relationship to his own powerful and influential theories of poetic imagination, cannot overlook the famous and bizarre prose introduction to 'Kubla Khan', strangest among all the clues that the poet has left :

In the summer of the year 1797 [*sic* : though almost certainly he meant to write 1798 : *Eds*], the Author, then in ill health, had retired to a lonely farm-house between Porlock and Linton, on the Exmoor confines of Somerset and Devonshire. In consequence of a slight indisposition, an anodyne had been prescribed, from the effects of which he fell asleep in his chair at the moment when he was reading the following sentence, or words of the same substance, in 'Purchas's Pilgrimage' : 'Here the Khan Kubla commanded a palace to be built, and a stately garden thereunto. And this ten miles of fertile ground were inclosed with a wall.' The Author continued for about three hours in a profound sleep, at least of the external senses, during which time he has the most vivid confidence, that he could not have composed less than from two to three hundred lines;

if that indeed can be called composition in which all the images rose up before him as *things*, with a parallel production of the correspondent expressions, without any sensation or consciousness of effort. On awakening he appeared to himself to have a distinct recollection of the whole, and taking his pen, ink, and paper, instantly and eagerly set down the lines that are here preserved. At this moment he was unfortunately called out by a person on business from Porlock, and detained by him above an hour, and on his return to his room, found, to his no small surprise and mortification, that though he still retained some vague and dim recollection of the general purport of the vision, yet, all the rest had passed away like the images on the surface of a stream into which a stone has been cast, but, alas! without the after restoration of the latter.

If this is accepted, then it seems that Coleridge had a 'vision' (how accurately is this word intended?) in which words and images were alike 'given', in parallel form. It appears that the process of 'composition' – a word that Coleridge himself pauses over doubtfully in the context – was in fact a transcription from memory, interrupted fatally by the person from Porlock. The notion that images and words should have been equally 'given', in 'parallel production', and in a dream induced by a drug, moves us a long way from 'secondary imagination' in its official, Coleridgean form. None the less, we are also a long way from 'fancy', if that is to be defined merely as an intellectual and mechanical rearrangement of sense impressions derived from the waking world. What Coleridge appears to be saying is that he transmitted 'Kubla Khan' rather than that he created it. But, where the transmission originated, and how far it depended upon the breaking down and recreating of 'reality' in Coleridge's unconscious rather than in his conscious mind, remains to be judged. Perhaps many people sometimes wake up with the sense of having written great poetry, composed great music, in their recent dream consciousness, but this seldom if ever with most of us gets transcribed.

If we look at Coleridge's 'the Ancient Mariner' with open minds on these questions of 'intention', certain features are, however, clear. A critic who suggests, as William Empson has done,* that the Mariner kills the albatross chiefly to make soup, and that the spiritual punishment of himself and the crew is therefore excessive, signifies a cheerful unwillingness to take the poem seriously at all. That we are indeed faced with a drama of betrayal and damnation, grace and penitence, seems too evident to require much defence. The poem cannot be assimilated to Christian theology by any direct process, yet the religious scheme is present throughout. The phrase 'O Christ!' occurs twice, jerked out of the Mariner first in horror and revulsion, as the universe becomes hell for him :

> The very deep did rot : O Christ !
> That ever this should be !
> Yea, slimy things did crawl with legs
> Upon the slimy sea.

and later in fear and wonder, as he sees the angelic presences who have been animating the zombie crew :

> I turned my eyes upon the deck –
> Oh, Christ ! what saw I there !
>
> This seraph-band, each waved his hand :
> It was a heavenly sight !
> They stood as signals to the land,
> Each one a lovely sight.

Mary is invoked twice, each time in the context of grace – first in appeal, when the ship of death becomes manifest ('Heaven's Mother send us grace !'), and later in praise, for release from torment :

> To Mary Queen the praise be given !
> She sent the gentle sleep from Heaven,
> That slid into my soul.

* William Empson, 'The Ancient Mariner', *Critical Quarterly*, vol. 6 (1964).

In other places, the religious references are more eclectic, with neo-platonism a frequent source. The Spirit who pursues the ship from the north is glossed in the poem's prose commentary in a manner referring us well outside Christian tradition for its source: 'A spirit had followed them; one of the invisible inhabitants of this planet, neither departed souls nor angels; concerning whom the learned Jew Josephus, and the Platonic Constantinopolitan, Michael Psellus, may be consulted. They are very numerous, and there is no climate or element without one or more.' And later, again in the prose commentary, there is a beautiful and quintessentially neo-platonic description of the *living* universe (though in saying this, we should never forget the great synthesis of neo-platonic and Christian ideas which took place in the early centuries of the church, so that the two traditions, while differing on certain important fundamentals, have never been very far apart): 'In his loneliness and fixedness he yearneth towards the journeying Moon, and the stars that still sojourn, yet still move onward; and every where the blue sky belongs to them, and is their appointed rest, and their native country and their natural homes, which they enter unannounced, as lords that are certainly expected and yet there is a silent joy at their arrival.'

With this in mind, we can (and must) attempt to trace the poem's central development, whether this is thought of as tentative affirmation, prophetic vision, or as a stream of suggestion flowing gently through fantasy. And here, the present critics should make clear, no doubt, that in this central development the poem is, in their view, evidently and specifically Christian. It is Christian in this sense: that it is written by a Christian; that its most characteristic ideas originate inside Christianity; and that the colour of feeling inherent in the power of the verse would not be found in any writer not profoundly influenced by Christian *experience*. We put the matter in this manner in order to safeguard certain other aspects which modify its Christianity, and defeat any attempt to read it as systematic Christian allegory, some of which have already been touched on. Again, it seems clear that Coleridge, who was not consciously allegorising, would have thought of the poem's truth as universal rather than as sectarian, and would have expected it to speak first to the imagination, and to the experience, of readers, not to their religious 'beliefs'.

Where, then, are the specific marks of Christianity? First, the albatross is welcomed as a guest, and offered friendship – which is why its betrayal cannot plausibly be glossed in terms of bird soup :

> At length did cross an Albatross,
> Through the fog it came :
> As if it had been a Christian soul,
> We hailed it in God's name.

The 'as if' suggests, of course, analogy rather than anything more definite, and it is obvious that the other mariners think of the bird merely superstitiously, hailing it as a good omen. When this view seems to be confirmed, yet the Mariner none the less kills it, they blame him not for betraying a living creature whom he has befriended, but for killing the bird that 'made the breeze to blow'. For this reason again, they praise him for killing the bird when a further reversal of weather appears now to prove the opposite :

> 'Twas right, said they, such birds to slay
> That bring the fog and mist.

No doubt this is the reason why, later, they simply die, but the Mariner himself is reserved for a different fate. This is nothing to do with a spectacular vengeance from a cruel deity (as William Empson seems to think) but is, rather, an indication of the poem's direction. We are to focus on the plight of the one man who is a moral agent, knowing good from evil, rather than upon the fate of many men excluded from spiritual insight, and so from spiritual life. The crew belongs, to use a phrase of Coleridge's already quoted, with the 'lethargy of custom' – with that majority among men who miss alike the beauty and the suffering of life, having no eyes to *see*.

The Mariner, however, who has *particularly* offered friend-ship to the bird, and established trust with it, commits evil in the fullest sense. The bird has come to recognise him, to receive from him, to respond when he calls to it, so the slaying is 'hellish' in the strict, Christian sense. The ancient world, Greek and Christian alike, had accepted duty to a guest as sacred, and believed that to harm a guest or indeed to fail to protect him from evil was a wrong crying to Heaven for vengeance. Above all, duty to a friend was sacred; Dante puts Brutus and Judas Iscariot together, in hell's deepest pit.

It could be argued, of course, that this duty to guests and friends did not extend to animals, yet man's Lordship of Nature is a profoundly Christian belief. The book of *Genesis* asserts it, and Christ himself said that not a bird falls to earth without his Father's knowledge. For centuries, the church had tended to ignore this aspect of its teaching to such a degree that St Francis's close relationship with creatures seemed, in the strict sense of the word, eccentric. Perhaps this was because the assumption had grown that animals have no souls, and, therefore, that callousness towards them is permissible; certainly a divine relationship between man and the creatures lower than himself had been very generally lost.

One feature of romanticism was the radical recovery of a sense of man's kinship with all creation, and of understanding that the fruit of the Spirit, love, joy and peace, is not divisible. Blake expresses this, simply and memorably, in 'The Little Black Boy' :

> Look on the rising sun ! there God does live,
> And gives His light, and gives His heat away;
> And flowers and trees and beasts and men receive
> Comfort in morning, joy in the noon day.

In Wordsworth, the unity of creation is everywhere asserted; and, in 'The Ancient Mariner', this insight is, more than anything, the poem's coherence. Because the albatross was really befriended, it was really betrayed; and the Mariner's punishment is precisely that of Macbeth. He passes into inner torment and dereliction, which is hell brought home to him. He cannot pray (one of the traditional signs of damnation), and, like Macbeth, he cannot sleep. When he tells of the killing of the albatross he *looks* demonic (Part I, final stanza), and he knows, as the other mariners do not, that he has done a 'hellish' thing. (The irony is that while the Mariner reports the phrase 'And I had done a hellish thing' as words said to him by his fellows, he alone knows the real meaning of the words, and their full truth.) Later, during his trance, he hears the dialogue between two spirits who direct the stricken ship : and, while these appear to belong to a universe more neo-platonic than Christian in concept, they bring home the moral in a directly Christian way :

> 'Is it he ?' quoth one, 'Is this the man ?
> By him who died on cross,
> With his cruel bow he laid full low
> The harmless Albatross.

> 'The Spirit who bideth by himself
> In the land of mist and snow,
> He loved the bird that loved the man
> Who shot him with his bow.'

The reference to the crucifixion balances the somewhat untheo-logical 'Spirit who bideth by himself', but the final two lines, with their image of a dance of delight and love between Creator and creatures that has been violated, are at once precise and profound. Perhaps the Christian understanding of the nature of evil has seldom been more simply and powerfully captured. There is a chain of love, including the Creator's love for the bird, and the bird's love for the man, which has been totally broken by the man. Towards the end of the poem, the community of all creation is again insisted upon, in lines which will look naïve or sentimental only to readers who wholly refuse the poem's imaged vision :

> He prayeth well, who loveth well
> Both man and bird and beast.

> He prayeth best, who loveth best
> All things both great and small;
> For the dear God who loveth us,
> He made and loveth all.

Prayer, to which we shall return, is the key concept, the word, and activity, which is the poem's key theme.

When the Mariner kills love, he commits the sin which cuts him decisively from God, and from the life of God, which *is* love, and puts himself in the self-alone, the absence of God, which is hell. Total change comes with the moment of murder, and Coleridge signifies this through a tellingly simple inversion. In Part I, we have read :

> The Sun came up upon the left,
> Out of the sea came he !
> And he shone bright, and on the right
> Went down into the sea.

This description, marvellously buoyant and compressed, of the day's ritual, returns, inverted, at the start of Part II :

> The Sun now rose upon the right :
> Out of the sea came he,
> Still hid in mist, and on the left
> Went down into the sea.

While a determinedly literal mind might deduce merely that the ship has now turned round and is going the other way, the evident force is that creation has turned round, the whole universe has turned round; and this indeed proves to be so. Arrest and fixity; dryness; horror :

> The very deep did rot; O Christ !
> That ever this should be !
> Yea, slimy things did crawl with legs
> Upon the slimy sea.

This, now, is the Mariner's 'world', and above all, he is

> Alone, alone, all, all alone,
> Alone on a wide wide sea !
> And never a saint took pity on
> My soul in agony.

Towards the end, the Mariner yet again stresses to the Wedding-Guest that the crowning horror of his suffering has been the absence, or the apparent absence, of God :

> O Wedding-Guest ! this soul has been
> Alone on a wide wide sea :
> So lonely 'twas, that God himself
> Scarce seemed there to be.

The universe dead and ghastly (a suicide's vision of reality?) is the Mariner's world after his sin. It belongs with Macbeth's world after the killing of Duncan, with the central quality of consciousness conveyed by T. S. Eliot in *The Waste Land,* and indeed with all visions of loneliness and madness in literature, whether specifically Christian or not, where these sufferings are linked, in whatever manner, with man's violation, or loss, of love. But the poem is also about redemption. The Mariner is released from his suffering not through anything he can do himself – above all, he cannot pray even – but through a moment's pure grace :

> O happy living things ! no tongue
> Their beauty might declare :
> A spring of love gushed from my heart,
> And I blessed them unaware :
> Sure my kind saint took pity on me,
> And I blessed them unaware.

'Unaware'. This word, often in the form 'unawares', was a favourite of Wordsworth's, and any determined student of the romantic sensibility could do worse than spend a few hours tracking it down. Here, it is pure grace : 'The selfsame moment I could pray.' With prayer comes release. The albatross falls away, and he can sleep. There is further penance to come, a strange doom of purgation, but the Mariner is no longer in hell. This release naturally calls to mind the moment in *Pilgrim's Progress* when Christian's burden of sin rolls away from him at the foot of the cross, since, though Coleridge is not an allegorist like Bunyan, his imaginative effect is most closely akin.

In 'The Ancient Mariner' Coleridge is moving on the plane of Reason as he defines it; he is depicting realities of good and evil, all probing well beyond the world of 'understanding'. The actual killing of the albatross is no more 'explained' than is the sin of Judas as recounted in the four New Testament accounts of it, or the sin of Eve and Adam as recounted in *Genesis*. 'The man said, "The woman whom thou gavest to be with me, she gave me of the tree, and I did eat." ' 'The woman said, "The serpent beguiled me, and I did eat," ' that is all : and, though Milton, in his dramatic presentation, tried to 'understand', tying himself in knots along with the rest of us, *Genesis* simply stops here. So, for Adam and Eve, there is expulsion, and loss of Eden, as God had decreed; they and their seed are to wander in exile for the rest of time. The 'truth' of the story in *Genesis* is, simply, the truth of it; men have eaten the forbidden fruit, do wander in exile, God knows why. Coleridge leaves the Mariner's motives likewise unexplained and mysterious; but they are met by the equally unexplained and mysterious operations of grace. The Mariner is in hell (as most men sometimes may be, and some men habitually) and, in human terms, he has no route back. Yet suddenly he sees the water creatures, and they are beautiful; in place of the rot and slime, the horror, there is a dance of delight. Love wells up in his heart; he praises (the moment is entirely given); above all, he blesses them, 'unaware'. 'The self-same moment I could pray.' The universe turns round again, and, for the world of death, a world of life is returned. The water creatures are still the same, in their own reality; it is the Mariner who has changed, or been changed.

Why does human consciousness sometimes inhabit a world of deadness and horror, where life is unbearable, sometimes rejoice in a world radiant with God? If there is one theme that links Blake, Wordsworth and Coleridge, it is this one, the mystery of joy, and dereliction, in the inner soul. All three poets are driven men, like the Mariner, with an urgent message of healing for their fellows to hear. Yet they know they will be dreaded and resisted, prophets unheeded; that most men will shun the tale they have to tell.

As one would expect, the romantics are keenly aware of different frames of reference, different interpretations, and the tension between joy and fear is at the heart of their *thought*. If God is really there to be seen clearly, why do many men miss him? Various traditional insights and guesses are explored. Many men perhaps lose the visionary gifts at adolescence, preferring the 'light of common day' to the wonder of God. Perhaps this loss is part of the harvest of sin, the original exile from Eden; perhaps it is loss of moral purity through deliberate sin. May it be that God preordains some men to the darkness and horror; that, in Blake's words, 'Some are born to endless night'? Or does God appear only when he wills, and then withdraw himself, coming and going to laws not yet revealed? In certain moods Wordsworth and Coleridge toyed with the thought that since we 'receive but what we give' in living, then, when our exuberance and energy fail, the world must go dead. Energy, which (said Blake) is both 'eternal delight' and 'from the body', may indeed be the fuel, the vision, of the soul. Yet *this* view risks locking men in psychic solipsism, and mistaking the mechanisms of human perception for the realities perceived.

It may be that the romantic poets had to declare their strong sense of election in differing fashions, since this sense of election was also their gospel for men. But had they, by grace or purity, achieved particular insight, or were they perceiving in strange, and maybe disordered ways? Were they saner than the excluded majority, or madder, were they driven by divine, or by demonic powers? When their universe went dead, had they sinned exceptionally? Or had their mind broken; or had they merely grown old? As the nineteenth century went on, and the optimism of the early romantics receded, their successors often gravitated to bizarre and consciously perverse modes of thought. Could the heavenly light be as capricious even as the erotic, sending poor driven, infatuated men quite out of their wits? 'La belle dame sans merci', will o' the wisp glimpses of divinity; what kind of life, and destiny, were these?

The distinctive character of 'The Ancient Mariner', we are saying, is that it is Christian in its implicit understanding of such questions as these. The mystery is a Christian mystery, and to this degree accessible; while 'good' and 'evil' are not 'explained', they are held under God. The poem offers a clear polarity between a universe where men pray and celebrate and love is paramount, and a universe where blessing is absent and horror prevails. In objective fact the universe is God's, and constant; but sin removes men to a vision where God is absent; to hell. Yet the Mariner receives grace, including the supreme grace of penitence, and is led back to a living, though wounded, destiny in the world of men. In knowing he has done a hellish thing, he makes grace possible; only failure to accept guilt could lock God finally out.

What, then, is the Mariner's destiny? In one sense he seems akin to any poet or artist, or any Christian, who, healed by grace, is driven to tell his tale. Freed from hell, he remains still in Purgatory, and is an object of terror to most whom he meets. The holy hermit is aghast, the Wedding-Guest afraid and reluctant; the Pilot's boy goes mad. The Mariner's destiny is not to start the voyage of sanctity and gradually to mirror holiness, but to remain visibly touched by hell, disturbing and disturbed:

> Since then, at an uncertain hour,
> That agony returns;
> And till my ghastly tale is told,
> The heart within me burns.

The Mariner exists for this 'uncertain hour', which is also the hour of this poem; the hour chosen by God when some other man must hear the tale. The other chief aspect of the poem, which we have not so far touched on, is that its centre is really the Wedding-Guest. At the start, he is picked out by the Mariner, and himself 'arrested'; there are strong suggestions of hypnosis and trance. He fears the Mariner, tries to shake him off, but is held by him; this is *his* moment, with no hope of escape :

> He holds him with his glittering eye –
> The Wedding-Guest stood still,
> And listens like a three years' child :
> The Mariner hath his will.
>
> The Wedding-Guest sat on a stone;
> He cannot choose but hear.

The Wedding-Guest's experience is, in this aspect, related to the Mariner's – especially at the point when, in a trance, the Mariner has heard the two spirits debate. Coleridge is dramatising the moment of encounter when, in the divine will, or the divine capriciousness, *this* man experiences the near approach of God. The encounter is unsought, it is an unwanted distraction, it is terrifying rather than comforting, but, just now, its moment has come. The Mariner's story, his destiny, is now for *this* man entirely, and everything romantic, and fantastic, will converge in its effect.

Coleridge, like Wordsworth, believed that most men are open on their God-ward side only occasionally; that normally, God's presence is ignored, or not even seen. But there are moments when a work of art springs to life, when a relationship crystallises, when something long known is *seen* suddenly – and, at such times, a response, a 'yes' or 'no' must be made. It is surely because Coleridge's poem dramatises this moment in images so bizarre, so altogether unearthly, that it can afford its moral to have the simplicity of a child's hymn. The last four stanzas of the poem, which in isolation may seem banal, rise from the poem with authentic, even with hypnotic power. The Wedding-Guest leaves the encounter not elated, but 'like one that hath been stunned/ And is of sense forlorn'. None the less, he rises 'sadder and wiser' – which is certainly something; a valuable, if apparently modest role for art itself?

10 MIGHTY HARMONIES: SHELLEY'S *ODE TO THE WEST WIND*

Today, poetry and indeed serious literature enjoy less popularity than the undemanding alternatives of television and film, pop literature and pop culture, as if in realisation of the fear voiced by T. S. Eliot in his *Notes Towards a Definition of Culture* (1948) that a 'mass-culture will always be a substitute-culture'. Even many serious students of literature in sixth forms, universities and elsewhere sometimes regard it as little more than an intellectual exercise, or as useful documentation for historical, political or social matters. And, though poetry, of course, *is* still read, the immensely rewarding habit of reading it aloud, listening to it, experimenting with sound, stress and meaning, has somewhat declined.

In such a climate it is not surprising that the startling dramatic effects of a poem like Shelley's 'Ode to the West Wind' frequently go almost unrecognised. But, when you do read the poem aloud – always an enriching approach, and one which investment in a tape-recorder can most usefully assist – you cannot fail to encounter the sheer power and intensity of feeling in the words. There are the striking vowel sounds ('fierce Maenad', 'the oozy woods'); the recurring alliterations ('azure sister of the Spring', 'grow grey with fear'); and the tremendous onomatopoeic energy – for example, the final line of the second section which culmi- nates in an immensely forceful placing of 'burst' before the desperate reiteration of the prayer, 'oh hear!' :

> Thou ... from whose solid atmosphere
> Black rain, and fire, and hail will burst : oh, hear!

It is not so much that sound adds to sense as that sound *is* sense. Those who complain of Shelley's supposed lack of visual imagination should first read, and listen – since it is only by entering the intense immediacy, the verbal precision of the poem, that its visual, as well as its aural, power becomes known.

Also, reading the poem aloud reveals how complex, yet controlled, the syntax really is, despite any first appearance of relaxed ease. It carries over from stanza to stanza, often delaying a key phrase until many qualifications and images attached to it have been given. In lines 15 to 23, for instance, 'The locks of the approaching storm' comes very belatedly, and the streaming head of hair is almost established long before the final words clarify just what such impressions have already strongly prepared us for and begun to create.

I

O wild West Wind, thou breath of Autumn's being,
Thou, from whose unseen presence the leaves dead
Are driven, like ghosts from an enchanter fleeting,

Yellow, and black, and pale, and hectic red,
Pestilence-stricken multitudes : O thou,
Who chariotest to their dark wintry bed

The wingèd seeds, where they lie cold and low,
Each like a corpse within its grave, until
Thine azure sister of the Spring shall blow

Her clarion o'er the dreaming earth, and fill
(Driving sweet buds like flocks to feed in air)
With living hues and odours plain and hill :

Wild Spirit, which art moving everywhere;
Destroyer and preserver; hear, oh hear!

The poem begins with an 'incantation': a word which is itself used later, and which is applicable to so much of Shelley's work. The speaker calls on the Wind as if it were some great Being, some Spirit from above. His apostrophe, 'Thou breath of Autumn's being', picks up this suggestion, adding to it the idea of creative power. But then, in stark contrast, 'the leaves dead/ Are driven' offers the reverse impression; and at once, as through the whole poem, we encounter a vivid illustration of the inevitable natural tension between life and death. The two magic words which follow, 'ghosts' and 'enchanter', take us already out of the immediate realities of the world to something beyond, striving towards that experience of transcendence which the whole poem desires.

The second stanza begins with a riot of colour, yet colour harsh and sickly : 'yellow, and black, and pale', with associations of jaundice and death; and then the final coupling of 'hectic red', where the red of the fallen leaves, blown along, unites hints of haste and fever. The power of 'Pestilence-stricken multitudes' makes us pause : three heavy long-drawn-out words, following the breathless, crowded, shorter words of the line before. Who are the multitudes? Are they people? What is the pestilence which has stricken them and which the colours have heralded? Now the note of invocation returns, leading on to 'who chariotest', with its image of a fire or sun god, magnificent, and bringer of death. As the wind blows the seeds to their winter resting places the words are of death and coldness ('cold', 'corpse', 'grave'), but the 'wingèd seeds' tell of hope and new life. When spring comes, the colours will be living, the corpse will be resurrected; in annual miracle the grave of the earth will prove to be a womb of new creation for the whole world above. Moreover, the autumn destroyer and the 'azure sister of the Spring' are not twin winds only; they are the same wind, manifest in different seasons and different moods. The cruel harbinger of winter has in it life as well as death; in the end, however obscurely, it tells of life through death.

So, although the thought may seem at this point akin to George Herbert's famous lines to the rose – 'Thy root is ever in its grave,/And thou must die' – the total effect is different. Herbert draws attention to the death which is inseparable from all life; yet he does it liltingly, in the music of hope. In contrast Shelley points to the hope of life inherent in all death; but paradoxically his tone is heavier, far more weighed down. Such an insight is clearly parallel to the central New Testament mystery: 'Except a grain of wheat fall into the ground and die, it abides alone; but if it die, it brings forth much fruit.' But we may find it also in pagan rituals of death and resurrection, and in neutral observation of the changing seasons. Some human intimation of a greatness not to be conquered by death always hovers; but, as T. S. Eliot's *Waste Land* was later to demonstrate, the polarity of hope and despair in this cycle is not easily restored.

So the speaker calls once more on the 'Wild Spirit'; and the key word is 'Wild', for it is this untamedness, this naturalness in the best sense, which is the poem's heart. In 'moving everywhere' the Spirit becomes universal, maybe omnipotent; not the leaves only but the whole creation become animate. The 'life' of Nature pervades this poem, not in Wordsworth's manner exactly (though there are moments when Wordsworth is not dissimilar), but through Shelley's re-enactment of a *felt* quality, expressed in verbal equivalents. Some god in nature, some elemental power, seizes him; some force to which even a rebel spirit can, and must, pray. Thus, in 'Destroyer and preserver', the Wind is not likened to a god but *felt* as a god; and if it is not the Christian God or any other god we could give a name to, it is indeed a real presence, an experience, before it begins to be a belief. As the first section of the poem ends, the prayer becomes more insistent, as we are led, through celebration of the Wind, to the movement when the speaker's identification, and alienation (already implicit), will become a spoken plea.

II

Thou on whose streams, mid the steep sky's commotion,
Loose clouds like earth's decaying leaves are shed,
Shook from the tangled boughs of Heaven and Ocean,

Angels of rain and lightning: there are spread
On the blue surface of thine aëry surge,
Like the bright hair uplifted from the head

Of some fierce Maenad, even from the dim verge
Of the horizon to the zenith's height,
The locks of the approaching storm. Thou dirge

Of the dying year, to which this closing night
Will be the dome of a vast sepulchre,
Vaulted with all thy congregated might

Of vapours, from whose solid atmosphere
Black rain, and fire, and hail will burst : oh, hear !

The second section of the poem continues the address to the Wind, both deepening and increasing the train of suggestions. Clouds are now added to leaves on the stream of the Wind's power; heaven is brought towards earth, in the image of a great tree from which the clouds have been shed or torn. 'Angels' is a splendid word, turning rain and lightning into elements – the crueller elements, with winter now lurking. With 'Bright hair' and the 'fierce Maenad', beauty and ferocity in unison, the implications of hair in 'tangled boughs' becomes clear, reaching a visual climax in 'locks of the approaching storm'. And, as our natural memory now drafts in the precise picture – the kind of cloud formation just before storm which we have all at some time witnessed – the entrancing image of a woman's wind-swept hair lies imprinted behind it, yet surges on with it also in one sweep of power.

As darkness closes in, the poem fills with foreboding and death ('dirge of the dying year'; 'closing night'; 'dome of a vast sepulchre/Vaulted with all thy congregated might/Of vapours'). Though still inseparable from the flying freedom of wind, the atmosphere is unbearably heavy, with 'solid' just catching the weight of the approaching storm before 'bursts' can release, with immense verbal violence, the 'Black rain, and fire, and hail', now too powerful to be any longer held. Then, as the speaker returns to his pleading, it is as if he is oppressed by his own weakness in the face of the Wind's strength: as if he feels himself in fact alienated from it, and even its victim, for all his yearning to share its abandon, for all the energy he lends it.

III

Thou who didst waken from his summer dreams
The blue Mediterranean, where he lay,
Lulled by the coil of his crystalline streams,

Beside a pumice isle in Baiae's bay,
And saw in sleep old palaces and towers
Quivering within the wave's intenser day,

All overgrown with azure moss and flowers
So sweet, the sense faints picturing them! Thou
For whose path the Atlantic's level powers

Cleave themselves into chasms, while far below
The sea-blooms and the oozy woods which wear
The sapless foliage of the ocean, know

Thy voice, and suddenly grow gray with fear,
And tremble and despoil themselves : oh, hear!

The poem moves to an interlude. The language becomes soft, the
images melt into each other, as in an impressionist painting.
There is the sensuous charm of summer days, calm relaxation,
with the beauty of 'old palaces and towers' intensified in the
inaccessible mystery of their own mirror images. In this spell, the
fascinating word 'overgrown' – gentle in sound but challenging
in meaning – suggests both extreme fullness, perfection in stasis,
and also neglect, decay and exotic ruin. 'So sweet, the sense faints
picturing them' : here, not too explicitly, is perhaps the thought
memorably expressed elsewhere by Shelley – 'Our sweetest songs
are those that tell of saddest thought.' The 'sense faints' : and a
faint (though its force appears here to be consummation) is also
loss of consciousness, the price of violent delights pursued too far.
At the very moment when romantic intensity perfects itself, the
propensity to swoon towards death, or it may be towards sickness,
makes itself known. Certainly we pass immediately, with an
almost dream-like transition, to the opposite, stormy mood of the

earlier part of the poem, all the more intense for its reappearance out of the summer calm. The description of the raging Atlantic marvellously captures the sheer power of the sea as it is cloven into chasms by the wind, levelled again, then itself levels all before it, even stirring terror into the strange vegetation of the undersea. (Here it is particularly worth noting the power given to 'Thy voice' by its isolation at the beginning of a line.)

It is interesting that, in a note on the poem, Shelley insisted on the accuracy of his visual observation :

The phenomenon alluded to at the conclusion of the third stanza is well known to naturalists. The vegetation at the bottom of the sea, of rivers and of lakes, sympathises with that of the land in the change of seasons, and is consequently influenced by the winds which announce it.

This is surely evidence that Shelley's imagination was far more exact than his detractors, and notably Dr Leavis, usually allow. Patrick Swinden elaborates the defence so well in his essay on this poem (*Critical Survey,* Summer 1973; reprinted in the Macmillan Casebook on Shelley, which he also edited) that we can do no better than quote from him, with a strong recommendation to read his analysis as a whole :

For myself I do not know how you get hold of an object like the fading of the evening star at dawn, or the motion of wind through dry grass, but in so far as it is possible I should say that Shelley has done it better than any other English poet I have read. Nor do I know what the discreteness of an object in its own nature and its own right really amounts to. The condition it suggests to me is of such metaphysical peculiarity that my mind finds it impossible to entertain the notion. If, however, objects exist in a shifting context of other objects, conditions of light and shadow, personal interest on the part of the individual who senses them and thinks about them, then I think Shelley reproduces very aptly the ways those objects, in those conditions, 'strike the sense'. I think he does so in the 'Ode to the West Wind'. But in the Ode there is much more than the accurate transcription of sense impressions. Shelley has impregnated his subject with philosophical speculations which are

interesting and of great importance to himself. The skill with which
he has fused the visible subject with the invisible thought, so that it
can scarcely be said that the one is simply an image or metaphor of
the other, accounts for much of the beauty and the complexity of the
poem.

IV

> If I were a dead leaf thou mightest bear :
> If I were a swift cloud to fly with thee;
> A wave to pant beneath thy power, and share
>
> The impulse of thy strength, only less free
> Than thou, O uncontrollable ! If even
> I were as in my boyhood, and could be
>
> The comrade of thy wanderings over Heaven,
> As then, when to outstrip thy skiey speed
> Scarce seemed a vision; I would ne'er have striven
>
> As thus with thee in prayer in my sore need.
> Oh, lift me as a wave, a leaf, a cloud !
> I fall upon the thorns of life ! I bleed !
>
> A heavy weight of hours has chained and bowed
> One too like thee : tameless, and swift, and proud.

In this fourth section we arrive at the moment which the
invocation seems to have been building up to from the start. The
speaker sees himself as lacking his own power, and needing the
Wind's. Yet he recognises in 'less free than thou' that, however
much power he inherits, however he changes, the West Wind will
still be god. Such recognition is reinforced by the shifting balance
between 'to pant beneath thy power' and 'share the impulse of
thy strength' – expressions which, though they read in context as
if synonymous, are directly at odds in emphasis; and 'O uncon-
trollable' is as much homage to the Wind as it is envy of its freedom from restraint.

As the speaker ponders, he looks back to his childhood when

he almost seemed to have the power he now misses so much. Yet was this illusion? Or blissful ignorance: the human sense of divinity, untested yet by time and real trial? Or was it that, in childhood, he was so close to being a spirit that to compete on equal terms with the Wind was nearly possible? Undeniably we are close here to the sense shared by Wordsworth that 'simple childhood sits upon a throne', that the child's supremacy is indeed a true intimation of immortality, not a mere illusion to be dispelled by adult knowledge, adult scaling down.

Wordsworth ponders the possibility that we arrive on this earth 'trailing clouds of glory', 'from God, who is our home'; but he never commits himself to pre-existence as a philosophic 'belief'. Shelley, as we have suggested, is even further than Wordsworth from the urge to speculate, being more purely concerned to invoke in words the experience itself. Yet in both poets there is a closeness to man's perennial sense of being a great spirit in exile from the greater and freer worlds to which he really belongs. And in both we find the sense that behind memories of childhood lies, not simply ignorance of adult realities, but closeness to that lost paradise which haunts all our lives. This poem, while not being in any way Christian, comes close to Christianity in its pervasive apprehension of ambivalent relationships with the power flowing through creation – at one with it in desire, but exiled in fact.

So, finally, we learn the reason for the prayer. From the start, description and mood have prepared us for this explanation, so that, when it comes, it is supported by the whole presence of the poem. The struggle for freedom has been too much for the speaker; the confidence of youth, now shattered, has turned to impotence and despair. There is a hint that this is the tragic destiny of a man flawed by pride, the inevitable punishment of the promethean urge to be not at one with the god by grace but, rather, the god's equal by right. Such hints are strengthened by 'too like thee', which recalls the myth of Eden. But the tone of the poem works against such implications, and 'tameless, and swift and proud' appear as the highest qualities in a man, not as his sins. The crushing of such qualities is not a punishment earned by rebellion, with the qualities to this degree 'unnatural'; they are the burden of mortality itself. 'A heavy weight of hours' . . . perhaps, after all, the child was as free as he seemed, when he seemed so; and divinity has been stolen from him simply by the passing of time.

The whole verbal power here is almost unbearable. (Again, one must *listen* to the words if one is to respond even to their visual effects.) 'Chained' and 'bowed' by age, by experience, by *life* (and this paradox is surely what the poem is all about), the speaker sees his failure in a brutally simple image : a falling, in his weakness, onto thorns, barbed product of nature. 'I bleed', he cries, in both pain and surprise; but the poem – almost impossibly – avoids self-indulgence (unless to be wounded, in need of help, nakedly praying to whatever god is felt to be present, is to be so described).

v

> Make me thy lyre, even as the forest is :
> What if my leaves are falling like its own ?
> The tumult of thy mighty harmonies
>
> Will take from both a deep, autumnal tone,
> Sweet though in sadness. Be thou, Spirit fierce,
> My spirit ! Be thou me, impetuous one !
>
> Drive my dead thoughts over the universe
> Like withered leaves to quicken a new birth !
> And, by the incantation of this verse,
>
> Scatter, as from an unextinguished hearth
> Ashes and sparks, my words among mankind !
> Be through my lips to unawakened earth
>
> The trumpet of a prophecy ! O Wind,
> If Winter comes, can Spring be far behind ?

In this final section, the speaker pleads to be like the forest, for both have autumn in their lives. He will be the voice of the Wind, if not the Wind itself. 'Make me thy lyre' is the recurring romantic image of the Aeolian harp, set up for the winds to breathe through, making music. It is the image of the poet as inspired, filled with divine spirit, and breathing out again divine tidings. And, as poet, he can turn .this very tragedy – defeat, capture, exile – into the rich song, 'sweet though in sadness', it is asking to be.

Thus the prayer reaches its climax, and now the tone is almost triumphant. 'Be thou Spirit fierce,/My spirit! Be thou me, impetuous one!' – literally, 'I will live in the god if he will live in me'. How close to Christianity! – but how far from it too, in that marvellously characteristic edge of rebellion, that determination not to *submit* as the price of the god's indwelling. The poet asks for his 'dead thoughts' to be driven 'over the universe'; but the thoughts are only as dead as the wind-blown seeds from which the poem set out. They grow in the dark, generate secretly, blaze up as sparks from the ashes. They reappear as this verse, 'masterful images', waiting new birth.

Shelley's poem has endured, so his prayer is answered. Words of hope *are* spread among mankind. The poem moves to its famous conclusion : 'If Winter comes, can Spring be far behind?' – lifting what might be a commonplace to the fire of sudden vision. Perhaps this is always one enduring role of poets and prophets : to convince us that great and sublime truths are true, despite a world's pain. They tell us that man is more than a 'poor forked creature'; that the endless human tug away from high destiny is a snare, a lie, when all has been said that can be said of time's ravages; that words remain things of power, and words do not lie. Like many great poems – perhaps most : in some senses perhaps all, through their formal perfection – Shelley's Ode witnesses to endless rebirth after death. The struggle itself is life as well as suffering. Poetry is part of the renewal of man himself.

Thou still unravish'd bride of quietness !
    Thou foster-child of silence and slow time,
Sylvan historian, who canst thus express
    A flowery tale more sweetly than our rhyme :
What leaf-fringed legend haunts about thy shape
    Of deities or mortals, or of both,
        In Tempe or the dales of Arcady ?
    What men or gods are these ? What maidens loth ?
What mad pursuit ? What struggle to escape ?
        What pipes and timbrels ? What wild ecstasy ?

Heard melodies are sweet, but those unheard
    Are sweeter; therefore, ye soft pipes, play on ;
Not to the sensual ear, but, more endear'd,
    Pipe to the spirit ditties of no tone :
Fair youth, beneath the trees, thou canst not leave
    Thy song, nor ever can those trees be bare ;
        Bold Lover, never, never canst thou kiss,
    Though winning near the goal – yet, do not grieve ;
She cannot fade, though thou hast not thy bliss,
    For ever wilt thou love, and she be fair !

Ah, happy, happy boughs ! that cannot shed
    Your leaves, nor ever bid the Spring adieu ;
And, happy melodist, unwearied,
    For ever piping songs for ever new ;
More happy love ! more happy, happy love !
    For ever warm and still to be enjoy'd,
        For ever panting and for ever young ;
    All breathing human passion far above,
That leaves a heart high-sorrowful and cloy'd,
        A burning forehead, and a parching tongue.

Who are these coming to the sacrifice?
　　To what green altar, O mysterious priest,
Lead'st thou that heifer lowing at the skies,
　　And all her silken flanks with garlands drest?
What little town by river or sea shore,
　　Or mountain-built with peaceful citadel,
　　　Is emptied of its folk, this pious morn?
And, little town, thy streets for ever more
Will silent be; and not a soul to tell
　　　Why thou art desolate, can e'er return.

O Attic shape! Fair attitude! with brede
　　Of marble men and maidens overwrought,
With forest branches and the trodden weed;
　　Thou, silent form, dost tease us out of thought
As doth eternity: Cold Pastoral!
　　When old age shall this generation waste,
　　　Thou shalt remain, in midst of other woe
Than ours, a friend to man, to whom thou say'st,
'Beauty is truth, truth beauty,' – that is all
　　　Ye know on earth, and all ye need to know.

To read the first two lines of this Ode is rather like walking into an old church or a quiet museum, which we have for a time to ourselves. They are calm and measured, yet richly luxurious. There is nothing jarring in their sound or, as it seems, in their sense.

But are they really as simple, as uncostly and effortless as they contrive to appear, or is this the deception of all calm places and sanctuaries? On a closer look the compressions and ironies are as striking as those in any metaphysical poem, yet they seem designed to direct attention away from themselves, to lull us, lotus-like, in their midst. There is the strangely poised use of language, apparent in almost every word of the Ode: 'unravish'd', for instance, setting up many possibilities, especially with 'still' in attendance; 'happy', subtly reversing itself through repetitions which, far from clarifying the meaning, cast it deeply in doubt.

The famous directness of the poem's ending may come, when we reach it, almost as a challenge – to go back, quite simply, and start reading again. If the meaning has seemed to flow over us, sensuous and undemanding, how has such a crowning illusion of art been achieved?

The opening address to the urn is a reminder that it has not only a maker whose imprint is on it, but foster-parents; again, that it is the bride in a marriage more enduring than any its human maker could have known. Does the artist recognise 'quietness' as a quality absent from his own endowment, so that his work must be surrendered into other hands than his for its perfecting? In its formal being all art may seem to belong with 'silence and slow time', with 'quietness' and the realm of contemplation; yet the passion which went to its making, like the scenes depicted on its marble surface, belong to living and suffering, to the ecstasy and the brevity of mortal men. As art, the urn incarnates human realities – though in its own cold perfection: yet the first line might apply, with hindsight, to the figures it depicts, as well as to itself.

'Bride': the urn is a 'bride' of quietness, and this is the initial image. Is 'quietness' a normal groom, offering its own known fulfilment; or for this match, is non-consummation the price to be paid? The word 'unravish'd' seems fraught with paradox: in everyday use 'ravished' is the word for rape, not for mutuality, yet it also means 'filled with ecstasy', unbearably fulfilled. The double edge of joy and darkness, desire and destruction, lurks in the word, as in the dionysian experience to which it refers. Again, 'ravished' can suggest being eaten away by suffering or illness, eventually by mortality, as if the price of excess is inseparable from the experience itself. The nearness of 'ravished' to 'ravaged' is more than phonic, yet it may, after all, be a foreshadowing, through death, of eternal bliss.

'Still unravish'd': 'still' might mean 'yet' – not yet ravished (is this good or bad, in context?) – or it might mean 'still' in the sense of 'serene'. Perhaps the bride remains 'still' (too passive for fulfilment?), or perhaps, for the bride of 'quietness', stillness

is the expected fulfilment. At the same time, 'still' can be
a property of art itself in its inner essence, which, as T. S. Eliot's
image of the Chinese vase brings out in *Four Quartets,* may
simply be life or motion so intense that it merely seems, as part
of its illusion, to have come to rest :

> Words move, music moves
> Only in time; but that which is only living
> Can only die. Words, after speech, reach
> Into the silence. Only by the form, the pattern,
> Can words or music reach
> The stillness, as a Chinese jar still
> Moves perpetually in its stillness.
> Not the stillness of the violin, while the note lasts,
> Not that only, but the co-existence,
> Or say that the end precedes the beginning,
> And the end and the beginning were always there
> Before the beginning and after the end.
> And all is always now.

Keats's Ode, as work of art, starts from such manifest opposites,
which are enriched in the ensuing images, but are never resolved.
In the second line we are reminded that the foster-parents have
indeed imprinted on the urn their own image. Like a stream,
'silence and slow time' have brought it down through the centuries
to ourselves. As men now look – Keats on the urn itself one early
nineteenth-century morning, we on his poem about the urn today
– time has done its habitual work of selection and enhancement.
The blessing of survival, of resilience, is inseparably part of the
beauty – 'antiquity, which in itself be venerable', as Sidney said.
Yet this very fact may be a deception, in Keats's later words, a
teasing – unless we accept that art is, in some insulated sense, its
own kind of truth. Will art not always lead us a dance (quite
literally), as the urn leads Keats here, until we are plunged into
creation, into disturbance, into ecstasy which is the beginning of
death? Perhaps any work of art is 'safe' only as long as we ignore
it; the danger sets in the moment that we attend. Then it will

lead us out of our torpid half-death, where half-life continues, into creation and recreation, the dangerous dance.

'Sylvan historian' : and, if the questions so far suggested lurk in the first two lines, before they are more fully explicit, we still have the illusion of ease, of refreshment, in reading on. The urn is an organic and living historian, sylvan, belonging to nature, to the world of green. There is a certain fascination in the way in which green enters and haunts this poem, even though the cold colour of marble is the sight Keats immediately sees : 'flowery tale', 'leaf-fringed legend', 'beneath the trees', 'nor ever can those trees be bare', 'happy boughs, that cannot shed/Your leaves', 'green altar', 'garlands dressed', 'forest branches'. As in Marvell, 'green' suggests deep sensuous fullness – not blood passion, but fruitfulness, rich repose. Yet it is as the world of the urn comes alive in the poet's imagination that spring enters, and it is as he withdraws that the chill and cold return. The green, which was there for the maker of the urn, and returns for us as we visualise, is not in fact a formal component of the work of art. The same paradox was marvellously expressed by Pope in *Windsor Forest,* though in a tone less elegiac than Keats's, a tone more attuned to resilient hope :

> The groves of Eden, vanish'd now so long,
> Live in description, and look green in song.

May it be that a 'sylvan' historian is superior (as the poem also says) to 'our rhyme' (just as in the next stanza 'unheard' music will be sweeter than 'heard', and so again to 'our' art) simply because nature, in this transmutation, remains always in flower? Wordsworth, we know, had hailed Nature, pure and simple, as supreme teacher :

> One impulse from a vernal wood
> Can teach you more of man,
> Of moral evil and of good
> Than all the sages can

and this was because Wordsworth was a religious man, talking of

God. Keats in the Odes, however, is a pagan man, talking only of beauty, so for him, nature itself bends to the deceptions of art. Is the word 'flowery' after all too much of a good thing? Does it sound too pretty, and tend to cloy? And if it does, is this intentional, as the cloying of 'happy', later in the poem, so evidently is? Is Keats already pointing to a *deliberate* quality of excess, which is known to be dangerous even while its enchantment holds? Certainly the rest of the stanza, which now depicts an incident that the urn captures, intensifies the Dionysian qualities we have already sensed. The pursuit is 'mad', the maidens 'loth', the ecstasy 'wild', yet in the intoxication something divine is present, so that one hardly knows whether these are men or gods. 'Tempe' and the 'vales of Arcady' suggest the morning of the world, youth and radical happiness, yet as so often, idyll and elegy, love and bereavement or betrayal, almost meet in cadence and mood. Is 'struggle to escape' an erotic game, intensifying joy in surrender, or is it the anguish of impending rape? Dionysus, god of dark instinct, of delusion and, sometimes, of destructive madness, is the god who offers his worshippers recovered innocence and lasting bliss. The word 'haunts' acquires a kind of floating suggestiveness, not to be separated from the total effect. The 'leaf-fringed legend' 'haunts' about the urn's shape, depending for its life, however, on the imagination of the watcher – who therefore becomes haunted and haunter both.

In fact, the whole life of the poem derives in one sense from the poet's willed decision to respond. The poet walks about the urn, examining closely, musing, as we now walk round and examine the Ode. Surely Keats would not have objected to close reading and detailed criticism, since it is precisely such attention to art that his poem records? Of all poets he would be among the least inclined, or entitled, to say 'we murder to dissect', since closeness of scrutiny is built into his creation itself. The legend haunts the urn, haunts Keats, haunts us through the poem, and you cannot hope to separate present from past, or cause from effect. But the process becomes violent in words, however luxurious its expression, as life *pours in,* torrentially, towards the stanza's end. Why then, is the poetic effect of the stanza so integrated, despite its move from 'quietness' to ecstasy? To say we have moved from the stillness of *form* to the intensity of *experience* is, manifestly, to oversimplify a complex effect. Perhaps Yeats's phrase 'Imagining in excited reverie' is a better clue, since it reminds us that the poet experiences the calm of art in conjunction with the excitement of the experience from which art is made.

If we ponder for a moment the stages by which Keats draws attention to this paradox, we notice one interesting fact. The paradox is true to some degree of all art, and by its nature must be; but Keats is unusually aware of having the nature of art itself as a main part of his theme. In this, he foreshadows Yeats, as well as many lesser late nineteenth-century aesthetes, and draws out hints already clear in (say) Shakespeare's Sonnets, and Pope's *Rape of the Lock*. It is worth recalling that the later aesthetes often tended to see the artist as priest, prophet, oracle, and even autonomous creator, transferring to *him* those central religious and Christian concepts which, in Wordsworth, had been trans-ferred in the first place to Nature, and to the artist only in his role as Nature's muse. It may be no accident that the heightened claim for a religious or quasi-religious role for art and for artists accompanied, in most of those who later made it, a loss of belief in religion itself. 'Art for art's sake' can perhaps be formulated as a precept only when art for God's sake, for Nature's sake, or for truth's sake, has failed to hold. Is it possible that art is in fact most divine, most like its maker, only when it serves a higher power? It certainly seems that the greater the claims art made for itself *per se* in the late nineteenth century, the less impressive it tended to become. Many have felt that for art to look into and worship itself displays the same kind of narcissism, and the same attendant vanity and triviality, that we encounter when a man looks into and worships himself. The very beauty becomes tinged maybe with something over-ripe, or simply implausible, reaching, as it does in some of Rossetti's poems and in many of Swinburne's, towards the 'feel' of day-dreams, self-indulgent fantasy, drugged escape. As most critics note, Keats was influential upon the later poets of escapism, and his Odes were among their chief texts. But Keats himself is never trivial, never in any important sense decadent; he is far closer to Shakespeare – to verbal luxuriance wedded to experience, and intensely alive.

It may be, in fact, that Keats captures the paradox of art at the point where it is totally rooted in experience, and has not started to become an alternative to experience, an anodyne, in its own right. Yet the main effect is undoubtedly a realisation of vacuum – a trap of verbal riches, a dead end. It is as if Keats's chief inspiration is that gulf, tormentingly uncrossable, between what men can dream of as possible, and what they know can possibly be. The words 'ever' and 'never' become near synonyms, as Keats bodies out in words a vision that falls somewhere, or nowhere, between the intensity of experience and the permanence of art. First, there was the man who made the urn, and who had the experience; his experience is now lost, along with himself. There were the 'men and maidens' whom he watched, and *their* experience; we can only guess now who they were. Perhaps the scene depicted on the urn was fiction, not a record? – and if so, does this matter, as long as the experience rings true? For our part, the reality is Keats's poem, not the art that he looked at, so further displacements stand between ourselves and the scene on the urn. In recreating the urn, Keats became artist, and his own life, and art, in unison, were thus touched off. His youthful life and suffering contribute to another pure moment, caught again in the form of a lasting work of art. As the urn journeyed, through time, until its encounter with the poet, so the poem has journeyed through time and changed, in its progress towards us. Is the 'fair youth beneath the trees' in some sense, now, Keats himself, crossed in love, dead before thirty, alive in his art? Such questions clearly submit to more than one answer, some of them far removed from the philosophy of the poet himself. And Keats keeps to his own rule : his poem has no 'palpable design' upon us, yet his art does, and must, have an intended effect. He offers us human experience arrested, yet arrested at maximum intensity, and fused with the vitality, as well as the fixity, of art. The unsolved riddle, of whether this 'is' impossible fulfilment or impossible frustration, is precisely the central force of the art. Ecstasy *is* ecstasy; it is not an urn, not a poem; it is an experience we can never recapture as it was. Again, art *is* art; it is not life 'really' frozen or 'really' eternal; its own being is in time indeed, and may have a stop.

Since these ideas are at the poem's heart, we can look at the remaining stanzas with them always in mind. The second stanza starts with 'sweet' and 'sweeter'. Is this deliberately cloying again, a little too much? Is the unheard music to be thought of really as music imagined (music heard in the mind), or is the suggestion that it would be sweeter if it could be heard, but it can't? Unheard melodies are silence, and the logic could be that no possible perfections can equal impossible perfections that we dream. Yet there is a suggestion also that it *is* the unheard melody that the poet attends to – so that, just as the urn was a better poem (in the first stanza) than any poem could be, now it is a better song than any possible song. But equally, if we accept that the unheard music is sweeter than any heard music, then, if it could be heard, it would surely cease to be so? Yet the sight of the urn has evoked it, for Keats's poem; as the poem in turn may evoke it for us.

Note that we have 'sensual', not 'sensuous' ear. This is not exactly saying 'not to the real ear', but 'not to the ear of sensuality'; so the contrast might be platonic, between higher spiritual truths and the gross earthly ear. Yet the final three lines of this stanza are profoundly sensuous as well as sensual, and the Ode denies any real effort to aspire to truths beyond sense. Note also that the lady on the urn, like the urn itself in the opening, becomes, for better or worse, a still unravished bride. Through this depiction runs the echoing aural play between 'ever' and 'never' – so accentuated, that it sounds out above the formal rhymes of the stanza even, setting up a mood of urgent nostalgia, barely held in check. The two words become in this play near synonyms; as if 'ever canst thou kiss' and 'never wilt thou love' resonate just under the words that we have.

'Do not grieve.' If he were alive, he would not have to grieve,

since he would soon attain; can the youth carved on the urn know
this? Or is it we who are alive who alone know this, so that 'do
not grieve' must be addressed obliquely to us? The elegiac tone
reverses the meaning, and the music of the stanza is full of grief.
Can we miss the half-implied image of Romeo and Juliet, dead
in the tomb together? – or, still more haunting, the moment
when Romeo, still living, believes wrongly that Juliet is dead?

> Death, that has sucked the honey of thy breath,
> Hath had no power yet upon thy beauty.
> Thou are not conquered : beauty's ensign yet
> Is crimson in thy lips and in thy cheeks,
> And death's pale flag is not advanced there.

In depiction, youth is eternally captured, yet 'thou canst not
leave' echoes in opposite ways. While it seems to say they are free
to be young eternally, it suggests too that they are frozen,
paralysed, deprived of even freedom to live. Is it better that the
lady should never fade than that he should ever attain her? –
'Do not grieve' is nearer to perpetual desolation than to fullness
of joy. 'Thou' and 'she' : but who, really? Is 'thou' a real man, or
the image depicted? Is 'she' a lady who once lived, fair and
transient, or the lady, fair and static, of the urn? We might be
reminded of Pope's Belinda, and of Clarissa's comment, 'and she
who scorns a man must die a maid'. Belinda too achieved an
unlooked for longevity, in Pope's poem, but no joy, as we know,
back in the realm of 'life'.

So, if the fulfilment of art is nearer after all to its foster-parents
than to its maker, how is the living artist, or his reader, to
respond? 'Ah, happy, happy boughs!'; 'more happy, happy
love'. This is not the 'happy' of simple happiness, nor of simple
wish fulfilment or sentimental self-indulgence, but the 'happy' of
ironic awareness – happy because totally lost. For Keats, moreover, the loss is not of something real in the past, a true arcadia,
but the loss of any place where love can ever be safe. The phrases
'cannot shed' and 'for ever warm' again suggest bondage or
paralysis, turning the stated joy towards near despair. It seems

closer to Sisyphus than to any real paradise (a youth teased by
the belle dame sans merci and left forlorn ever after? – an artist
doomed to remain for ever unknown?). In fact, the image of
delirium or hangover in the final three lines comes near to
clarifying the previous emotion, even though it is apparently
offered as contrast of the sharpest kind. The 'for ever', four times
repeated, surely says 'never' : yet the poem's own music, rich and
still apparently uncomplicated, again offers a verbal experience
of the sensuous pleasure which its meaning denies.

The word 'breathing' is especially interesting : explicitly, it
suggests that the lovers on the urn have transcended 'breathing'
men; but, if so, in what way? They are not more spiritual, more
rarefied, since they are a suspended *simulacrum* of sensuality :
and, of course, they are *not* breathing; which is to say, they are
not human; not alive or real.

The next stanza is in some ways the most elusive of all. We are
back again with 'green', and with a richly animate landscape,
once more brought to life by the poet's imagination working on
the figures on the urn. The heifer is 'lowing' – again perpetually,
and again in a music that cannot be heard; yet now, it is the
music of frozen imminent slaughter, of enduring fear. He too
remains suspended, ever to be killed, never killed : a perfect
mirror image, or complement, to youth and love? The 'little
town' is unknown, anywhere or nowhere, and, permanently
empty, it will never know why. All its inhabitants are elsewhere,
and for ever will be, yet the poem contrives to make the 'little
town' an almost breathing presence, rich with a lasting, a
'wondering' quality, akin to art itself. For all we know, the town
may not be depicted on the urn even; perhaps the poet infers its
existence, and so creates it himself? If so, it is created to be
envied, as well as pitied – for the strange calm and stillness that it
is fated only to know.

At the end of the penultimate stanza of the Nightingale Ode,
the word 'forlorn' sounds out, returning the poet from luxurious
daydreaming to emptiness, which the final stanza further elaborates and explores.

> The fancy cannot cheat so well
> As she is famed to do, deceiving elf.

It seems that the poetic faculty, so described, is not the creative and even revelatory faculty known to Wordsworth and Coleridge, but something more akin to eighteenth-century 'fancy', to the mind's power of inventing concepts with no exact equivalent in the realm of the real.

In our present poem the word 'desolate' has a very similar effect. Coldness returns, the urn turns back to marble, the green vanishes (almost literally — it turns, through 'trodden weed', to nothing, as we look). 'Attic' means Greek, but suggests also 'arctic'; 'attitude' is fair like the youth, but posed, and artificial, and dead. 'Overwrought' fuses the Bacchic excess of the scene depicted with awareness of cold marble, and perhaps of cold artifice in the actual process of art. The word 'silent', attached to 'form', seems to become merely reproachful, as if the art is, after all, silent, and the 'ditties of no tone' are known, now, as mere illusions in the poet's own mind. 'Cold pastoral' : it seems as if the teasing, so richly elusive, has itself turned to weariness and disappointment, to mere didactic tone. Indeed, the poet confesses to being teased 'out of thought' — the very thought which the poem has evoked, and, effectually, *been*.

After this, the final stanza restates, in more formal ambivalences, the weight of regret. 'When old age shall this generation waste' : all living things are 'wasted', yet 'generation' remains the word of life. The urn, which belongs neither to waste nor to generation, speaks, however, to both of them, and so remains a friend to man. But even here there is still equivocation; what kind of a friend is art, when all is said? 'Thou shalt remain in midst of other woe/Than ours' — is this the promise of endurance, but in a necessarily tragic world, where nothing endures?

Yet 'friend', which must be partly ironic, cannot be wholly so, or why should Keats offer us art, and why should we receive it as a gift? What the urn says, or appears to say, is something which, though familiar to Platonists and Christians in their own particular contexts, is hard at this climax of the poem to gloss. 'Beauty is truth' : are we to understand that whenever we sense beauty, we have truth present? (in other words, that experiences, not systems of ideas, are truth). But then, truth is beauty; and what is 'truth'? We recognise beauty when we encounter it (*pace* a few linguistic philosophers), though can we give it so confident a name? Might the words mean that whatever we call 'true' *is* beautiful, as if sordid, and ugly, and dismaying things might prove lies? Or is the urn, then, merely riddling, as friends themselves sometimes do?

The final two lines present a scholarly problem because of the differences of punctuation in different manuscripts; whether the part of the sentence starting 'that is all' is to be taken as the urn or the poet speaking remains open to conjecture. But, however we interpret, a deliberate ambiguity seems built in. Is 'beauty' truth because it passes on, in art, from generation to generation, or because it is a quality in transient experience which satisfies while it lasts? Or is 'beauty' the only truth we can be sure of, because anything else claiming the word is less substantial, and in the end less real? Above all, why is it 'all ye need to know'? Though this final phrase suggests consolation, or at least revelation enough, we cannot escape the fact that these things are precisely not among the poem's affirmations.

Might formalists ultimately decide then that, since 'beauty' and 'truth' do reside in Keats's poem, in evident union, we can invoke the poem itself to explain what it means? We have received a certain structural perfection and verbal richness. Perhaps, after all, these are truth enough?

APPENDIX: HINTS FOR 'DATING'

This more generalised section is intended for students new to literature, and we would underline the cautions already expressed in the Introduction about its use. Students might read it with a good anthology of English verse beside them, so that they can check (and question) the generalisations against the poems themselves. The best anthology for this purpose is the *New Oxford Book of English Verse, 1250–1950* (1972), chosen and edited by Helen Gardner. Serious students will also find it useful (and pleasurable) to browse in the fuller Oxford anthologies devoted to each century: *Seventeenth Century Verse* (chosen by Sir Herbert Grierson and G. Bullough, 1914), *Eighteenth Century Verse* (chosen by David Nichol Smith, 1926) and *Nineteenth Century Verse* (chosen by John Hayward, 1964). If the study is being conducted in class or with groups of people, then a cheaper and more compact anthology might be used. Penguin provide both an anthology of English verse as a whole and period anthologies, all or any of which will serve.

(1) 1600–1660

This first period to concern us is marked by ornateness of style and complexity of content. In drama the distinctive features are often called 'Jacobean', in verse 'metaphysical'; the period itself spans the reigns of James I, Charles I and the Commonwealth. It is interesting, and even odd, that the Civil War, and its sequel in the radical political experiments of the 1650s, introduced no literary innovations to compare with the immense changes of the Restoration decade.

If one looks back to the Elizabethans, the most obvious new

development is in the lyric. The metaphysical lyric ceases to be as consciously 'poetic' as its forerunners. In diction and syntax it becomes conversational and often dramatic, owing more to the soliloquies of *Hamlet* (say) and to Shakespeare's dramatic verse generally than it does to the majority of Elizabethan lyrics, including Shakespeare's. In theme, it acquires complexities of thought and wit of a kind seldom found earlier (though Shakespeare's Sonnets could be instanced as a partial exception, and his 'The Phoenix and the Turtle' might be regarded as an archetypal, as well as a very early, 'metaphysical' poem. In fact, Donne was writing in the 1590s, though his poems were not published or generally known until much later. The exact nature of the influences working between the young Donne and Shakespeare's later style must remain conjectural.

It is important to note, at the outset of our discussion, that the 'metaphysical' poets were not a 'school' in their lifetime, and that they did not apply this label to themselves. The term was coined later, by critics largely hostile; and, in so far as it suggests that philosophical thinking was a chief concern, it is clearly misleading.

One evident difference between the Elizabethan and the metaphysical lyric is that the latter is clearly not written, give or take an exception or two, to be set to music. The rhythms are less regular, the verbal sounds less mellifluous, the images less conventional and predictable, than we usually find in poems written with music in view. Again, there is seldom the repetition of emotional pattern from stanza to stanza which is found when one recurring tune is in question; rather, the metaphysical poem frequently includes intellectual arguments or series of arguments which span the poem. The whole tone and mood may change, or develop extreme ambivalences, from verse to verse, and the poem may be marked by unpredictable transitions, by unexpected local strokes of wit and complexity.

The new images include many drawn from science, from mathematics, from geographical exploration and from the whole range of preoccupations of the age they belong to. The older allegorical or emblematic images now co-exist with very novel imagery, so that they appear startling in context, even if familiar in form. For any analogous development we have to look perhaps to the early years of the present century, when a number of 'modern' poets rejected the stylised, poetic language and diction of the late Victorians for more experimental modes. At both of these periods there was a feeling that poetry had perhaps become too set apart from 'life', too much a game, with its face turned to formal beauty; and a conviction also that the formal existence of art could, and should, encompass every real experience of men.

As we would expect, there is continuity as well as difference, and no clear-cut break with the past is made. The metaphysical poets continue to draw on the traditional images of courtly love, and especially on those relating to man's search for ideal beauty, truth and goodness in love, whether sacred or profane. But whereas, in most of the Elizabethans, such themes are characterised almost always by stylised elegance, the metaphysicals tend to use them in individual and even quirky ways. Poised often between assent and irony, their poems become part of an exploration, a voyage to probe, and clarify, the experiencing and unresolved 'self'. Donne's love poems are, in some ways, as much a game (or war?) with the lady as are those of the Elizabethan courtiers, yet the rules, and the tone, change as he goes along. Certainly there are in the earlier poems exquisite balances of tenderness and cynicism, honesty and profession, anguish and banter, passion and seduction; but there is nothing of that flux and uncertainty, that naked intensity, which we find in Donne. Often, indeed, a metaphysical poem generates uncertainty of tone as its main impression. Is Donne's 'Extasie' a defence of spiritual love, or a complex seduction; or does it assimilate and transcend all such possibilities, to become something else?

The metaphysical lyric often shares with its Elizabethan forerunner the use of the 'conceit', which Helen Gardner has defined as 'a comparison whose ingenuity is more striking than its justness, or, at least, is more immediately striking. All comparisons discover likeness in things unlike: a comparison becomes a conceit when we are made to concede likeness while being strongly conscious of unlikeness.'* But, as she also points out, the metaphysical conceit takes on a new *rigour*; it is on the whole less ornamental, and more extended, than Elizabethan conceits: 'In a metaphysical poem the conceits are instruments of definition in an argument or instruments to persuade. The poem has something to say which the conceit explicates or something to urge which the conceit helps forward.' One could add that in a metaphysical poem the conceits are very frequently linked with an elaborate and often continuing argument or pseudo-argument which fuses its own strange and unprecedented quality with the unlikeness, rather than the likeness, of the comparison used.

The complexity of metaphysical poetry is sometimes talked of chiefly in intellectual terms. It is linked with an age of rapidly changing values when the new science and the new empirical philosophy, associated at first with Bacon's name, impinged on medieval scholastic philosophy and theology, As Donne put it: 'The new philosophy calls all in doubt.' This flux of values is invoked to explain the exploratory quality of the verse, its uncertainty of tone and direction, its habitual juxtaposition of old and new, its restlessness, its propensity to fierce and often outlandish argument. The humanism deriving from Greek and Christian thought merges with the new scientific humanism, which is more purely optimistic in social implications than Christianity, more prone to stress man's power and inventiveness than his sin. Could it be for this very reason, even, that the taint and horror of sin and death, at this very moment of their banishment from much formal thinking and philosophising, return in the literature of this period (as they do) with particular power? Critics have pointed out that the sense that death is inherently tragic is apt to appear especially strongly in imaginative literature at times of greatest human optimism; and again, that the attempt to see man as indeed a godlike being, entering his inheritance, usually, opens up particularly ironic and satiric explorations of the gulf

* Introduction to her Penguin Anthology, *The Metaphysical Poets* (1966).

still to cross. The Renaissance, we should remember, had thrown up its own religious ferment between 'protestant' and 'catholic' — a clash between basically differing images of God and man, in which political and intellectual and social motivations rapidly crossbred.

In the middle ages it had been a commonplace to envisage man as part of a created hierarchy, combining higher and lower elements in himself. The highest created beings were the angels, purely intellectual beings, without flesh or mortality, who were also immediate agents of the providence of God. It should not be forgotten that they were conceived as moving the physical as well as the spiritual universe; before 'gravitation' substituted a material model, motion in the universe was ascribed to the actions of Intelligences, enacting the will of God. Under the angels came man, and under man the brutes and animals. The brutes and animals were purely 'sensible' (the word used to describe the domain of the five senses) : which is to say that they were motivated not at all by intellect or by moral characteristics, but lived wholly by instinct, and were made mortal — made to die. Man himself, combining an immortal and intellectual being with a mortal and instinctual body, had to find his own laws, and role, halfway between the two. Half brute and half angel, he was made for eternity, and sealed most particularly in God's image by the coming of Christ. Perhaps it was natural for him to locate his moral being in terms of hierarchy and of the ultimate superiority of soul and mind to body in the scheme of things. This would account for the platonic colouring of much thinking, inside as well as outside Christendom, and the mutation of Christendom itself to a more gnostic dualism (in appearance, at least) than its central teachings allowed.

During the seventeenth century this mode of thinking was far from being displaced or superseded. It finds, indeed, what is possibly its finest expression in the poetry of Milton, not only in the early *Comus* (1634) but in *Paradise Lost* also (1665–6). It was, however, modified and in some ways cast in doubt by the newer scientific modes of thinking, with the angels as a special point of dispute. Perhaps it is no surprise that the seventeenth century became particularly preoccupied with the problem of *how* angels manifest themselves to men, apparently clothed in bodies, at precisely the time when many of the phenomena usually ascribed to 'Intelligences' were passing to the impersonal realm of scientific 'law'. Again, it may not be surprising that, while the scholastics fell into disrepute along with the whole realm of 'metaphysical' philosophy (thinking about being, essence, eternity, and questions beyond purely material frames of reference), the main school of poets attracted the label 'metaphysical' to describe their intense intellectual preoccupations and effects. The 'metaphysicals' continually allowed old and new to co-exist, in ways that might or might not intend irony but which certainly underlined the character of the times as a flux.

The metaphysicals may be recognised by their use of ideas at their particular cultural crossroads; but they can also be recognised, and studied, from quite other points of view. The 'metaphysical' complexities are sometimes seen chiefly as a psychological phenomenon, an exploration of the inherent paradoxes of love and of religion as these things are in fact experienced by men. On this showing earlier writers had been more attached to systematic structures and dogmas; the metaphysicals differed in putting experience first, and all thinking in a second and exploratory place. The Elizabethans, certainly, in their love poems had tended to stylise in a tradition deriving from Petrarch, from medieval courtly romance and from other ascertainable sources and traditions, and had seldom attempted novelty for its own sake. The lady is always beautiful, sometimes supremely so; she is often identified with a goddess or with Beauty itself. The descriptions run to spun gold, quiet pools, roses, and many emblems, with the allegory of love seldom far out of sight. These poems were written mainly by courtiers, men highly sophisticated and experienced, and well aware of the gulfs between poetic profession and sober fact. The man who presents himself as the lady's slave, in danger of dying for love of her, in sober fact inhabited a very masculine world. The banter of love, its deep seriousness and ever-lurking dangers, mingle with enchantment; many of the songs could be sung on Twelfth Night in Orsino's court. How serious or playful, how deeply felt or how tinged with cynicism they are, would sometimes be known only to the poet and to his lady – if, indeed, with any certainty, to them.

How, then, do the metaphysicals differ? They are not less serious, not less tormented, not less complex (least of all that!); but they probe the psychology of love with a new clarity – a new naked intensity, perhaps. Attention is deflected from the courtly show and imagery to the inner world of experience, which then dramatises itself in wholly novel, and indeed calculatedly unexpected, modes. The metaphysicals habitually explore, first and foremost, their own tortured and turbulent feelings, giving to the lady's real or supposed beauty second place or often no place at all. The lady is complimented no longer chiefly because she is a goddess but because she makes a man feel godlike; the turbulence in her lover's heart is *her* praise. Courtly and platonic images remain, but shorn of autonomy and requiring always the test of particular mood and tone. Some of the new images are, by former standards, wildly 'unpoetic' – limbecks, compasses and the like. Attention focuses on complexities of human heart and head, on the difficulty a man may have in distinguishing sincerity from libertinism, high platonic devotion from dreams of seduction, even when – or especially when – his emotions burn with intensest power. Explorations so complex that critics, with no hope of victory, wage war around them have become a hallmark of these poems' teasing and often irresistible hold on the modern mind.

In its detail the metaphysical poem often proceeds by way of a tortuous argument, inherently absurd yet reflecting strange and unmistakable truths of love. As Eliot said, thought is felt, and feelings are reflected upon, yet neither thought nor feeling seems an end in itself. These poems were written, as it happens, by men who combined deep resources of passion (religious as well as erotic) with an impulse to articulate, to explore immediately and sensuously in words, that seemed never to rest. With Donne in particular, the poem often strikes us as coming from the white-hot moment of experience, and miming, or even fulfilling, its own immediate theme. Yet a moment's reflection shows that this is indeed an illusion; the gulf between experience and finished art is never so effortlessly leaped.

During this period the main themes of poetry are highly personal. By and large, it is not a great age for political poetry, nor is it an age of theological poetry in any abstract or social sense. The situations we repeatedly encounter are a man's relationship with a woman or with his Creator – or sometimes, as in Marvell, with nature, but in its cultivated form. The metaphysicals were profoundly religious as well as profoundly sensual and sensuous, and it is no surprise that the Christian paradoxes are marvellously expressed and explored in their work. This is one of the periods when we find many great poems, both of love and religion, but all with their deep roots in the experiencing self. Intense awareness of guilt and of death forms a continuous backcloth, a stark and often majestic fixed point in the restless scene.

These poets are also men in whom a fascination with words, with wit, paradox and ingenuity as inherent challenges and pleasures, was inseparable from their entire sense of life. Perhaps there never have been other poets who could be more easily mistaken for mere intellectuals, mere lovers of words and of games with words, yet in whom these characteristics, though real enough, were less valued or employed as ends in themselves.

A further point to note is that most of these poets did not think of poetry as their main vocation. Like some of the Elizabethans, they wrote chiefly to please themselves, their friends and their mistresses; most of their poems were not published during their lives. If asked what they 'were', they would not have answered 'poets'; they would have said clergymen, courtiers, politicians, as the case might be. They did not have a sense of bardic mission or a calling to prophecy. In this they are akin to most of the Elizabethans, but differ sharply from the three great poets who were to dominate the period following their own : Milton, Dryden and Pope.

Do they in any way resemble the romantics? In one obvious way perhaps they do. Like the romantics, they were intensely personal poets. But they did not, like the romantics, formulate distinctive claims for poetry, and imagination, as modes of revelation. Very obviously, they valued wit, logic, intellectual and verbal play more highly than the romantics did. And in imagery and syntax metaphysicals and romantics are poles apart. They differ also – again, despite certain affinities – from the later nineteenth-century symbolists and from those twentieth-century moderns who acknowledged debts to them, including T. S. Eliot. While the metaphysicals share with many modern poets a conscious preference for ambiguity and ambivalence, as modes of exploring experience, they do not *consciously* use images for their resonances as the symbolists do. It is worth remembering that their particular kind of verse attracted hostility from the neo-classical writers and indifference from most of the romantics; only in our own century have they been recognised as great poets and come into their own.

None of what has been said should be taken to imply, however, that they were amateurs; few poets have been more skilled as craftsmen or had a finer metrical sense. The notion that their poetry is metrically rugged or unaccomplished is highly superficial – as anyone may discover from the discipline of reading it aloud. In their own way, they took poetry extremely seriously, and were no doubt formidably critical of themselves. The fact that they wrote for their peers may explain a certain love of obscurity and a frank willingness to accept intellectual toughness as pleasurable in itself.

It is important to add that the metaphysicals were not the only poets in their period, though they were the greatest and by far the most distinctive. More traditional kinds of verse were also being written at that time. A line of more song-like love lyrics can be traced from the Elizabethans, through Lovelace, Ben Jonson, Herrick and others, to the Restoration writers, and notably Rochester. The 'school of Ben' was in some way influenced by the metaphysicals, and there are several poems by Jonson himself

(read, for example, his 'Epitaph on S.P., A Child of Queen
Elizabeth's Chappel') which, if come upon out of context, would
most likely be ascribed to a 'metaphysical' in any dating test. In
the more traditional lyrics, the Chloes and Phyllises, the shep-
herdesses and nymphs, the pastoral descriptions and emotions,
are handed on, through the earlier seventeenth century, from the
Elizabethans to the court of Charles II. In the later seventeenth
century they at times acquired a peculiar flavour of coarseness
and cynicism which is immediately recognisable, and is one sign
of the striking transition from 'metaphysical' to 'Restoration' wit.

(2) 1660–1740

The decade following the Restoration was one of decisive change.
Just occasionally we can point with hindsight to a date – 1530,
1660, 1789, 1914 – when a very basic cultural transition occurs.
Usually it affects the whole mood and thinking of a generation as
well as the arts individually, and in retrospect marks a conscious
break with the past. Naturally, such changes have their roots in
the years preceding them, and there is continuity in many
aspects of life in the years that follow. To a historian cut-and-
dried generalisations are bound to seem superficial, but for those
charting the history of taste, or 'dating' poems, they have a
pragmatic usefulness as 'clues' that lead in the right direction far
more often than not.

The Restoration of the monarchy was not in itself the most
significant factor, though it played its part in the ensuing mood;
after the turmoil and growing uncertainty of the revolutionary
1650s most men were ready to enjoy stability again. Undoubtedly
the most important factor was the new science, which began now
to affect every aspect of thought. The era of scientific thinking,
associated previously with Bacon, crystallised and consolidated
round the names of Newton and Locke. Newton's 'law of
gravitation' came to be seen not only as a scientific endorsement
of the religious belief in divine and ordered creation, but also as a
proof of man's godlike mind and future power. From now on,

man could hope first to understand and then to improve and modify creation, making the kingdom of Nature subserve the kingdom of Man. Pope's famous couplet about Newton, conceived first as an epitaph and later incorporated into the *Essays on Man*, is witty but in no sense ironic in intention; its thought was echoed again and again for a century or more :

> Nature and Nature's Laws lay hid in night;
> God said, 'Let Newton be !', and all was light.

There are famous tributes to Newton in Thomson and again in Wordsworth's *Prelude*; Blake was isolated, as well as early, with his contrary report.

The new science created a climate in which observation and logic came to be seen as the sole reliable guides to 'truth'. Bacon attacked the whole tradition of medieval scholasticism, likening it to a web spun by a spider out of itself. His own new, scientific epistemology found no place for metaphysics, and relegated even 'faith' to its own sphere, in isolation from 'reason'. Empiricism eventually received definitive expression in Locke's *Essay Concerning Human Understanding* (1690), and during the eighteenth century Locke joined Bacon and Newton in a formidable trilogy of 'moderns'. There was a general belief that human reason had now come of age, accompanied by a resolute determination to prune English prose of its recent imaginative extravagances, and to make of it a medium suited to rational discourse. Inevitably, this movement also influenced poetry, and the arts generally; all things gothic, baroque and ornamental yielded to classicism.

One remarkable effect was upon religious thinking. The split between religion and science, threatening throughout the sixteenth century and erupting in the Galileo crisis, suddenly seemed to be resolved in a new alliance between the two. If order on the scale discovered by Newton could be found in every corner of the universe, did this not prove, and continually demonstrate, the first Great Cause? God's imprint on his works, as Mind, became a truth of observation and deduction; 'the works of nature everywhere sufficiently evidence a deity', as Locke somewhat tepidly said.

This new alliance between religion and science told against scepticism, but eventually it told still more against religious fervour and mysticism. Though Anglicans did not accept (and, indeed, bitterly opposed) the deist position, none the less deism greatly coloured Christian thought. Much of the past was written off as superstitious, priest-ridden and irrational, and Scripture itself was seen as second best (if that) to Nature as the revelation of God. God himself became a Great Designer, known through reason. Whether such a God can long attract worship, or even interest, was perhaps insufficiently probed.

That all the arts were affected, and notably literature, is an aspect very easy to see. There was a determined move by the Royal Society to take prose as a medium for scientific and empirical discourse, and to refine and simplify punctuation, sentence structure and syntax with this end in view. Prose of the ornate, metaphysical kind was explicitly rejected; even the great Authorised Version of the Bible took on an archaic appearance in a comparatively short time.

But the desire for clarity, for prose-strength and logic, extended also to poetry, which now gravitated towards classical or rational moulds. The metaphysicals began to be condemned for their riot of fancy, their extravagance of metaphor and expression: qualities more akin to the old superstition than to the new judiciousness – or so it now seemed. Metaphysical wit was defined, in Lockean terms, as 'false wit' : that is to say, as a play of fancy in defiance of observation and sense. To Samuel Johnson, indeed, it seemed near to madness, a mere disorder of the intellect – possibly pleasing but misleading and even dangerous in the end. Perhaps we should not be surprised to find that Cowley was the metaphysical poet whom the eighteenth century found most acceptable : Cowley, the most pseudo-classical, the most tediously long-winded, the most wedded to 'sense'.

In contrast, 'true wit' (as Pope called it) became admired and celebrated as an ally to judicious thinking and to large human truths :

> True wit is Nature to advantage dress'd.
> What oft was thought but ne'er so well express'd.

True wit, though chiefly a stylistic grace when described so, was closely related to a whole view of life. In essence it reflected a desire not to invent new notions, to make new discoveries or to shine strange new lights on experience, but to find the most polished and memorable words for truths that endure. In this period the notion of 'originality', like that of 'enthusiasm', shared the taint of eccentricity. When these qualities reappeared in literature, as they did in the middle years of the eighteenth century, they usually had an edge of conscious defiance of their age.

Not unexpectedly, this period in which men congratulated themselves on great and definitive advances in science was one, also, which resisted further implications of change. The great men – Bacon, Newton, Locke – were indeed innovators, equal to or (most said) greater than the giants of the ancient world. (In his *Battle of the Books* and elsewhere Swift ironically savaged the 'moderns' in defence of the 'ancients', yet the very need for such satire tells its own tale.) But, now that the work was done, men could enter their heritage, not expecting to add to or subtract from the culture thus finely mapped out. In practical terms the main task was to comb the past for those moral and rational truths which had in some sense been known to all men at all times, and to restate this common heritage with elegance and wit. Such truths were to be disentangled also from the accretions born of ignorance; all superstition, priestcraft and divisiveness was to be purged.

That these new directions affected every department of life is apparent in literature, and not least in poetry, through the very conscious ambition to wed content to form. Each 'genre' was a classical equivalent to a mode of human experience, a fitting vehicle for certain truths and approaches to truth. Dryden and Pope both wrote elegies, lyrics, odes, philosophic poems and epics as well as mock-epic satire; Pope's first poems were cast in the pastoral mould.

The belief that civilised progress was a natural concomitant to intellectual enlightenment produced the 'gentleman' and the 'lady' as natural moral ideals. Great value was placed upon manners, upon style and appearance, as the outward and visible signs of inner wholeness and poise. The 'gentleman' ruled his life by universal precepts, striving to emulate and excel in all graces of civilised life. He would seek to control wayward instincts and emotions by reason, and to achieve courtesy towards others, whatever his personal moods. Ideally, he would be a man of learning, familiar with the current enlightenment in all its parts. He would hope to converse in the coffee houses on every topic of importance: arts and sciences, philosophy and religion, politics and morality, opera and drama, Milton and Locke.

In 1711–12 the ambition to consolidate a classical society reached new heights in *The Spectator* of Addison and Steele. The journal's twin objects were to make the age more moral, and to make it more philosophical. Its methods were urbane ridicule and unremitting good sense. In effect the notion of the 'gentleman' was moved further than ever from that of class description and nearer to that of a classical moral ideal. One clear aim was to civilise the rising middle classes, transmitting to them the virtues of a truly cultured élite.

As one would expect, an age so dominated by reason threw up its own opposites, long before the full-scale romantic revolution swept it away. Doubtless, any age which believes not only that man is capable of perfection but that he has virtually attained it, must become particularly aware of how far short the reality falls. As Basil Willey puts it, in *Eighteenth-Century Background* (1946): 'if you worship "Nature and Reason", you will be the more afflicted by human unreason; and perhaps only the effort to see man as the world's glory will reveal how far he is really its jest and riddle.' In the seventeenth century, Hobbes had been on hand with a view of man diametrically opposite to the one that was soon to prevail. In *Leviathan* he depicted the ground of all life as material conflict, enacted in the consciousness of man himself. All life was traced to laws of material causation, and all morality to permutations of self-interest and fear. This philosophic materialism, while being very generally deplored and rejected, was always available for purposes of satiric critique. In Rochester's powerful 'Satire Against Mankind', as in Swift's *Gulliver's Travels,* Pope's 'Moral Essays' and *The Dunciad* and many other places, man's depravity is played off, most complexly, against his rational ideals. Again, the Restoration Comedies, probing the superficial glitter of a polite world, found bleakly coarse and brutal behaviour just beneath. Every man a lecher, every wife an adulteress, every husband a cuckold – from such assumptions the wit and sparkle are made to flow.

And, at a slightly different level, this age which exalted the gentleman as a cultural ideal of universal application also became fascinated by the 'noble savage'. As if in counterpoint with its main insight into human behaviour, it explored the quest, through primitivism, for 'natural man'. Paul Hazard (whose two books, *The European Mind,* 1973, and *European Thought in the Eighteenth Century,* 1965, remain among the best introductions to the period) traces this tension between 'gentleman' and 'noble savage' as a major theme. He relates the noble savage partly to travellers' tales, with their accounts of virtuous and contented pagans untouched by civilisation, and partly to the question, 'Where shall happiness be found?' Just in so far as the ideal of civilisation failed, or seemed to fail, to produce happiness, so the other ideal of unsophisticated innocence might become attractive. Primitivism sometimes (as arguably in Book IV of *Gulliver*) was used for satire, and sometimes as a basis for alternatives to classical man. The strong strand of primitivism which can be found earlier in Montaigne and Milton, and later – in full strength – in Rousseau and the romantics, flowed strongly also in the Age of Reason itself.*

* We would stress again that these contrasts seldom appear in the very clear form that generalisations such as these may suggest. Christian belief – which posits that man was created good, fell into evil, but is redeemed potentially – cuts across the view that he is either 'naturally' bad or competitive (Hobbes), or that he is 'naturally' good. Again, the tradition of thinking which derived from

How do such trends directly influence poetry? – in numerous ways. The optimistic humanism of the period is matched by the ambitions and achievements of its three major poets, Milton, Dryden and Pope. In particular, the recovery of classicism made inevitable the reintroduction of the epic – that genre most attuned to celebrate man's achievement and greatness – along with its inevitable concomitant, the mock-epic, with its use of the epic apparatus and tone to deflate and mock. The three major poets all entertained the highest ambitions for their art and their use of language as well as for their themes. They were public and bardic poets in a way that the metaphysicals had not been, and their dedication to poetry was complete. Milton wrote to 'justify the ways of God to man'; Pope, in a near quotation, to 'vindicate the ways of God to man'. Dryden's aim was to celebrate, and fight for, political order, to vindicate Charles II as the chosen servant of God.

Political themes not only reappear in poetry but they do so majestically. *Absalom and Achitophel* is possibly the finest poem ever to have been inspired by particular, and passing, political events. When we turn to religion we find that there is another sharp break with the metaphysicals, not in the faith itself (of course) but in the treatment that it now normally receives. In place of personal explorations of religious experience, personal prayers and discoveries, we find great and public explorations of the nature and destiny of Man. When planning *Paradise Lost**

Locke co-existed with platonism, so that 'reason' was not solely used in an empirical sense. The Cambridge Platonists in the later seventeenth century, and the third Earl of Shaftesbury in the early eighteenth century, kept alive a platonism where 'Reason' was 'the candle of the Lord'. This may be discovered in Pope and Thomson, as in many other eighteenth-century poets, long before it flowered in Coleridge and Wordsworth, and became a challenge to Locke.

* Milton was born before Marvell and, in his 'Nativity Ode', was a clear metaphysical. It must be stressed again that 1660 is not a magic date; *Paradise Lost* existed as an idea as early as 1640, while some metaphysical poems, in Helen Gardner's selection, have dates as late as 1691.

Milton expected to write the greatest poem the world had ever known. This hope was grounded in his intention to use the greatest of forms, the epic, and to match it, by grace, with the greatest of themes. The account of the creation, fall and redemption of man was as remarkable as anything celebrated by Homer or Virgil, but had the immense added merit of being God's revealed truth. Characteristically, Milton realised that he could, even so, achieve his aim only if he nurtured the great linguistic gifts which he knew to be his by dedicated discipline, and only if he attained outstanding moral purity in his personal life. It is also characteristic that his neo-classical ambitions extended to the English language, which he hoped would acquire added dignity and power. In Shakespeare English had proved a suitable medium for tragedy, the second greatest of the 'genres', but it still had no epic to match those in Latin and Greek. *Paradise Lost* reaches, among other things, towards grandeur and sublimity of utterance, matching in this comparable developments in music, architecture, painting and the other arts. Milton leaves behind the blank-verse usage of the Elizabethan and Jacobean dramatists, in favour of a more latinate vocabulary, syntax and style. As it turned out, the Miltonic usage was to influence blank verse for the next two centuries; only Browning (perhaps) completely evaded the new, 'epic' tone.

By a paradox already noted as normal, this age of epic was also an age of satire. But, while Dryden and Pope in our day are thought of first and foremost as satiric poets, we should not forget that in their lifetimes they were acclaimed chiefly as the translators of (respectively) Virgil and Homer. Their own satire, moreover, is only partly 'mock' heroic; it also embodies the highest civilised ideals. At the same time we should bear in mind that these three great poets were only partly 'typical'. The period which they embody they also evade. Milton was fiercely protestant, a puritan of the puritans, and also a platonist; in his bones the empiricism of the century had no place. Dryden became a Roman Catholic by choice, and Pope was born one; both belonged to the minority and repressed faith which Locke's 'reason' mocked. Whatever doubts may be expressed about the sincerity of Dryden's conversion or the depth of Pope's sectarian allegiance, the demoralisation of poetry by rationalism had little effect upon them. Only in the minor poets do we detect any latent unease. There can be no doubt that, while Dryden's *Religio Laici*, Pope's *Essay on Man* and 'A Universal Prayer', are influenced by 'reason', they are influenced by it in no petty or reductive way. Any attentive reader of Pope, in particular, is bound to detect, beneath the poet's deep sense of life's tragic mystery, the profound influence of Catholic forms of worship and faith.

One final note on the heroic couplet, which in this period is the dominant verse form. The metaphysicals had frequently used this form (as well as the octosyllabic couplet), but always in its 'open' mode. Meaning and sense had most usually spilled over from couplet to couplet, drawing attention away from, not towards, the poetic form. It was Dryden who first decisively 'closed' the couplet, so that each couplet (with rare exceptions) has a shape of its own. Again and again after this, couplets are epigrammatic or otherwise detachable – even when they belong to so complex a whole as *The Rape of the Lock*. It was not until the young Keats rebelled against the 'rocking-horse couplet' (his phrase), and wrote *Endymion*, that 'openness' of the pre-Dryden kind was restored. By and large, a student encountering the 'closed' heroic couplet out of context can think of 1660 to 1817 or so as its most probable period of origin. But this, of course, must be checked against other evidence; and there are a few notorious traps. Marlowe could write heroic couplets that sound Augustan:

> It lies not in our power to love or hate,
> For will in us is overcome by Fate

and, later, some of the Victorians closed the form again. It is worth remembering, too, that Goldsmith, Cowper and others wrote many rhyming couplets after 1740, yet in their work some hint of the changes which are now finally to concern us can usually be found.

(3) 1740–1850

What is 'romanticism' ? Few words have been used in wider and more paradoxical senses, as O. A. Lovejoy's famous essay 'On the Discrimination of Romanticisms' demonstrated.*

Since the poets of the 1740s and onwards are sometimes described as 'pre-romantic', this period seems a fitting place to start. The challenge is to notice those aspects of 'romanticism' which make a distinctive appearance in the 1730s and 1740s, and to distinguish them from the more radical later innovations that the word most often signifies today.

Thomson's *Seasons* (1726–30) is an early and seminal instance. It is the first use of Miltonic blank verse in a major poem, and a forerunner of the great influence that Milton's style was to have for a further century and a half. But, whereas Milton himself was concerned with the epic, Thomson's purposes are less clear-cut. In essence, his poetry describes and reflects upon the natural world, moving easily from personal rapture to abstract thought. At best, he achieves a sense of epic grandeur and even sublimity, but some element of uncertainty haunts the style. Behind the offer of hitherto unknown truths now proclaimed and celebrated, the reality is often a dressing-up of moral commonplaces in bardic garb. The result can seem outlandish and odd, even when charming; T. S. Eliot compared it with a solemn game. We readily notice that the philosophising is amateur and the structure rambling; there is nothing analogous to the compression or the complexity of *Paradise Lost*. In Thomson the main attempt might be described as a meeting of empiricism and platonism : an

* 'On the Discrimination of Romanticisms' (1924), in *Essays in the History of Ideas* (1948); reprinted in *English Romantic Poets: Modern Essays in Criticism,* ed. M. H. Abrams (1960).

ambition to bring Locke and Shaftesbury together in a single frame. Such a description does less than justice, however, to Thomson's deep love of nature and to the charm and power with which this is often conveyed.

From the 1740s onwards many poets followed Thomson's formula, but none with comparable success. Young's *Night Thoughts* (1742) is the most extended instance but, despite splendid passages, it fails as a whole. The structure is loose and the sensibility morbid; Young's personality, which pervades the poem, is hard to endure. Akenside, Cowper and others wrote very fine passages, but their poems, as wholes, fail to stand up. Since the poet's personal mood and tone rules the structure, the results seem garrulous and lacking in edge. These poets fail, not through their lack of intelligence, but through their inability to integrate; thought becomes abstract and divorced from one total effect.

None the less, Thomson's *Seasons* does, in one particular, introduce a major, and continuing, romantic theme. For a long time poetry about Nature had tended to fall into two main kinds. There was the 'pastoral' tradition, notably influenced by Shakespeare's last plays and by his festive comedies, which offered an idealised and stylised rural world. Often this was seen as an alternative to or as an escape from courtly or urban corruption, or as a search for innocence or youth or love, slightly to one side of time. It could produce love poems with a genuine striving for rural peace and innocence, or – with varying shades of transition – thoroughly sophisticated and corrupt parodies in the same genre. In Milton's 'Il Penseroso' the desire for solitude and contemplation predominates : a note which Gray, Collins and other poets of the mid-eighteenth century took up.

The other tradition of 'nature' poetry runs alongside this, and in pastoral overtones often overlaps. From the pleasances of medieval courtly romance, Spenser's enchanted landscapes, through Portia's Belmont, Marvell's gardens and Milton's Paradise, civilised nature – God and man in harmony – had been a continuing ideal. God's original gift of Eden, which Adam and Eve were to cultivate, is the prime archetype of nature and art in an alliance for good. The garden is an emblem, a reminder of Paradise, and a civilised pleasure; its harmony and enchantment still speak to man of his highest good. The tradition appears again in Pope's early pastorals and his delightful *Windsor Forest,* where the celebration of England, and of progress, is an added note.

Where then is Thomson genuinely novel in his treatment of Nature? – clearly, in his choice of *wild* nature, of scenes untended by man. He writes of rocky or mountainous regions, far from man's habitation, of storm and tempest, snow and desolation, winter and death. The human onlooker exults in a power which both defies and threatens him, yet which also confirms him in his pride as God's favoured son. Behind Newton's God, deduced by reason and admired in abstractions, there is the felt presence of a God of majesty and power.

From this point onwards, the eighteenth-century poets started to seek out mountains and desolate, dangerous places, and to encourage feelings deeper and stranger than those in 'reason's' writ. The poets of the 1740s began to write of graveyards, of melancholy nurtured in solitude, of ancient ruins and splendours, and to find in these their inspiration and delight. Such poetry crossbred with prose, especially in the 'gothic' novel, and inaugurated a tradition which spread and ramified, and which still goes on. But, before we leave Thomson, one thing needs to be noted : he did not invest 'feeling' with cognitive authority as Wordsworth later did. Wordsworth is prefigured, indeed, in the themes and in the exhilaration; but 'reason', whether Locke's or Plato's, remains the one path to truth. To this degree, 'feeling' has not yet broken through all barriers and claimed its own validity as revelation of God.

The signs of 'pre-romanticism' are usually located in the 1740s, perhaps because articulate opposition to the classical now enters the scene. Pope starts to be referred to as a 'cold formalist' and to be instanced as an over-intellectual poet, lacking in warmth. Though heroic couplets indebted to Pope were still fashionable, a more relaxed, more sentimental mood begins to prevail. In Goldsmith and Cowper blank verse and heroic couplets become almost interchangeable as a vehicle for leisurely, good-natured rambles about life and thought. In style we are reminded always of Milton and Pope respectively, but the 'feel' of this period differs markedly from both. The poetry is civilised, warm-hearted, often sentimental, even when satire (if we except Churchill and Johnson) is its chief concern.

In a survey such as this we can do no more than list the main innovations of the 1740s. There was the rediscovery first of Spenser and then of the Ballads. These proved fruitful influences upon poets turning now to the charm of the exotic and wonderful: precursors, in this, of Wordsworth's 'old, unhappy, far-off things/And battles long ago'. The finest of the mock-Spenserian poems is unquestionably Thomson's 'Castle of Indolence', which imitated not only Spenser's allegorical method but also his languid and luxurious diction, and his delight in the marvellous; there is, moreover (students of dating should remember) conscious archaism of style. The 'Castle of Indolence' greatly pleased Keats, influencing his Odes as well as his 'Eve of St Agnes'; in this way it became a potent presence also for the Victorians. One could, indeed, argue that poets such as William Morris and Dante Gabriel Rossetti are closer in spirit to Thomson than was Keats himself. There is, in this kind of romanticism, a suggestion of a deliberate indulgence, of escapism – a cult of 'the wonderful' as an alternative to life rather than as an insight – which sets it slightly apart from true romantic seriousness, of whatever kind.

In the 1740s 'melancholy' became a favoured theme – again pointing the way to Keats's Odes. The most famous instance is Wharton's 'Pleasures of Melancholy' (1748), where the morbidity seems strangely poised between sickness and sport. Better to languish a prisoner in Siberia, we are told, exiled from love and hope and perpetually snowbound, than to achieve almost any other delight that fancy might shape. Is Wharton serious? Perhaps he scarcely knew himself; yet the desire for solitude, for wildness, for frustration even, can pierce very deep. The pleasure in solemn moods, in loneliness, in escape from the busy scenes of men to a private world of heightened, if morbid, sensitivity and musing, haunts poetry at this time. We find it in the 'graveyard' school, of which Gray's 'Elegy' is the most famed example, and in Collins's 'Ode to Evening' : a poem whose fluid images and shifting syntax look forward to Shelley's style. These themes were not, of course, novel, nor without recent precedent; yet their obsessive quality looks forward rather than back. Perhaps the melancholy Jacques, and Hamlet, are the truest precursors, in that morbidity and incipient madness certainly lurks in *them*. We may recall also the young Milton's 'Il Penseroso' and Pope's beautiful and often neglected poems of melancholy, 'Eloisa to Abelard' and 'Elegy to the Memory of an Unfortunate Lady' (both first published in 1717). None the less, the 1740s bring melancholy themes into prominence, in that we now find them in the poetry almost wherever we look.

What, then, happened in the later 1780s and the 1790s that must make this later period the one from which we date the next decisive revolution in English culture? Not English culture only, indeed, but European culture – with the French Revolution providing the most quoted date. It is certain that about this time there was a cultural change at least as great as that associated with the 1660s, and arguably bigger than any previously known in the history of man. C. S. Lewis took this view in his inaugural lecture at Cambridge, 'De Descriptione Temporum' (1955), where he expounded the steps by which he had 'come to regard as the greatest of all divisions in the history of the West that which divides the present age from, say, the age of Jane Austen and Scott'. He points to the French Revolution, the romantic revolution (now often so describing itself) and above all perhaps to the Industrial Revolution, with its inauguration of technology and its accelerating quest for the new. In particular, he instances the rejection of an hierarchical and structured view of creation in favour of ideas that brought democracy and, later, egalitarianism to the cultural fore. The pattern of 'rulers' and 'ruled' yielded to the rhetoric of co-operation, keenness, campaigns for 'independence', and eventually to the fragmented culture, and world, as we know it today. Again, he points to the fact that, in art, qualities such as novelty and originality (and, he might have added, enthusiasm) which had before been suspect become honoured and prized ideals. He suggests, finally, that it was the triumph of machines, more than anything else (the theory of evolution not excepted), which made the dogma of 'progress' so irresistible in the modern world. In one sense 'progress' had been a renaissance and scientific assumption for several centuries, but it had lacked concrete and proliferating evidence to bolster its claims. It was the existence of machines, each more efficient (and, in this sense, 'better') than the last, which turned 'progress' into an apparent fact of life. Lewis suggests that the belief in 'progress' then transferred itself, however illogically, to all of our thinking, whether about poetry, religion, philosophy, politics or anything else. If this assessment is right, then the romantic period as we meet it in poetry is connected with the distinctive evolution and emergence of 'modern man'.

Not everyone will agree with 'De Descriptione Temporum', and perhaps it already wears a dated look; the collapse of optimistic humanism was taking place in Lewis's lifetime, and already we may have lived through a further decisive cultural change. But, certainly, the extent of the romantic revolution cannot be underestimated, nor the permanence of many of its effects. In Blake, for instance, we encounter an extreme rejection of the eighteenth century, and an equating of scientific empiricism with a 'universe of death'. Blake believed that in reducing religion, poetry and the human spirit to mere intellectualism the empiricists had locked mankind in a small prison house. In sharp contrast, he asserts the supremacy of the creative imagination, not only in the making of art but also in the perception of ultimate truth. We encounter God, not through abstract reasoning and deduction, but through a direct awareness of him in his works and in our own hearts. Blake's temperament was that of a mystic and, with Wordsworth and Coleridge, he contributed to a powerful reassertion of *experienced* divinity in nature and, above all, in man.

To attempt an exposition of Blake's thought would be impossible here (though a functional synopsis will be found in Chapter 7 above). Blake's outstanding affinities are with the primitivists, and the social utopians, whose debt to him – and to Rousseau before him – is well known. Romanticism is sometimes almost equated with primitivism, and we should guard against making this particular mistake. As Professor A. O. Lovejoy points out,* primitivism was only one strand of romanticism (and, we may add, it was only one strand of Blake's thought). The German romantics, who were the first to employ the word romantic to describe themselves, explicitly deny a dichotomy between 'culture' and 'nature' of the primitivist kind. They assert the immense importance of will and of self-disciplined effort, both for the modern artist and for the modern man. Their hope was that the full range of human experience and imaginations might find expression, and they expected tension and complexity, not simplicity, to result if this were achieved.

When we turn to the three or four key English romantics, one common and vital emphasis is clear. In Blake, Wordsworth and Coleridge, the appalled perception that man has been reduced, and diminished, by Lockean empiricism leads to a new philosophy, a new psychology and a new type of faith. Coleridge, the most influential thinker of the school, rechristened 'reason' (in Locke's usage) 'understanding', and used the word 'Reason' more as Plato had done. 'Reason' is a direct perception of beauty, truth, goodness in creation, a supersensuous perception accompanying, but transcending, the evidence of the 'senses five'. Naturally, this led him on to the mystery of perception and of basic human psychology, and to speculations which are briefly expounded in our study of Wordsworth (Chapter 8 above). In essence, these three poets believed that man is never so divine as when he is creating, and that his creations are themselves symbols, and evidence, of the great truths that they tell. Just as God created the external universe, so man creates the cultural world; in both is to be discerned the nature of divine creation.

* On the Discrimination of Romanticisms'.

It will be apparent that, when so many cross-currents meet, there is no simplifying; notoriously, definitions of romanticism can seem to cancel each other out. What we can risk saying is that the romantics have influenced our cultural life so extensively that many men with no interest in poetry are, unknowingly, their heirs. A pattern could be traced between English romanticism and modern existentialist philosophy; important and as yet unpublished research on this is now being done. Certainly, modern psychology is, in its insights, often deeply 'romantic'; the ideas of Jung and of Blake can most usefully be compared. Otto's *Idea of the Holy* (1923), a seminal work of modern theology, is continuously and explicitly indebted to romantic ideas. More important, it is the romantic poems themselves that influence many men, even more than their 'content'; their power is to evoke, not merely to state, the truths at their heart.

Yet, if the romantics influenced much that is most vital in subsequent religious thinking, their influence has also pulled in quite other ways. Their appeal to deep feeling, personal experience, came as a liberation; yet it could lead to another solipsism, another prison, if carried too far. Suppose that feeling goes dead, and one is left derelict? Even Wordsworth and Coleridge knew and recorded such moods. And in Keats we find the torment of romanticism when it comes adrift from religion and explores the gulf between what men can dream of as possible and what they sense can possibly be. In Keats's Odes, the tradition of melancholy inherited from the eighteenth century takes on a new intensity as it becomes, not aesthetic luxury, but an image of inner despair.

It is important to remember that the romantic poets influenced most of the major Victorian novelists, and that these dramatise the complexities, and often the snares, in the quest for 'oneself'. Many fictional heroes and heroines set out on the romantic voyage to 'fulfilment', but encounter contradictory circumstances, inner contradictions, tragic defeats. The psychic intensities released by a cult of 'feeling' often turn morbid, as Mario Praz traces in his *Romantic Agony* (1970), a now classic work. Both in fiction and in life we encounter men wrecked by their intensities, or lapsing from high idealism into destructive boredom and fear. The inner tensions between idealism and dissipation, love and lust, religion and diabolism, which Dostoievsky charted so powerfully, have their progeny in much violence, torment and absurdity in life and literature today. Perhaps it is no surprise that C. S. Lewis should consider romanticism chiefly as an enemy of 'old' Western culture, despite that passionate commitment to religion and to mystery which is one of its strongest strands.

Is there any sorting out of such riddles? Not in any purely theoretical way. Fortunately the poems of Wordsworth and Coleridge, Blake, Keats and Shelley are still at hand, to keep our questions, at least, anchored in certain real texts.

'We are all romantics now.' Is there any truth in this? In so far as we value our independence and judgement, our right to experience and, if need be, to suffer, then perhaps there is. But it is worth recalling that the Christian tradition, which includes these values, has also long fostered them, however obscured by dogma they have sometimes been allowed to become. It seems likely then that, while modern despair and absurdism and even secularism can claim in some sense to be 'romantic', they ought to recognise themselves as morbid mutations, not as true heirs. The romantic poets, who fought for a divine view of man against eighteenth-century depredations and reductions, cannot be made patron saints of the greatest reductions of all.

In fact the great romantics were all, in one way or another, profoundly religious, and would have made little sense of a view of life divorced from wonder and praise. They were also, in the most important sense possible, profoundly classical; few writers have been more directly indebted to the Greeks. We should not allow their strong, and passionate, reaction against seventeenth- and eighteenth-century neo-classicism to blind us to their deep affinities with the original classicism itself. Few poets have been more influenced by Plato than Wordsworth and Coleridge; few poets have been more enchanted by paganism than Shelley and Keats.

The early and great romantics were rebelling, in fact, against empiricism and neo-classicism in their *recent* forms. Because intellect had been abstracted from wholeness, and exalted at the expense alike of man's soul and his senses, the casualties had included true religion, as well as sheer bodily joy. It was this tradition which they regarded as cold and repressive, as an enemy of instinct and as a threat to the individual's right to know and explore and fulfil himself as a whole. The true villains were empiricism, with its reduction of philosophy, religion and man himself to mere intellectualism; and science, with its propensity to abstract man from Nature, and Nature from God.

In so far as the real dislike of the romantics was for the dehumanisation implicit in such developments, their real hatred was not for the ancient paganism, but for the secularism to come. What they reacted against in the tradition which they inherited was not those aspects which had produced a new flowering of classical beauty, but those aspects which threatened beauty itself. If they could see modern secularism in its ugliest forms they would surely recognise it as the disaster which they did their best to avert. If they could be shown modern cults of instinct and self-fulfilment, adrift from religion, it is unlikely that they would acknowledge any responsibility for them.

FURTHER READING

Students wishing to study more deeply the poems and poets dealt with here are recommended to turn first to the appropriate Macmillan Casebook. Each of these gathers together a selection of early reviews and critical material, and presents an anthology of the best modern critical essays; there is also in each a very useful Select Bibliography. The Casebook volumes relevant to this present study are :

Donne, *Songs and Sonets,* ed. Julian Lovelock (1973).
The Metaphysical Poets, ed. Gerald Hammond (1974).
Milton, *Paradise Lost,* ed. A. E. Dyson and Julian Lovelock (1973).
Pope, *The Rape of the Lock,* ed. John Dixon Hunt (1968).
Blake, *Songs of Innocence and Experience,* ed. Margaret Bottrall (1969).
Wordsworth, *The Prelude,* ed. W. J. Harvey and Richard Gravil (1972).
Wordsworth, *Lyrical Ballads,* ed. Alun R. Jones and William Tydeman (1972).
Coleridge, *'The Ancient Mariner' and Other Poems,* ed. Alun R. Jones and William Tydeman (1973).
Shelley, *Shorter Poems and Lyrics,* ed. Patrick Swinden (1976).
Keats, *Odes,* ed. G. S. Fraser (1971).

There is no Casebook on Dryden; we suggest that students turn first to Mark Van Doren's *John Dryden: A Study of His Poetry* (1946); B. N. Schilling (ed.), *Dryden: A Collection of Critical Essays* (1963); H. T. L. Swedenberg (ed.), *Essential Articles for the Study of John Dryden* (1966); and L. I. Bredvold, *The Intellectual Milieu of John Dryden* (1934).
Students seeking fuller guides to criticism of all these poets

should turn to A. E. Dyson, *English Poetry: Select Bibliographical Guides* (1971), each of which is accompanied by a commentary.

For the literary history of the period, we would suggest the volumes in the *Oxford History of English Literature,* which achieve a consistently high standard.

For intellectual background, we refer readers to works mentioned in the text, and especially to :

Basil Willey, *The Seventeenth-Century Background* (1934), *The Eighteenth-Century Background* (1946), and *Nineteenth-Century Studies* (1949).

R. L. Brett, *The Third Earl of Shaftesbury* (1951).

Paul Hazard, *The European Mind* (1973), and *European Thought in the Eighteenth Century* (1965).

M. H. Abrams, *The Mirror and the Lamp* (1973).

Students wishing to acquaint themselves with the history of literary criticism in the present century, and its various shifts of emphasis, might start with the chapters on 'Literary Criticism' in C. B. Cox and A. E. Dyson (eds), *The Twentieth Century Mind,* three volumes (Oxford University Press, 1972). Suggestions for further reading are also offered there.

Readers wishing to consider the basic justification for literary studies could best turn, in our view, to Helen Gardner, *The Business of Criticism* (1959), and C. S. Lewis, *An Experiment in Criticism* (1961). Northrop Frye's *Anatomy of Criticism* (1957) is a fascinating, if theoretical, book for more advanced students and, with W. K. Wimsatt's *The Verbal Icon* (1973), is widely and highly admired. Cleanth Brooks's *The Well-wrought Urn* (1949) remains one of the best and most balanced defences of 'practical criticism', both in its theory and in its practice.

INDEX

This index includes all proper names, and all poems referred to in any detail; poems will be found under the name of their author. Certain key themes are also listed, but others run too pervasively through the text to be abstracted. Students wishing further to trace the development of thought might find it useful to compare the views of the poets discussed in this book on the topics we have omitted because of the multiplicity of references: notably art, death and rebirth, freedom, God, Heaven, Hell, imagination, love, nature, primitivism, reason, revolution, science.